Degradation

Degradation

What the History of Obscenity
Tells Us about Hate Speech

Kevin W. Saunders

NEW YORK UNIVERSITY PRESS
New York and London

NEW YORK UNIVERSITY PRESS
New York and London
www.nyupress.org

References to Internet websites (URLs) were accurate at the time of writing.
Neither the author nor New York University Press is responsible for URLs
that may have expired or changed since the manuscript was prepared.

Library of Congress Cataloging-in-Publication Data

Saunders, Kevin W.
Degradation : what the history of obscenity tells us about hate speech /
Kevin Saunders.
p. cm.
Includes bibliographical references and index.
ISBN 978-0-8147-4144-3 (cl : alk. paper) — ISBN 978-0-8147-4145-0 (e-book)
1. Hate speech. 2. Obscenity (Law) 3. Pornography. 4. Hate speech—United States. I. Title.
K5210.S28   2010
364.15'6—dc22   2010027857

Manufactured in the United States of America

10 9 8 7 6 5 4 3 2 1

Contents

Acknowledgments

I wish to thank Elizabeth Glazer, Shubha Ghosh, Koji Higashikawa, Mike Hoffheimer, Frank Ravitch, Fred Schauer, Al Storrs, and James Boyd White for their comments on, exposure to, or discussion of the issues raised in portions of this book or for reactions to earlier work leading to this effort. Thanks also to the reviewers, who contributed important suggestions to the New York University Press, and to those at the Press itself. The library staff at Michigan State University College of Law also provided valuable research assistance, and recent graduate of the College of Law Christina McDonald is to be thanked for her cite checking.

The Michigan State University College of Law provided summer research and sabbatical support for periods of time devoted to this book. Thanks also to the University of Oxford's Centre for Socio-Legal Studies and Wolfson College for their hospitality and support during that sabbatical.

An early version of the approach to the history of obscenity presented herein was published as "The United States and Canadian Responses to the Feminist Attack on Pornography: A Perspective from the History of Obscenity," in 9 *Indiana International & Comparative Law Review* 1 (1998).

Lastly, as always, thanks to my wife, Dr. Mary Scott, and our daughter, Molly Saunders-Scott, to both of whom this book is dedicated.

1

Introduction

This book is ultimately about hate speech. That may not be obvious from the first half, which is a discussion of the history of how societies have accepted pornographic depictions or have rejected those depictions through lists of banned books or antiobscenity laws. Yet obscenity is a useful way to talk about racist, sexist, or homophobic speech. It stands as a sort of metaphor for hate speech, but like the best of the metaphors for hate speech, it is something more than simply a metaphor. In order to see this, we need to examine what bans on obscenity, or other reactions to pornography, have been all about. When this is understood, we can see that obscenity concepts can be useful in analyzing just what is wrong with hate speech and the factors that speak to a word's or phrase's being acceptable or unacceptable.

Because there is sometimes confusion between pornography and obscenity, some clarification may be helpful in reading what follows. *Pornography*, from Greek for the writing of or about prostitutes, includes all sexual writing or images. *Obscenity* has a somewhat different meaning, focusing on repugnance or offense. For sexual images and in legal contexts, *obscenity* attaches to those depictions of sex that may be proscribed by law. In nonlegal contexts, it may more broadly encompass acts or expressions that are morally objectionable. Thus, pornographic images are not necessarily obscene. Most societies tolerate some sexual images, not only as a legal matter but as a matter of morality and aesthetics. Images or descriptions become obscene when they are considered shameful or morally, or even legally, objectionable. As a result, precisely the same sexual image, though always pornographic, may be obscene in some societies and eras and not obscene in others.

Before proceeding with an examination of the nature of obscenity, it would be useful to consider the use of metaphor in discussing hate speech. The most powerful aspect of Charles Lawrence's work on hate speech is that part that treats it as an assault.[1] His description of the physical impact of hate speech is extremely forceful: "Psychic injury is no less an injury than being struck in the face, and it is often far more severe."[2] Elsewhere, Lawrence speaks of more direct physical effects. Racist epithets "produce physical symptoms that temporarily disable the victim, and the perpetrators often use these words with the intention of producing this effect."[3]

Richard Delgado and Jean Stefancic are more explicit regarding the injuries that may be caused by racist speech. "Hate speech is not merely unpleasant or offensive. It may leave physical impacts on those it visits. . . . The immediate, short-term harms of hate speech include rapid breathing, headaches, raised blood pressure, dizziness, rapid pulse rate, drug-taking, risk-taking behavior, and even suicide."[4] Mari Matsuda makes similar points in her work.[5] The most drastic of these impacts, an increased likelihood of suicide, was documented in a 2004 study. In an article evocatively subtitled "Hate Speech Predicts Death," Brian Miller and Joshua Smyth presented their study of the correlation between suicide and membership in an ethnic group subjected to hate speech. Their conclusion was that "[e]thnic immigrant groups subjected to more negative ethnophaulisms, or hate speech, were more likely to commit suicide. This pattern was obtained even after taking into account the previously established association between immigrant suicide rates and the suicide rates for those ethnic immigrant groups in their countries of origin."[6]

When these authors speak of hate speech in terms of assault, it seems to be as more than simple metaphor. It is more than the whole world's being like a stage or hate speech's being *like* an assault. Hate speech, for them, is literally an assault. That is what makes it far more powerful than the ordinary metaphor. And that is why this book requires an extensive discussion of pornography and obscenity. That discussion provides the basis for arguing that hate speech is the current obscenity, although not necessarily in a legal sense. Rather, the conclusion is that what obscenity was all about in the past now applies to racist and sexist speech rather than to sexual images.

Before laying out the direction of this effort, I want to recognize a certain disability in addressing this topic. I am not a member of a minority group that has commonly faced, at least in my lifetime, racial invective. Nor have I been subjected to the sexist speech faced by many or most women. Although I find such speech distasteful, I do not feel the effects of such speech in the same way as its target groups do. Thus, I might be seen as offering, in that sense, unqualified or uninformed views.

I recognize that members of minority groups or women do not need me to validate their feelings or reactions. When I turn to the discussion of the factors that may make the use of a word offensive in some contexts and not so in others, my analysis is unaffected by personal impact. If those who have been so affected feel differently, I certainly do not intend to criticize or diminish that response. I do hope that my analysis provides something to think about. But if a reader has thought about it and still finds more offense in a situation in which I might find less, then I have simply failed to appreciate the personal impact the language in question may have visited on that reader.

One of the distinctions I offer in the second part of the book is the use-mention distinction. That distinction recognizes a difference in using a word and talking about a word. This distinction is most commonly recognized by the use of quotation marks or italics. When a word is present without quotation marks or italics, it is most commonly being used. When there are quotation marks or italics, the word is more commonly being mentioned or talked about. I suggest that there is more likely to be reason for offense when a word is used than when it is mentioned. Ascribing a racial epithet to an individual is more offensive than talking about that word. The difference may be more or less clear. The statement "The word 'nigger' is the most offensive word in the American vernacular" mentions the offensive word, and one would hope it is less a ground for offense than using the same word to address or describe an individual. The statement "The best label to attach to you is 'spic'" technically seems to be a mention of the racist word, but it is clearly intended as a use of the word.

I mention the distinction here, well before the discussion of racist speech, because it is one I intend to be guided by in the later chapters. Although I do not *use* racist or sexist words in this book, a book on hate speech can hardly avoid the *mention* of those words. Again, if this distinction does not lessen the offense some may find in the language, my apologies. But look again at the mention of a racial epithet in the preceding paragraph. I hope the reader sees that in statements about language, rather than about people, there is less reason for offense.

Now, as to where the book is headed, in the first part, I look at the history of how societies have treated sexual images. I show that in the classical era, the Greeks were very accepting of sexual images, while as Socrates was to find out, blasphemy and heresy were punishable even by death. The same is true of pre-Christian Rome. But with the onset of the Christian era there is a change. There was certainly the continuation of punishment for heresy, but at least certain instances of sexual depiction came to be proscribable. It is clear that this was not true for all sexual images. As Fred Schauer presents it, from the first Christian banning of a book as heretical in 325 CE for the next one thousand years, religious censorship increased, while secular bawdiness was uncensored.[7] Schauer sees a turning point in the invention of the printing press in 1428, because of the increased availability of books to all classes. But even then, there was no concern over secular bawdiness. The increased concern was over the need for the Church to protect itself from attack. As Schauer points out, Boccaccio's *Decameron* was placed on the Church's list of forbidden books, not because of its sexual content but because of the identity of those who were sexually active. In a later edition, when the clergy was changed to the laity, monks to conjurors, nuns to noble women, an abbess to a countess, and the archangel Gabriel to a fairy king, the book was no longer forbidden.[8]

Although Schauer finds an increase in public demand for limits on obscenity that did not touch on religion or politics in the last part of the seventeenth century, he says the courts were not in line with the movement, rejecting the prosecution of a purely sexual book in the first decade of the eighteenth century. In 1727, a conviction was upheld for publishing a book titled *Venus in the Cloister or the Nun in Her Smock,* a book about lesbianism in a convent.[9] Though the book was still religious in terms of the actors, Schauer suggests that the religion factor is insignificant, since the actors were Roman Catholic rather than clergy of the Church of England.[10] Although he cites a reasonable basis for that conclusion in the comments of one of the judges, the Catholic Church and the Church of England may not have been so far apart, other than in their views on the pope, as to lessen the impact on the officially recognized church. On the other hand, the work was translated from a French work written as a Protestant tract.[11] And the attorney general at trial argued that there was a common-law offense to be found in that which, separately from an attack on religion, is against morality, arguing not that all immoral acts are indictable but that those that are destructive of morality in general and affect all the king's subjects are offenses of a public nature properly addressed by the courts.[12]

Schauer counts about three obscenity prosecutions per year through the first half of the nineteenth century,[13] still seemingly a rather small number. The great increase in prosecutions occurred in the United States in the latter part of that nineteenth century. There seemed to be little public call for limits through the Civil War, but in 1872 Anthony Comstock began political and prosecutorial activities that over the next forty years led to the destruction of 160 tons of obscene material and the imprisonment of over thirty-six hundred persons.[14]

The question then becomes one of why sexual images have been treated the way they have in these eras. I argue that the differences are explainable in terms of the impact of sexual images as statements regarding the place of humans between the divine and the animals. In a culture in which the gods were themselves sexual creatures, there was no debasement of humans in depicting them in sexual situations. Once God becomes a singular, nonsexual being, showing humans in sexual acts is depicting humans as on the animal side of a divine/animal divide. This, at first, cuts mostly against the depiction of clergy in sexual acts. Whatever may be the status of the common person, the clergy must be held out as more godly. Sinning laypeople in the *Decameron* may be acceptable, but sinning priests and nuns were not.

As humans start to find our place in nature, during the Enlightenment, we became more comfortable with our, at least partially, animalistic nature. Darwin, however, later was taken by some people as telling us that we are nothing but animals. It is that revelation that came with the great increase in obscenity prosecutions, particularly in the late nineteenth through the first half of the twentieth centuries in the United States. It is as though society expressed itself in denial of Darwin's claims by proscribing the depiction of humans engaged in animal or such nondivine activities.

This recasting of the treatment of pornography and obscenity indicates that obscenity is not really all about sex. It is about the placement of humankind in the hierarchy of the animal, humanity, and the divine. It is about degrading humankind not only to less than divine but to something that is in a sense less that human, an activity shared with the animals.

Harry Clor expresses a view that is in accord with this approach. He says that obscenity is "a degradation of the human dimensions of life to a subhuman or merely physical level."[15] That clearly is a denial of the higher order of humanity and a reduction to the animal level. With regard to public display, Clor suggests that we bar from public view acts that are governed by animal urges, rather than the human spirit, or at least acts for which the observer will experience only the subhuman aspect.

> There are certain bodily acts which will tend to arouse disgust in an observer who is not involved in the act and is not, at the time, subject to its urgencies. What the observer sees is a human being governed by physiological urges and functions. Now, to the participants, the act . . . can have important personal and supra-biological meanings. But the outside observer cannot share the experience of these meanings; what he sees is simply the biological process.[16]

That is, we see the act on the animal level, not on the human level and certainly not as an aspect of the divine. .

If obscenity is about degradation, what should be its focus today? Most of us are comfortable with our sexual side. We also recognize ourselves as being animals, even if we hold out aspects that distinguish us from the rest of the animal kingdom. Sex may no longer be degrading in the sense just presented. So what does depict a person as less than human? I contend that racist, sexist, and homophobic speech do. They clearly state a belief in inferiority, a position that the target is, in some sense, less than fully human. Hate speech may be, if not in a legal sense, then at least in a conceptual sense, today's obscene depictions. At least, however, it offends for the reasons that obscene material offended in the past.

If hate speech is today's equivalent of obscenity, or is offensive for the same reason that obscenity offends, then the body of law that has grown up around obscenity may provide insight into the analysis of speech that may or may not qualify as hate speech. Obscenity has been the law of offensive degradation. If society wishes to sanction what is the current offensive degradation, hate speech, then some guidance in that effort may be found in obscenity law. That is the focus of the second half of this book. The legal test for obscenity, with factors addressing intent, offensiveness, and value, is applied to incidents of potential hate speech. In addition, the obscenity doctrine that finds objectionable material presented to children that might be acceptable for adults is examined in the context of racist, sexist, and homophobic speech.

The conclusion is not that hate speech should necessarily receive the same legal treatment as obscene speech; that is, this effort is not a call for legal sanctions against hate speech. It does, however, recognize the possibility that such proscriptions may at some future time come to exist and, if that happens, provides guidance for the application of the future law. Additionally, there are treatments of hate speech outside any criminal restrictions. Among the most common are limits on speech in the workplace. Looking at what makes obscenity objectionable may provide insight into which workplace incidents should lead to the loss of a job or some other penalty. Whatever choices society may make regarding the sanctioning of hate speech, careful analysis is required to make sure that the sanctions are reasonably applied. It is my hope that the examination of obscenity law provides some framework for that analysis.

2

Pornography, Life, and the Gods in the Greek and Roman Eras

The noted journalist and author David Loth begins his discussion of pornography in the ancient world by saying, "For as long as man has had literature he has had pornography but most of the time he didn't know it. Among the ancients sex was unashamedly joyous, in reading as in practice."[1] Although the passage applies to even older civilizations, Loth is also addressing the Greek and Roman worlds. The point might be made instead by saying that, though there was a recognition that the material was pornographic, there was none of the shame or disapproval that is the hallmark of obscenity. Pornographic images celebrated sex, and therefore they were not hidden away. As art historian Peter Webb puts it, in concluding his section on the classical world, "The Classical world celebrated the joys of love-making as a vital, guilt-free, and often sacred activity, and to this end they devoted much of their finest literature, painting, sculpture, and decorative art."[2]

What was it about the classical cultures that led to this wide acceptance of sex and sexual depictions? Although we may now have come again to a fairly widespread acceptance, there was an extended period, after the end of the classical era, in which there was lesser acceptance. That is not to say that pornography disappeared, but public art became less sexual, and sex and pornography came to be accompanied by a shame that was not present for the Greeks and Romans. To see the basis for the change, I first look to art, sex, and religion in Greece and Rome.

The Greek Arts

The sculpture and pottery of classical Greece often conveyed a pornographic theme. Vases and other forms of pottery were decorated with sexual scenes. Given the continued existence of over thirty thousand Attic vases and the likelihood that most did not survive, it seems no exaggeration to suggest that the output was, as Robert Sutton puts it, "comparable in relative scale to contemporary mass-market media."[3] Interestingly, most of the output of sexually explicit pottery seems originally to have been exported to the Etruscans.[4] Nonetheless, the home population also fully accepted sexual scenes and were themselves consumers of the products.

The major difference between these pieces and modern "adult material" is more technological than thematic. Although the classical pieces lack the animation of a film, their subject matter is the same and is as varied. Pieces of pottery still in existence serve as examples. A cup found in the Louvre is said by Peter Webb to depict "a wild orgy with various types of intercourse depicted in vivid detail."[5] An accompanying photo justifies the description, with scenes of females in congress with two male partners. Even accepting the claim of Kenneth Dover that vase painters who showed two or more couples having intercourse in the same scene may have been engaging in some form of pictorial convention,[6] the sexual activity among the individual pairs, or more accurately threesomes, is explicit. Dover provides other descriptions and photos of vases, cups, and bowls depicting characters with exaggerated erect phalluses and cavorting in rites honoring the god Dionysus.

The role these pieces of pottery played is of interest. Clearly, they may have been part of Dionysian rites. No less would be expected of a phallic cult and a concern for fertility. In addition to these cultic rites, it has been suggested by Harvey Alan Shapiro that the pottery was intended for "all-male symposia," a lofty title for the stag parties that they seem to have been.[7] Webb also notes that pottery was the most common gift given in Greece and suggests that many of these gifts would have been given by men to hetaerae, the courtesans of the era.[8] A natural theme for such a gift would focus on sexual intercourse. On the other hand, it has been claimed by UK barrister, author, and parliamentarian H. Montgomery Hyde that similar representations of various forms of sexual intercourse were found "even . . . on the bottoms of children's drinking bowls and plates, so that they could have something amusing to look at when they were having their meals."[9] Further, the Danish scholar Poul Gerhard provides photos of two Attic cups from the period 490–480 BCE as evidence for the claim that ordinary domestic articles were decorated with pornography.[10] Whatever the uses of the pottery, they seem to bear out the claim of Webb that "[l]ove and its sexual expression were vitally important to the Greeks and did not involve feelings of shame."[11]

The literature of the time was also rather open regarding sex. Greek society was very tolerant of sexual themes in the arts. As D. H. Lawrence reportedly said, "some of Aristophanes shocks everybody today, and didn't galvanize the later Greeks at all."[12] This is hardly surprising, given the origins of Greek drama in the festivals honoring Dionysius, festivals centered on fertility, with phalluses in prominence, and often developing into orgies.[13] Although the content of the plays does not contain the explicit material of a modern adult film or even of the pottery of the time, they are sometimes somewhat bawdy. That can be seen in Aristophanes's plays *Lysistrata* and *The Clouds.*

There are, of course, somewhat differing translations of Aristophanes's *Lysistrata,* but the plot concerns an agreement by the women of Greece to refrain from sex with the men, until the men reach a peace agreement among the city-states. In Douglass Parker's translation,[14] in one scene, the male and female characters all remove their tunics.[15] Although they do appear to have still worn undergarments, not wearing tunics would have made the situation more obvious later in the play when Kinesias staggers onto stage "in erection and considerable pain."[16] The males in the chorus are similarly affected, and a variety of characters end up on the stage trying to conceal their states of excitation. When a delegation from Sparta arrives, they show that they are in the same state by throwing their cloaks open, exposing their phalluses.[17] The play also personifies Peace in the person of "a beautiful girl without a stitch on," who, when she appears, contributes further to the men's excited condition.[18]

In Robert Henning Webb's translation,[19] when a Spartan herald arrives in Athens, an Athenian official asks the herald if he is Priapus in the flesh and goes on to suggest that the Spartan is hiding a weapon under his cloak. When the herald is asked about the state of things in Sparta, he replies, "Shparta iss rampant . . . ja, und her allies . . . Dere iss a gross uprising eferyvere!"[20] When a group of ambassadors later arrives from Sparta, the Chorus asks about their condition. The Spartans throw open their cloaks and respond, "Vy do you esk? Vat need of vords to zay? Your eyess kann tell you how it shtands mit us!"[21] The Athenians, in response, throw their cloaks open, showing that they share the same discomfort. Rather than Peace, in the Webb translation the goddess Appeasement appears "clothed in smiles."[22]

Lysistrata is not the only play with such sexual content. In William Arrowsmith's translation of Aristophanes's *The Clouds,* the character Strepsiades at one point is said to raise his phallus to the ready.[23] Later the same character repeats his action while threatening another character with, "I'll sunder your rump with my ram!"[24] In both cases the reference to a phallus is not to an actual phallus but to a symbolic leather thong the actor wore. Arrowsmith does point out that there is dispute over whether the actor did actually wear a thong, but he believes the text makes sense only if such a prop was employed.[25] The argument that there was no phallus worn is based on the appearance of Aristophanes as a character earlier in the play,[26] when he delivers a monologue in which he describes the play: "She's a dainty play. Observe, gentlemen, her natural modesty, the demureness of her dress, with no dangling thong of leather, red and thick at the tip, to make small boys snigger."[27] Even if a thong was not employed in *The Clouds,* the demureness claimed by Aristophanes seems to have been meant as counterpoint to the common usage of the leather phallus in other Greek plays.

Later in *The Clouds,* the characters Philosophy and Sophistry are rolled onto the stage in large gilded cages. They are described as human from the shoulders down and fighting cocks from the neck up. Arrowsmith again recognizes a debate over their form, but the contention seems to center on whether the characters had any nonhuman aspects.[28] As far as the human portions are concerned, Philosophy is described as "large, muscular . . . , powerful but not heavy, expressing in his movements that inward harmony and grace and dignity which the Old Education was meant to produce."[29] Sophistry, by contrast, is "comparatively slight, with sloping shoulders, an emaciated pallor, an enormous tongue and a disproportionately large phallus."[30]

Bella Zweig, in her study of Aristophanes's plays, describes a number of scenes, including a scene in which an adolescent female displays her genitals to an older man, who "paws the girl's breasts and genitals while . . . negotiate[ing] her price" and another in which a male character handles "the goods," two young nude females in piglet masks, as he negotiates their price.[31] Zweig concludes, seemingly quite reasonably, that "[i]f these were contemporary scenes, there would be little doubt that they were culled from pornographic movies." She does note that male actors clad in padded costumes that included breasts and buttocks may have played the female roles,[32] which might have detracted from the pornographic impact, without affecting the literary pornographic content. She also notes, however, that the roles may have been played by hetaerae,[33] and she says, "The characters that represent desirable abstractions, such as Treaties, Peace, or Reconciliation, would hardly be subject to the ridicule that a costumed male actor would naturally evoke. A real hetaira, nude or suggestively dressed, and who already embodies male sexual fantasies, would more aptly dramatize the pleasurable attainability of the personified goal."[34] She concludes that there was nothing preventing hetaerae from playing these roles and that given the comedic enhancement achieved by females in the roles, it is equally imaginable that women did play these nude characters.[35]

Although it has been noted that Aristophanes's play *Lysistrata* was subject to customs seizure during the first thirty years of the twentieth century and was considered obscene by the U.S. Post Office, as recently as 1955,[36] it was most likely not a result of the language of the script itself but of plates that often accompanied the play and depicted some of the scenes. Nonetheless, it shows how bawdy some performances of the play may have been.

Adding to the sexual depictions in art and the sexual content of literature, phallic symbols seemed to be ubiquitous in ancient Greece. They could be found on street corners, where people could pray for fertility,[37] and it seems, as Richard Posner concludes, that "every Athenian home had a statue of Hermes, with his penis erect, before its front door."[38] These phalluses played an important religious role. Phallic worship may have come from the Egyptians,[39] but it was not uncommon among other early religions. In Dionysian rites, giant wooden phalluses were carried in procession to the temple and would be straddled by nude women attempting to assure fertility.[40]

This mix of religion and sex was also present in temples to the goddess Aphrodite. The temple in Corinth was said to have had in excess of one thousand hetaerae dedicated to the goddess, and the city grew rich off the visitors who came to avail themselves of the pleasures to be found there. This was not just commercial sex, since, according to Vern Bullough, "[i]f the girls prostituted themselves for money, part of which they donated to the temple treasury, this . . . could be an act of piety since it was a thanks-offering to the goddess of female beauty, maturity, and fruitfulness."[41]

Greek Life

The acceptance by the Greeks of pornography in the arts and strongly sexual themes in drama may be seen as mirroring their views on sexual activity in real life. It is important to recognize that most of what is known about Greek sexual custom is really the custom of Athens, with some additional knowledge of Sparta.[42] It is also possible that there is some skewing from the fact that our knowledge comes from literature and the arts, which, as Posner has pointed out, may reflect life in the intellectual and artistic subculture and may not be reflective of even Athenian society as a whole.[43] Nonetheless, it seems accepted that, as H. Montgomery Hyde says, "the Greeks thoroughly enjoyed sex in all its sundry manifestations and felt not the slightest sense of shame about it."[44]

The conclusion that the Greeks were so sexually free is actually applicable only to males and noncitizen or slave females. The females of the citizen class did not enjoy the same freedoms. Among the citizen class, girls were kept at home, while the boys attended school at the gymnasium. A citizen girl remained at home until she entered an arranged marriage that was seen as a contract between the girl's father and her husband to be.[45] After marriage, she lived in her husband's home, again remaining in the home except for religious or other special occasions. There seemed, then, little opportunity for citizen females to engage in premarital or extramarital sex, and indeed, if such sex did occur and was discovered while in progress, the father of the girl or husband of the woman could kill the adulterer without penalty or could recover damages or have the violator prosecuted.[46] The honor of men was heavily invested in the chastity of the women of their households.[47] Despite these restrictions, it is suggested by David Cohen that "some women were thought to buy the favors of young men, and some men to acquiesce in the financial advantage they might gain from their wives' infidelity."[48]

So, with females so sequestered, how did males gain the reputation for such openly sexual behavior? After all, the boys of the citizen class were also kept from their counterpart females, and marriage occurred later in life for males than for females. The key is that the restrictions did not apply to noncitizen females. Males had other outlets. There was a slave class in Greek society, and slaves could be used for sexual purposes. There were also prostitutes and the higher-class courtesans, or hetaerae. ·

The Greek male had few restrictions. Demosthenes is said to have said, "We keep courtesans as mistresses for pleasure. . . . Whores we pay for daily service, but wives we have for legitimate child bearing and looking after our domestic property reliably."[49] If a man was married, his duties to his wife did not include fidelity. He had to provide support for his wife, engage in sexual relations with her,[50] and not bring another woman into the household.[51] Beyond that, married and single men were free to satisfy their sexual urges, as long as their sexual partners were not the daughters or wives of citizens. There were taboos against incest, laws protecting young children, and what amounted to property rights for citizens regarding the women of their household, but most other activities were acceptable.[52]

A word should be said about the hetaerae. They seem to have been more sophisticated than citizens' wives, hardly surprising given the sequestered life the daughters and wives of citizens led. In addition to sexual sophistication, they were likely to be artistically and intellectually superior to the higher-class wife.[53] These hetaerae are also the women who are known from the era, with history having recorded their names, while making little to no note of the women who were citizens.[54] They were also often of great beauty. It is said that when the hetaerae Phryne of Thespiae was put on trial for the capital offense of corrupting the youth of Athens, her advocate became concerned that he was losing the case. He had her stand up in court, and he then tore off her robe to, as Hyde describes it, expose "her beautiful breasts and figure . . . to the public view."[55] Such beauty convinced the judges that the defendant had been divinely endowed by Aphrodite, and they found her not guilty. Reportedly, following her acquittal, a decree was promulgated prohibiting the introduction of such evidence by advocates in any future cases.[56]

With marriage some years away, the one outlet available to citizen youths for sexual relations with someone of the same social class was a homosexual relationship,[57] and the Greeks considered the desire of unmarried men and youths for boys and of unmarried men for youths to be a natural desire.[58] There were, of course, homosexual opportunities to be found with male slaves and prostitutes, but the children of citizens, the gymnasium boys, were also possible targets for seduction.[59] The homosexual relationship presented no problem for the older and presumably aggressive partner, but it was another matter for the younger, submissive youth or boy. Playing the submissive role did not fit well with future citizenship. The submissive partner's role was not bragged about, could not continue into the manhood of a citizen, and was minimized by the use of standing interfemoral intercourse.[60] If, however, the boy, or for that matter a man, accepted money for his participation, he would lose his citizenship rights.[61]

The Gods and Sex

The sexual activities of the people of classical Greece were matched, or perhaps exceeded, by the sexual exploits of the Greek gods. Zeus, the mightiest of the gods, was a rapist and adulterer. As already seen, prostitution in some cases had a religious significance, as when practiced at the temple of Aphrodite. Certainly, any festivals dedicated to the god Dionysus are reasonably characterized by David Loth as "wild sex orgies."[62] Sex went well with religion.

The gods of the classical Greek era were not like the modern God of the Christian, Jewish, or Islamic worlds.[63] In the first place, while the "always will be" nature of the existence of monotheism's God may have been believed to apply to the Greek gods, the "always was" part, especially in terms of supremacy, was not present. The gods were actually a third iteration. The first "beings" were Mother Earth, or Gaea, and Father Heaven, or Ouranos, who have been characterized as not really seeming to have been alive.[64] They were followed by the Titans, or the Elder Gods, who were said to have been of great strength and of enormous size. They were led by Cronus and his sister/

queen Rhea. Eventually Cronus was overthrown by his son Zeus. The Titans were then banished, with the exceptions of Atlas and Prometheus, who had taken the side of Zeus in his battle with Cronus.

Cronus had obviously not been omnipotent, another difference with the later Christian view of God. Neither, it seems, was Zeus. At least when it came to his relations with the other gods, Zeus may have been the leader, but he was not in complete control. In various instances, he and other gods took different sides, some helping one human faction, and others another in a battle among those humans. Zeus also seems to have been somewhat in fear of his wife/sister Hera, who took revenge on the various lovers of Zeus. Although the revenge was always taken on the lover, rather than on Zeus, Zeus did not have the power to stop her, other than through his guile or by taking steps to counter her actions.

Although Zeus may have been the chief god, there were a number of other major gods. Of course, there was Hera, his sister and wife. Zeus and Hera also had offspring, Ares and Hebe. Athena was said to have been the daughter of Zeus alone, not the daughter of Zeus and someone other than Hera but actually the daughter of Zeus alone, having sprung from him full grown. Hephaestus, the god of the forge, was also possibly of single parentage, being either the son of Zeus and Hera or of Hera alone.[65]

Other gods were also offspring of Zeus. Aphrodite is sometimes said to have been the daughter of Zeus and Leto, a daughter of the Titans Phoebe and Coeus, but it is also sometimes said that she sprang from the foam of the sea.[66] Whatever may have been her origin, she later married Hephaestus, who may have been a half brother, a stepbrother, or of no relation. Apollo and his twin sister, Artemis, were also said to be the children of Zeus and Leto. Another god, Hermes, was the son of Zeus and Maia, who was the daughter of the Titan Atlas.

There were also other siblings of Zeus and Hera among the Olympians. Poseidon, the god of the sea, was the brother of Zeus and Hera. He married Amphitrite, the daughter of the Titan Ocean. Poseidon was also said to have a human lover, Tyro, who bore him twin sons. Hades, the god of the underworld, was another brother of Zeus. He, too, was married; his wife, Persephone, was the daughter of Demeter, who was herself the daughter of Cronus. Hades would then seem to have married his niece, hardly shocking in a world ruled by a brother and sister who were also husband and wife. Hestia, or Vesta among the Roman gods, was yet another sibling. She was the goddess of the hearth and was, like Athena and Artemis, a virgin goddess. The combination explains the Roman Vestal virgins tending the sacred fire.

There were also a number of lesser gods. Eros was the son of Aphrodite. Hebe, mentioned earlier, was the goddess of youth. She married Hercules, who was said to be the son of the human general Amphitryon but who was "in reality" the son of Zeus and Alcmene, the wife of Amphitryon.[67] Dionysius and Castor, and perhaps Pollux, may also be considered to be among the lesser gods.[68]

This complex family life presents a different setting from the life of a single and omnipotent God. The Greek gods had husbands and wives, as well as offspring. They were clearly sexual creatures, and the fact that humans are also sexual creatures would not serve to distinguish humans from the gods. Human sexuality would not place humanity on the side of the animals and strongly differentiate humans from the divine, since there was no such divide between the gods and even the animals. Of course, what may be best established is that the gods had sexual relations within marriage. That would differentiate them from the animals and could lead to the conclusion that marital sex did not put humans on the animal side of a divine/animal split, but it might have said little about sex outside marriage.

The response to that limitation is already seen, somewhat, in the previously discussed offspring of Zeus with Maia and Leto. But Zeus was a far more promiscuous figure than the few relationships already presented indicate. Many Greek myths have as a subject the dalliances of Zeus and the acts of jealousy those relations inspired in Hera.

One of the better-known legends is the relationship between Zeus and Leda. Leda was the wife of the king of Sparta, with whom she had two mortal children, Castor and Clytemnestra, who later became the wife of Agamemnon. Zeus visited her in the form of a swan, and from that interspecies (or inter-god-human) sexual relationship resulted Helen of Troy and Pollux.[69] Here, too, not only was the chief god a sexual being but the relationship was with a human. Furthermore, the god took the form of an animal in order to enter into the sexual relationship. The sex act was one of god and human but also, in a strong sense, involved an animal. A culture with such a legend cannot have seen much difference between humanity and the divine, nor with the animals, when it came to sexual activity. Sex certainly could not be seen to differentiate humans from the gods, when the act was between a human and a god. It also could not speak to a divine/animal divide, in which sex served to differentiate the two, when the god took the form of an animal to engage in the sexual relation.

To recount just a few other relations between Zeus and human women, Zeus had relations with Aegina, resulting in a son named Aeacus, and with

Alcmene, resulting in Hercules. There was also Semele, a princess of Thebes, resulting in the god Dionysus, the only god without two divine parents.[70] Zeus's relationship with Aniope, another princess of Thebes, resulted in Amphion and Zethus. Amphion later married Niobe, the daughter of Tantalus, the founder of the royal house of Atreus and said to be another mortal child of Zeus, although we are not told by whom.[71]

Some of these additional relations of Zeus also involved interspecies, or even god-human-animal acts. Zeus changed Io, described as a princess, into a white heifer in order to hide his relationship from Hera. (He does eventually change her back into human form.) Zeus changes himself into a bull in order to carry off Europa, the daughter of the king of Sidon, to Crete. In another case of a human changed to an animal, Hera changes Callisto into a bear, after Callisto's son Arcas is born of Zeus. Hera later brings the bear/human Callisto into contact with a grown Arcas, hoping that Arcas will kill her. Zeus counters Hera with another transformation, this time not by changing them between animal and human but by changing them both into star formations, Callisto into the Great Bear, Ursa Major, and Arcas into the Little Bear, Ursa Minor.[72]

Animals, People, Gods, and Mixes Thereof

Zeus's practice of changing into a swan or a bull and the metamorphosis, at the hands of Zeus or Hera, of humans to heifers or bears are not the only examples of gods or humans changing to some other form. Other humans who were turned into animals include Nisus and Scylla, a father and daughter who were both turned into birds. Humans even turned into plants. Clytie pined for the sun god and was changed into the sunflower,[73] which turns to follow the sun across the sky. Dryope, seemingly as punishment for having harmed a tree, grows bark and roots, becoming a tree.[74] There were also humans who became gods. Glaucus, a fisherman, turned into a sea god with a body ending in the tail of a fish.[75] Tithonus, the husband of Aurora, goddess of the dawn, was made immortal by Zeus at Aurora's request; although in an ironic turn he was not given the attribute of remaining youthful.

Even these examples may not be the strongest demonstration of the blurred lines between god, human, and animal. They were, after all, changes from one form to another. Better examples may be found in beings that were some combination of gods, humans, and animals. There are a number of examples of entities that were part god and part animal, which or who have been included as among the lesser gods.[76] The Gorgons were dragonlike, with two of the three of them being immortal.[77] The satyrs, including Pan, the son of Hermes, were part god and part animal as well, having goat horns and hooves.[78] The centaurs were half human and half horse but are included among the lesser gods.[79] Of the centaurs, only Chiron appears to have been immortal, and even he was allowed by Zeus to die because of permanent suffering from being accidentally wounded by Hercules.[80]

There were also mixes of humans and animals. The Selini were part human and part horse. They walked on two legs, but the legs had the hooves of horses, and they had horse ears and tails. The Minotaur was half bull and half human, the result of a sexual relationship between Pasiphae and a bull. The Sphinx was said to have had the shape of a winged lion but the breast and face of a woman.[81] Somewhat hard to place is Erechtheus, the first king of Attica. It is said that he lacked human ancestry and that his form was only half human.[82] It is also said that he was born of a dragon, that his lower half was that of a dragon,[83] and that he was the son of Hephaestus and was raised by Athena.[84] From this, it seems unclear what combination of god, human, and animal is properly assigned to him.

There were also mixtures of differing animals. For example, Pegasus was a winged horse who sprang from the blood of a Gorgon. But combinations of animal species seem less troubling. They do not blur the lines between god and animal or human and animal, and they do not then have anything to say about the relationship between humanity and the divine.

The greatest human heroes were often of divine ancestry. Achilles, the Greek hero of the Trojan War, was descended from the gods on both sides. His mother was Thetis, who was a Nereid, a water nymph considered to be among the gods of the waters. His father was King Peleus, who was a grandson of Zeus by Aegina.[85] Achilles was the slayer of the Trojan Hector and Prince Memnon of Ethiopia, who was himself the son of the goddess of the dawn.[86] Although Achilles was mortal, he was almost invulnerable. He eventually was wounded fatally in the heel, the one part not protected by his mother's almost total immersion of her child in the River Styx. Aeneas, a hero of the other side said to be outshone only by Hector, was also the son of a goddess, this time Aphrodite.[87] Though on the losing side, he escapes with the help of Aphrodite and, after a journey that rivals that of Odysseus, lands in Italy and founds the city of Rome.

Not only did the descendents of gods engage in the combat of the Trojan War; the gods themselves at least took sides. Not surprisingly, Aphrodite was on the side of the Trojans, as were Ares, Apollo, and Artemis. Hera, Athena, and Poseidon sided with the Greeks. Zeus, favoring the Trojans but fearful of disagreeing with Hera, took a largely neutral stance.[88] Ares, the god of war, rather than settling for cheering for his chosen side, actually engages in combat. He was driven back to Olympus, after being bloodied by Diomedes, who would have been unable to defeat the god without the help of Athena.[89]

The royal houses of Greek city-states also found their origins in the gods.[90] The royal House of Thebes, the family of Creon, Oedipus, and Antigone, was descended from Zeus, through his union with Io. Zeus later entered the family tree again; his union with Semele produced Dionysus, a cousin of Oedipus through both of Oedipus's parents, Laius and Jocasta. The House of Atreus, the family that produced Agamemnon, Menelaus (whose loss of Helen to Paris started the Trojan War), Orestes, and Electra, also found its origin in Zeus. The family descended through Tantalus, a son of Zeus. Turning to Athens, the first king of Attica is, somewhat disputedly,[91] said to be Cecrops, the half man, half dragon, thought to have had no human ancestor, without any mention of what his ancestry was, or alternatively thought to have been an ordinary man.

The split between the human and the divine is again blurred. The difference between human and god seems almost to be quantitative, rather than qualitative. There are gods, and there are humans, but there also those who are descendants of gods and humans. Those hybrids are better than humans; they are stronger, braver, and larger than life. They are also the founders of the royal houses, and through the veins of their descendants godly blood flows. These descendants of the gods, and indeed the gods themselves, do not behave differently from ordinary persons. They are simply more epic in their actions.

Another interesting aspect of the culture of Greece, speaking to this lack of strong lines between humans and animals, if not between the gods and either other group, is the tradition of animal fables. The most well-known fabulist was Aesop.[92] His fables involve animals of various sorts displaying human characteristics. Some, such as "The Ant and the Grasshopper," simply demonstrate, through the animal figures, characteristics that would be beneficial or harmful for humans. In that fable, the grasshopper spends the warmer months frivolously, while the ant is hard at work, storing up food for the winter. When winter comes, the grasshopper has no food and is in danger of starvation. When it asks the ant for help, it is rebuked for its lack of industriousness. The animals serve only as stand-ins for the human virtue of hard work as opposed to idleness, and the blurring of the human/animal line is rather limited.

"The Tortoise and the Hare" makes a similar point. In that fable, the tortoise, in response to ridicule from the hare, challenges the hare to a race.

When the hare takes an early, and seemingly commanding, lead, it decides to take a nap. While the hare is asleep, the slow but steady tortoise passes him and wins the race. Again, there is not much attribution of human characteristics, but there is the lesson that a steady effort may be more successful than a stronger but intermittent performance.

Another fable that comes closer to attributing human characteristics to animals is the fable of "The Fox and the Grapes." In it, the fox makes a number of attempts to reach grapes hanging on a high vine. When the fox's attempts all fail, the fox concludes that the grapes are sour anyhow. The fox, therefore, copes with his failure in the way a human might.

Other fables show planning by animals that seems human in its design. In "The Fox and the Crow," the crow is on a branch eating a piece of cheese it has found. The fox hatches a plan to obtain the cheese for himself. He flatters the crow, and once the crow's ego is sufficiently inflated, the fox requests to hear a song. When the crow begins to sing, the cheese falls from its mouth and is eaten by the fox. "The Mice in Council," from which the phrase "to bell the cat" comes, involves forward-looking planning by mice to protect themselves from the cat by putting a bell around the cat's neck, which would warn them when it came near. The fable also shows another human characteristic, when there is reluctance of all the mice to perform the potentially fatal and certainly difficult task.

The gods even play a role in the fables. In "The Frogs Who Desired a King," a group of frogs become discontented by their seemingly happy and peaceful life. They believe life would be better with a king to rule over them and ask Zeus to send them such a ruler. Zeus puts a large log in the pond and tells them that it is to be their king. The frogs fear their king but soon discover that it is inert. They tell Zeus they need a king that moves, and he sends them a large stork that proceeds to devour them. When they call on Zeus to save them, he tells them that they have to face the consequences of what they requested. While also involving the gods, the fable demonstrates the human characteristics of the inability to leave well enough alone and teaches the lesson of being careful what you wish for.

This may seem like a topic with an at best tenuous connection to the thesis of this chapter, but it has more relevance than at first appears. Joyce Salisbury, in her work *The Beast Within: Animals in the Middle Ages*, says that "[i]t is most likely that any society that sees a close relationship between humans and animals, that sees a parallel between species, will produce fable-type stories that explore the metaphorical relationship."[93] This, then, is further evidence that, in the view of the Greeks, there were not significant differences in character not only between the gods and humans but also between humans and animals. All three shared characteristics, and neither sex nor the depiction of sex served to place a chasm between the gods and humans and to put humans more in alignment with the animal than the divine.

Roman Life and Arts

Roman society borrowed heavily from the Greek, with some facets derived from the Etruscans, so it is not unexpected that their attitudes toward sex, both in life and in the arts, were similar to those of the Greeks. In the theater, sexual themes were treated with at least as much toleration as in Greece. Richard Beacham, in his study of Roman drama, finds similarities between the performances given by Etruscan actors in Rome and the Greek phallica, phallic ceremonies aimed at assuring fertility.[94] He also points to the existence of the oversized phalluses of terra-cotta figures similar to the Greek examples and found in areas of Italy colonized by the Greeks, concluding that in early Rome there were performances of suggestive dances of the variety he characterizes as found at modern "stag-parties."[95]

Later Rome continued in its liberal treatment of sex. Beacham says that the Floralia festival performances were known for their license and naked female performers.[96] The treatment of sex in the theater seems, in fact, to have gone beyond the Greeks. Beacham reports on the faithful reenactment in late Roman theater of the story of Pasiphae concealing herself in a false cow so as to be mounted by a bull.[97] He also says that, in the third century, it was ordered that all sexual scenes in performances be actually performed, rather than simulated.[98] Posner makes a similar assertion regarding the Roman theater, noting that "[w]omen appeared on the stage, as actresses and dancers, often in the nude and sometimes performing sexual acts."[99]

As with the Greeks, the Romans mixed the arts, religion, and fertility. The Romans, too, had an annual fertility festival, the Liberalia, involving a huge phallus carried on a chariot and crowned with a flower garland, with the procession followed by a sexual orgy.[100] The frescoes of Pompeii depict all varieties of sexual intercourse,[101] and that decor was not limited to brothels. Peter Webb says that "[t]he walls of the Imperial Banqueting Hall in Nero's Golden Palace were decorated by the finest artists in Rome with scenes of couples making love. The Emperor Tiberius had his palace on Capri hung with erotic pictures."[102] Both brothels and "respectable" dwellings contained erotic paintings,[103] and there seems not to have been a difference in erotic content in the two venues.[104] There was also a domestic industry producing pornography, centered around the city of Arezzo.[105] The subject matter of all this material may have carried over from the Greeks, who occupied parts of Italy,[106] but it is also clear that the Etruscans had their own erotic arts, perhaps themselves influenced by their Greek contemporaries,[107] and the two sources may have influenced the Roman era.

The literature of the Roman era also had its sexual side, with two of the best-known extant works being focused on sex. A description of Ovid's *The Art of Love* again shows the treatment of love and sex as joyous and unshameful. Hyde says that *The Art of Love* "has been described as perhaps the most immoral work ever written by a man of genius, though it cannot be called by any means the most demoralizing, since it is entirely free from any morbid feelings."[108] Perhaps the acceptance of this sort of literature is called into question by the fact that the emperor Augustus banished Ovid from Rome. Augustus seems to have had at least stronger moral pretensions than others of the time, but he may have been more influenced by his belief that Ovid's writings had led to rebellion by his daughter Julia.[109] After the deaths of two of Julia's husbands, the results of arranged marriages, Augustus tried to force a third marriage to his stepson, whose divorce he had forced to that end.[110] When Julia refused, Augustus seems to have blamed Ovid. It has also been suggested that Augustus was motivated by a concern that Ovid's work would undermine marriage, an institution he had been trying to promote as a matter of public policy.[111] The first explanation would not speak to a distaste for this sort of literature, and the second seems to be a concern over secondary effects.

Whereas *The Art of Love* is more a guide to seduction, Petronius's *Satyricon,* also a classic of the era, is more purely pornographic. Again in the words of Hyde, "the *Satyricon* is unsurpassed on the seamy side of Roman provincial life in the first century of the Christian era. The author describes in considerable detail, which leaves little to the imagination, every sexual deviation from oral copulation . . . to sodomy . . . and the defloration of little girls."[112]

The actual sex life of the Romans was at least as open as, and on some fronts more open than, that of the Greeks. The pederastic culture of the Greeks was not to be found in Rome, but it was less a necessity, since Roman women were not sequestered as Greek women were. Although married women were expected to remain faithful, men were not. Married women were out in the world, however, and were, according to Posner, even sometimes said to "have had a considerable and frequently indulged taste for adultery."[113] The increased worldliness of Roman women and their participation in public life also meant that there was not the same need for hetaerae, although these mistresses/courtesans certainly existed in the Roman world too.

The increased availability of women of even the upper social class did not completely eliminate the practice of pederasty. There was both male and female prostitution, commonly centered on bathhouses, which involved both adult and child prostitutes, so homosexual acts with children did occur.[114] The emperor Hadrian also had a very public relationship with a boy lover named Antinous, and when Antinous died, Hadrian had him deified, and he was widely worshiped.[115] But the cult of pederasty did not carry over from the Greeks.

Turning to the Roman gods, we find analogs to or renaming of the Greek gods.[116] The Romans had their own gods, before adopting the Greek gods, but they seem not to have had the same sort of personalities. As the classicist Edith Hamilton puts it, "It was a simple matter to adopt the Greek gods because the Romans did not have definitely personified gods of their own. They were a people of deep religious feeling, but they had little imagination. They could never have created the Olympians, each with a distinct, vivid personality."[117]

Prior to the adoption of the Greek gods, the Romans had the Numina. The early Romans did not need beautiful and poetic gods but had a group of practical gods with no stories attached, no real personalities, and even no gender identified.[118] There were Numina attached to the various aspects of home life, and families had ancestor spirits to protect the household. Two of the Numina, Saturn, who was associated with planting, and his wife, Ops, who was the harvest helper, eventually became identified with the Titans Cronus and Rhea. From there, it was easy to adopt the rest of the family, with changes of name. Zeus became Jupiter, and Hera became Juno. Poseidon became Neptune; Aphrodite, Venus; Artemis, Diana; and Athena, Minerva. And as already indicated, Hestia became Vesta. Apollo managed to keep his Greek name. Each of the Olympians had a Roman counterpart, coming complete with their personalities and adding a richness to the lives of the gods that had been lacking in earlier Rome. As with the Greek royal houses, there was also a tie between the gods and the legendary founder of Rome; Aeneas was the son of Venus.

For the Romans, then, as for the Greeks, there was a parallel between the lives of their adopted divine immigrants and the lives and arts of the people. The gods were sexual, and the sexual activities of human beings did not, then, serve to distinguish them from the gods. Neither did sexual depictions of humans or the public display of sex serve to depict humankind in a way that might be seen as purely animal and far removed from the divine.

Sex, Pornography, and the Failure to Degrade

Before moving on to a summary of the lessons to be learned from this examination of Greek and Roman culture, there is one cultural movement to be examined. Despite the history of open and celebratory sexuality in the life of the individual and in public art in classical culture, it has been noted that in both Greece and Rome there was a philosophical development that could have led to the renunciation of the sexual attitudes present in those polytheistic cultures. The Stoics led this movement, not so much out of a religious sentiment regarding sex but out of a belief that humankind is better off rejecting sensual pleasures of all sorts and participating in eating, drinking, and sex only to the degree necessary for survival. James Brundage describes this philosophical school:

> The Stoics considered sex a special type of pleasure. Sexual enjoyment was in itself morally indifferent, they believed, but they considered that men make poor use of their time when they occupy their minds with such matters. Sex, like wealth, was not a worthy goal for reasonable adults to seek, and the pursuit for sexual pleasure was not conducive to a healthy morality. . . . The truly wise person . . . cultivated a sober and reserved demeanor; he abstained from sex and other lower concerns, such as eating and drinking, beyond the minimum essential for bodily health.[119]

Many of the Roman legislators were Stoics, and some sexual restrictions did begin to creep into Roman law.[120]

But the views of the Stoics were not the views of the majority. As put by a seeming admirer of the views of the Stoics and of moralists in general, the Irish historian William Lecky,

> [A] broad chasm . . . existed between the Roman moralists and the Roman people. On the one hand we find a system of ethics, of which when we consider the range and beauty of its precepts, the sublimity of the motives to which it appealed, and its perfect freedom from superstitious elements, it is not too much to say that though it may have been equalled, it has never been surpassed. On the other hand, we find a society almost absolutely destitute of moralising institutions, occupations, or beliefs, existing under an economical and political system which inevitably led to general depravity, and passionately addicted to the most brutalising amusements.[121]

Thus, despite any philosophical movement to the contrary, an accepted and open sexuality was a characteristic of Greek and Roman culture. It is an atmosphere that differs starkly from life among the later monotheistic Christians, and it seems to be a difference that is the result of a different view of the nature of the relationship between humans and God or between gods on the one hand and humans and animals on the other. This claim may gain additional backing from the fact that the positions of the Greek moralists had to be preceded by a renunciation of the legendary sexual deeds of the gods.[122] The tie between the behavior of humans and gods was not denied by the moralists. Rather, to make humans more moral or more stoic, to remove human behavior from the camp of the animal, it was necessary also to move the behavior of the gods from that camp. Only then could the argument that humans ought to be more restrained in their sexuality have any force.

This is brought home in an explanation by Roger Scruton of Plato's position on sex and love. In discussing Plato's distinction between erotic love and sexual desire, Scruton says that in Plato's view

> our animal nature is the principal vehicle of sexual desire, and provides its overriding motive. In desire we act and feel as animals; indeed, desire is a motive which all sexual beings—including the majority of animals—share. In erotic love, however, it is our nature as rational beings that is primarily engaged, and, in the exercise of this passion, altogether finer and more durable impulses seek recognition and fulfilment.[123]

For Plato erotic love could flourish only if desire could be eliminated. This view may be seen in the later work of St. Augustine and rests on the human/animal or the divine/human/animal issue at the heart of this book. Plato took a position in favor of separating humans from the animals in order to address his concern, but Plato was not the average Greek. For those who accepted the Greek gods, and for that matter the Roman gods, sex and other pleasures in which the gods engaged would not have been seen in the negative light of the Stoics or of Plato. If not only animals but also gods were sexual, sex could hardly be seen as bad or degrading.

The Greeks' and Romans' tie to the gods, in their emulation of the sexual activities of the gods and in not seeing sex or its depiction as making humans more animal than divine, can also, perhaps, explain the difference between the acceptance of sexual activity of males and that of female citizens in Greek society. Athena, Artemis, and Hestia were all virgin goddesses. Especially in Athens, the city to which Athena was so central and from which we draw much of our understanding of Greek culture, the virginity of Athena could well have led to a difference between males and females with regard to chastity. Males, drawing guidance from the example of Zeus, might have seen an active sex life as godlike and certainly as not degrading themselves to the animal level. Females might have emulated Hera, the queen of the gods. She would have been a different sort of role model. Hera was no Zeus with regard to sexual exploits and was noted mostly for the jealous revenge she inflicted on the lovers of Zeus, but she was not a virgin goddess. She was, of course, the mother of at least some of the children of Zeus, and Athenian women certainly were allowed to be sexual partners to their husbands. There is not really indication of extramarital sexual activity on her part, other than the possibility that Hephaestus was her child alone, at least in the sense of not being the child of Zeus. However, if Athena could be the child of Zeus alone, springing from him full grown, it seems that Hephaestus could be the child of Hera alone. Whatever guidance women might have drawn from a link to Hera, the link to the other goddesses, especially to Athena, would have led to chastity, at least outside marriage. For women, sexual activity could be seen as separating women from the goddesses. Being separated from the goddesses and being identified with animal sexuality instead of divine behavior could have caused female sexuality to be seen as degrading. This discussion of the possible reasons for the difference between the acceptance of male and of female sexuality is not to deny any roots such a difference might have had in males' asserting a property interest in their wives or daughters or in the sexual insecurities of men or in the interest in certainty in parentage for a man's heirs, but it does offer an interesting consideration.

There was no sexually obscene material in Greek and Roman culture. There was a great deal of pornography that was quite explicit in its nature, but obscenity requires more than sex. In the more modern view, obscenity turns on how "hard core" the sex is. But the sexual depictions of Greece were every bit as hard core, at least to the degree that the available technology allowed, so it is not the amount or nature of the sex that made the difference. Pornography becomes obscenity not only when it becomes sufficiently explicit but also when it becomes offensive and when it appeals to a prurient interest. The Supreme Court, in its attempt in *Roth v. United States* to define obscenity, quoted the American Law Institute's Model Penal Code. The Court said it saw no significant difference between case law analysis of the concept and the definition set forth by the ALI, which said, "A thing is obscene if, considered as a whole, its predominant appeal is to prurient interest, i.e., a shameful or morbid interest in nudity, sex, or excretion, and if it goes substantially beyond customary limits of candor in description or representation of such matters."[124]

In Greek and Roman culture, sexual depictions were not offensive and certainly did not appeal to a shameful or morbid interest. What reason for offense would there have been? What would have been shameful or morbid about an interest in such depictions? Although many people would ask the same questions in the current era, in the classical era the religious beliefs of the time make for easy answers: there would not be offense, and the interest would not be shameful.

In antiquity, sex did not serve to distinguish humans from the gods and place them on the animal side of a divine/animal distinction; hence, society did not equate sex and pornography with obscenity or shame. True, at least the more advanced animals are sexual creatures, and true, humans engage in activities that are at least similar to those of the animals. But the gods engaged in the same activities. Sex simply did not define a chasm between the divine and the animal. Without that chasm, the sexual activities of humans did not serve to put humans on a lower level than the gods. Sex did not emphasize any animal, ungodlike nature of humans, and its depiction was not obscene.

If sex did not put humans in the camp with the animals and separate humans from the gods, depictions of human sexuality could not be degrading. Such depictions were simply of activities enjoyed by all but plants and the lower animals. They were not degrading, and without this degradation, there could be pornography, but there could be no obscenity. Sexual depiction could be a part of public art and not the closeted arts of later eras. However, as discussed in the next chapter, when God is seen as a single, nonsexual entity, sex comes to place humans on the animal side of the divine/animal split. Sexual depictions then may be seen as degrading images of humanity, focusing on the animal side of our natures and divorcing us from the divine.

3

The Arrival of Christianity

With the arrival of Christianity, Europe faced a profound change in the nature of God. For the Greeks and the Romans there had been a host of gods and goddesses, who were in many respects like humans. They had healthy appetites for food, drink, and sex. With a multitude of gods, there was interaction not only between gods and humans but also among the gods. Those interactions had a great deal of similarity to interactions among humans and even to some degree among the animals, and there was not a great chasm between the gods and humanity, or again even with the animals. There were entities that were the result of sex between mortals and gods. There were half-human, half-animal beings and even gods with animal characteristics. The place of mankind in the universe was not troubled, because the differences between or among the categories were not so stark. Gods, humans, and animals had much in common, and our human activities, including our sexual activities, did not place humans on either side of some divide between the gods and the animals or really distinguish us in any major way from the gods, other than in our mortality, or from the animals. We, the gods, and the animals all had the same appetites, and in satisfying those appetites we were not engaged in anything shameful.

The Christian God is of a different nature. The Christian God, like the Jewish God, is not one among many. The Christian God is a unique individual, even if one believes in three aspects represented in the Trinity. That God does not have others of similar type with whom to interact. That God is certainly not sexual and would seem to have no need for other appetites. The ascendancy of that God had to work a profound change in the view of the relationship between God, humanity, and the animals. We could no longer all be similar entities, and one of the differences would be in our appetites. Our appetites separated us in our nature from God and showed more of a similarity with the animals.

At the same time, the story of the creation of humans had us created in the image and likeness of God. That similarity to God was not physical and was not in a shared level of knowledge or of power. It had to be a spiritual similarity.[1] We shared in godliness not in our bodies but in our spirit. But our bodies, and the needs of those bodies, separated us from God and corrupted the shared spirituality. Because we had bodies, we were also like the animals, despite the likeness of our spirits to God. We were reminded of this belonging in part to the animal side of a divine-animal divide when we experienced and when we fulfilled appetites like those of the animals, appetites that God did not experience.

Richard Posner, in his book *Sex and Reason,* recognizes that the Christian belief in a degree of divine nature in humanity would be corrupted by the existence and needs of the body:

> Man is a degenerate version of God, the degeneracy consisting not only in pride and envy and other spiritual flaws but also in the possession of a body that is prone not just to decay but to every sort of shame and indignity. The body . . . should be clothed, ideally at all times; for it is a shameful thing, a thing to be concealed, not flaunted in the manner of the Greeks and Romans. And bodily activities should be confined to those that are necessary.[2]

The nature of a noncorporeal God, one without appetites, made the existence of our needs to eat, to drink, and to eliminate and the existence of our sexual urges a measure of just how far we were from the divine nature and how close we were to the animals.

The early Christian Church faced the task of distinguishing humans from the animals. If we were to share in the divine nature, we would have to establish a difference between God and the animals and show that humans did not belong on the animal side of that divide. Joyce Salisbury studies the relationship between humans and animals in the Middle Ages, and it must be remembered that the Middle Ages were still early in the development of the Christian Church and its impact on the culture of Europe:

> When early Christian thinkers established what they believed to be clear categories that separated animals from humans, they were not only making a theological statement of humanity's dominance over the natural world, but they were actually defining what it meant to be human. And as in so many things, it was easier to define humans by what they were not— animals—than by what they were.[3]

This helps to explain why, as Peter Brown says, "[i]n the early sixth century, Caesarius of Arles was genuinely appalled that human beings should dance through the streets of his city, bearing the great horns of the stag and uttering the calls of wild beasts."[4]

Perhaps the greatest concern regarding this relationship between man and animal was sex. Our other appetites, though shared by the animals and not by God, did not otherwise weaken the connection to God. Eating and elimination may have been signs of nondivinity, but sex was seen to weaken divinity in a way that eating or elimination did not. The distinction between man and the animals, the distinction on which the claim to some connection to the divine could be made, was in the ability of humans to reason. But it was believed that sex weakened that distinction and, for the period in which one was engaged in sex, diminished that ability to reason.

Joyce Salisbury explains the Church's view:

Augustine as early as the late fourth century established the notion that during sexual intercourse "there is an almost total extinction of mental alertness; the intellectual sentries . . . are overwhelmed." If sexual intercourse banished reason, and if reason were the defining quality of humans, then sexual intercourse was bestial and threatened one's humanity. . . . The irrational passion implicit in the act of intercourse led Thomas Aquinas to say that "in sexual intercourse man becomes like a brute animal" and that insofar as people cannot "moderate concupiscence" with reason, they are like beasts.[5]

The Gnostic Julius Cassianus echoed similar sentiments, noting that humans become like beasts when engaging in sexual intercourse.[6] This sort of Gnostic view seems to have had more influence on the development of sexual thought in early Christianity than did the views of the Jewish culture from which the religion had sprung.[7]

Even if the other activities we share with the animals were of theological concern, they could not be banned. We, like the animals, eat and eliminate, but these activities are necessary for survival of the individual and must be allowed. Although they must be allowed, however, going beyond what is necessary for survival could be criticized as ungodly, as giving in to animal urges. Thus, gluttony could be seen as sinful.

Sex, on the other hand, is not necessary for the survival of the individual. Virginity or continence could be encouraged as a way to separate the individual from the animals and further the connection to the divine. Sex is necessary to the survival of the species, and it could not be banned altogether. Indeed, any completely celibate community will eventually die out. Not all members of the community must be celibate; there must be enough reproduction to provide for new members of both the community and the species. As shown by the difference between the need to eat and gluttony, however, the need for and role of sex could be limited. Sex could be limited to reproductive purposes, and not everyone needed to be engaged in reproduction. Nonprocreative sex and, for that matter, sex outside marriage spoke against any nature that mankind might share with God.

This concern over the place of humanity between God and the animals is also demonstrated by the literature of the early Christian era. The observation in the preceding chapter that the distinction between the gods, humans, and animals was not as strong in the classical era as in the Christian era was supported by the number of entities that were not uniquely of one status, for example, by creatures that were part human and part animal. In a new religious culture in which there was a chasm between God and the animals, stories of half-human, half-animal creatures would place humanity more on the animal side of that chasm. In particular, any stories of a change in status between human and animal would be troubling.

Tales of species metamorphosis often were based on sexual episodes, again showing the connection between man and animal in the engagement of both in sex.[8] Even without the sexual connection, stories of species ambiguity or metamorphosis would still be of concern to the place of humankind. This concern led to criticism of these pagan stories by early Christian scholars such as St. Ambrose, St. Augustine, and St. Thomas Aquinas,[9] and this criticism spoke to a new concern over the status of humanity.

The Church's Teachings on Sex
General Teachings from St. Paul to St. Augustine

The Christian Church, at its earliest stages, could be viewed as a cult of virginity. As Oxford fellow Robin Lane Fox says, "From its very beginnings, Christianity has considered an orderly sex life to be a clear second best to no sex life at all."[10] Fox says that St. John, in his Revelation, saw "a heaven positively teeming with virgins, 144,000 of them, he said, men who were singing to their harps and had never defiled themselves with a woman."[11] To believers, it would be a strong incentive to abstinence.

Fox says that a "primary source of this 'madness' was Jesus himself."[12] In Mathew 19:12, Jesus is said to have commended those who are "eunuchs for the sake of the kingdom of heaven," and most people took that to mean continence rather than castration. Adding fuel is Luke 20:35–36, in which Jesus says that in the next life those who are worthy neither marry nor are given in marriage. For believers, either deciding that what was good in the next life must be good in this one or believing that that next life was nearly upon them, it was a short step to abstinence in this life. Again adding to the incentive were the examples of the virginity of Jesus and of his mother, Mary.[13] On the other hand, James Brundage notes a lack of comment on sex in the Gospels and concludes that "this silence implies that Jesus was relatively uninterested in the subject."[14] He concludes also that Jesus accepted traditional Jewish beliefs on marriage and the family but placed more emphasis on love as the important element in marriage.[15]

St. Paul may well be the most important early influence in this area. Peter Brown says, with regard to St. Paul's teachings on marriage and particularly on his letters to the Corinthians, that his missive had a "distinctly lopsided quality."[16] St. Paul in his epistle to the Corinthians addresses their belief in sexual abstinence, even among married couples. With regard to abstinence, he says that it is an ideal but that not all will be successful. Those who cannot remain abstinent should marry so as not to engage in sinful extramarital sex; marriage and sex within marriage may not be wrong, but they are not the ideal.[17] Fox says that "[a]lmost every subsequent author took Paul's remarks out of context and made a strong passage even stronger."[18] Although later writers may have strengthened St. Paul's remarks, those remarks were already fairly strong and clearly had a great deal of influence.

Peter Brown calls chapter 7 of St. Paul's First Epistle to the Corinthians "the one chapter that was to determine all Christian thought on marriage and celibacy for well over a millennium."[19] Brown, too, notes Paul's acceptance of marriage and of intercourse within marriage, but it is an acceptance of the institution and act as a defense against a worse state, the potential for immorality that attempted abstinence might bring. As St. Paul says, "it is better to marry than to be aflame with passion."[20] Thus, marriage was a very different institution for St. Paul than for his non-Christian contemporaries. According to Peter Brown, "What was notably lacking, in Paul's letter, was the warm faith shown by contemporary pagans and Jews that the sexual urge, although disorderly, was capable of socialization and of ordered, even warm, expression within marriage."[21] Paul's was not a positive view of marriage;[22] its role was to help Christians ward off desire.[23] And again in Brown's words, it "left a fatal legacy to future ages."[24]

St. Paul was not the only Apostle who was at least said to have preached chastity, and some seem to have gone beyond what St. Paul suggested. In the Acts of St. Andrew, he is said to have broken up marriages at the highest levels of society, telling a married woman that marriage is "foul and polluting" and that renouncing sexual relations could restore the fall of man.[25] Other texts took a similar turn. Fox discusses the stories of St. Thomas the Apostle:

> By the mid-third century, "Acts" of St. Thomas were available, composed by an author, probably a Syrian, who did show signs of an extreme enthusiasm for sexless living. He invented some startling stories of the Apostle's impact on the nobility of western India, how one wife had run out of her husband's bedroom . . . and how another couple saw Jesus in their bedroom on their wedding night, explaining that sex was foul and that marriage should never be consummated.[26]

Fox says that these texts, which he categorizes as "apocryphal," were no less read and known than the orthodox texts and that as time passed their "dubious origins" were easily forgotten.[27]

Among the later writers whom Fox may have been thinking of as taking St. Paul's comments out of context were the leaders of the Encratites, who insisted on perfect chastity inside and outside marriage.[28] The rationale for that limitation is particularly relevant to the thesis of this book. The Encratites also abstained from eating meat and drinking wine. Peter Brown ties the abstentions to sexual abstinence: "These abstentions were intimately linked to the constitutive act of sexual renunciation: for the eating of meat was held to link human beings to the wild, carnivorous nature of animals, as intercourse linked them to the sexual nature of brute beasts."[29] Here was the logical extension of the need to place humanity on the divine side of a divine-animal split. Just as a monotheistic God does not have occasion for sex, that God needs no physical sustenance. Sex and eating put us on the animal side.[30] Whereas sex might be foregone altogether, eating is necessary but certainly can be limited, although it is not clear why adopting the diet of an herbivore, rather than a carnivore, keeps one closer to God.

Particularly important as an advocate of chastity was Tertullian, who lived in the late second and early third centuries. He renounced sexual relations with his wife and argued that sex, even within marriage, is incompatible with Christian virtue. Brundage describes the views of Tertullian: "He argued that coitus causes spiritual insensitivity: sexual intercourse drives out the Holy Spirit, and this deprives sexually active couples of the benefit of divine counsel."[31] Brundage says that this sexual revulsion extended to women themselves: "Women, Tertullian declared, are the devil's door: through them Satan creeps into men's hearts and minds and works his wiles for their spiritual destruction."[32]

Despite radicals such as Tertullain and the Encratites, Brundage finds the Christians of the second and third centuries to have been accepting of marriage and of sexual relations within marriage: "St. Clement of Alexandria (ca. 150–ca. 200) enunciated the majority view when he taught that it was as wrong to condemn marriage as it was to seek indiscriminate sexual pleasure."[33] While the majority may have accepted marriage and sex within marriage,[34] the orthodox also believed in limiting the role of sex in marriage. Again in Brundage's words, "For St. Justin Martyr in the early second century, marital sex was designed to produce children: faithful Christians either married in order to have offspring or else lived in complete continence. His contemporaries and successors reiterated this theme time and time again: marital sex was legitimate when employed for procreation but not when indulged in for pleasure."[35]

In the era just before St. Augustine, St. Ambrose and St. Jerome continued to express this low regard for marriage and sexuality. St. Ambrose's thinking centered around the virgin birth of Christ and the way in which Christ lived his life as an example of perfection in human nature as well. Peter Brown describes the position of Ambrose: "The absence of sexual desire in the circumstances of Christ's own conception and in Christ's own human flesh was not, for Ambrose, simply a prodigy, incapable of imitation by others. Rather, Christ's sexless birth and unstirred body acted as a bridge between the present, fallen state of the human body and its future, glorious transformation at the Resurrection."[36] St. Jerome believed that sex and salvation were in hopeless conflict. He believed that even within marriage sexual intercourse was evil and unclean and that Christians should avoid sexual activity.[37] Although marital intercourse might occur, and was certainly necessary for procreation, it should be infrequent, sober, and without desire.[38]

Perhaps deserving the most credit or blame for the early Christian views on sex is St. Augustine, writing in the early fifth century. Interestingly, in his view of life in the Garden of Eden, he takes a more liberal view compared to earlier writers. It was commonly taught that sex was the result of the Fall. Only after Adam and Eve had eaten the forbidden fruit did they realize they were naked and cover themselves. Thus, it could be believed, prior to the original sin, there would have been no sexual desire or sexual intercourse. Augustine took the position that there would have been sexual intercourse in the Garden aimed at the producing of children. It would be a "calm but blissful activity," and the mechanics would be at the behest of the will, "rather than in the spontaneous and insubordinate way the male organ is presently 'moved' to sexual intercourse."[39] That is, it seems, there would be sexual intercourse but no sexual desire.[40]

Nonetheless, St. Augustine found sexual intercourse problematic, even if it would have existed in Eden, and again it was, at least to a degree, an issue of lust. Posner sums up Augustine's view:

> [O]riginal sin . . . is transmitted from generation to generation in the very act of conception. Nonmarital sex is sinful even when procreative, because God has ordained marriage as the exclusive channel for licit sexual activity. But even in marital sex, positions and caresses designed to enhance sexual pleasure are sinful, for such pleasure is unnecessary beyond the bare minimum required to produce penetration and ejaculation.[41]

Thus, not to be sinful, sex should emulate as much as possible that which would have occurred in paradise. It may exist as a matter of necessity, but it should not be any more exciting than is necessary. Once again pointing to the difference between human and animal, Posner sums up the view: "Since it is the nature of man as distinct from beast to conform his bodily functions to his rational needs, the illicit forms of sexual activity are not merely wrong; they are unnatural."[42]

Clerical Celibacy

Clerical celibacy is not solely the invention of the Christian Church. Robin Lane Fox notes that some pagan cults required more from religious leaders than their cultures required of the ordinary person. Some were served only by virgin priests or sexually inactive women.[43] Perhaps the best-known example is the Vestal Virgins of Rome. Vesta, the virgin goddess of the hearth, home, and family, had her fire tended by virgins who were taken into the temple before they were ten. The Vestal Virgins served for at least thirty years, when, at a time past likely childbearing age, they were allowed to leave the temple and marry.[44] Outside the Vestal Virgins and a few other cults, prolonged virginity, as opposed to some period of abstinence before engaging in religious practice, seems to have been rare. There were, as Fox says, "a few exotic 'Oriental' cults [that] went further and required priests who were physically eunuchs,"[45] but generally this practice was disapproved

in Greece and Rome. Again in the words of Fox, "Outside these few, contro-
versial priesthoods, abstinence and asceticism were urged as lifelong ideals
of behavior only by some of the schools of philosophy."[46] These Stoic schools
were concerned not so much with divine commands regarding religion as
with overcoming desire generally, and their beliefs did not reflect the practices of those in their societies who were not so philosophical in their views
on life.[47]

The practice of celibacy among the Christian clergy became far more
widespread, but it took a great deal of time to establish. Fox says that St.
Jerome drew on pagan philosophy in arguing for virginity among Christians, and Christians too believed in a period of abstinence before approaching God, with St. Paul arguing for such abstinence before periods of intense
prayer.[48] Given this tie of abstinence to prayer and to approaching God, it
seems a logical extension for the belief of some pagans in a virgin priesthood
to carry over to Christian clergy. Indeed, Brundage finds the sentiments in
favor of celibacy for the clergy to be grounded in Pythagorean beliefs, along
with Encratite perceptions of an "incongruity between sexual activity and
participation in the sacred mysteries of the Christian liturgy."[49] Fox, however,
insists that the belief was not simply a carryover from pagan religions, noting the facts that Christians would have considered pagan cults demonic and
that the Christian teachings on virginity came from those who had no close
contacts with these pagan cults.[50] Father Edward Schillebeeckx, on the other
hand, finds these ideas widespread in the area in which Christianity emerged
and probably influential in the development of the Christian view.[51]

According to Schillebeeckx, in the apostolic era the church official would
be a married man, a father who governed his family well and had been chosen for his leadership qualities to be a priest or bishop,[52] but eventually celibacy would take hold. Father A. W. Richard Sipe, in his study of Christian
celibacy, finds the origins for that practice among the clergy in two quotations from the New Testament. He cites to Mathew 19:12, in which Jesus says,
"and there are eunuchs who have made themselves eunuchs for the sake of
the kingdom of heaven. He who is able to receive this, let him receive it."[53]
Not surprisingly, he also finds support from St. Paul, citing 1 Corinthians 7:7,
in which St. Paul writes, "I wish that all were as I myself am. But each has his
own special gift from God, one of one kind and one of another."[54] Neither of
these seems to be a command to commit to celibacy, and indeed, Sipe says
that the passages are more a grant of permission to remain celibate; it is seen
as a fact of religious psychology that the religious experience may simply
make some people incapable of marriage.[55] It seems that the religious experi-

ence would be sufficiently strong for some people to leave them incapable of marriage, and that is the sense in which they would be eunuchs.[56]

Christ was said to have been celibate, but that was not necessarily the case for the Apostles. In fact, Sipe finds it significant that even St. Paul wishes that all were as he is, not as he was, and Sipe says that St. Paul writes like a man who had experienced marriage before taking on a celibate life.[57] The Apostles were not all or, according to Sipe, even mostly celibate, and St. Peter had both a wife and a family.[58]

The noncelibate practice of the first pope seems to have persisted in the early Church. As Sipe says, "The list of popes who fathered future popes reads like an Old Testament lineage recitation: Anastasius I (399–401) begat Innocent I (401–417); Hormisdas (514–523) begat Silverius (536–537); Sergius III (904–911) begat John XI (931–935)."[59] If the children of those of lesser rank are included, the list of popes fathered by clergy grows to include Theodore I, Damasus I, Boniface I, Felix III, Anastasius II, Agapitus, Marinus I, John XV, and Adeodatus I.[60]

Sipe traces a history of well over one thousand years for the establishment of celibacy in the clergy, even if we begin counting the passage of time with the Spanish Synod of Elvira of 305, in which those in holy orders were forbidden to marry.[61] That Synod also required a priest who was already married to stop engaging in intercourse and to be excommunicated if he should father a child.[62] The force of that decree was limited to Spain and was rejected for application elsewhere at the Council of Nicaea in 325, although the Council did adopt a rule forbidding a person to marry after receiving any important office in the Church.[63]

It is only in 1022 that Sipe finds a complete ban on marriage and concubinage for all the clergy, as a result of Pope Benedict VIII and the Synod of Pavia.[64] A further decree that any children born of clergy would become serfs, with the provision enforced as part of the imperial code of King Henry II, reveals two aspects of this rule. First, it indicates that full obedience was not expected to occur. Second, it may be seen to have had a not fully religious motivation. It, again according to Sipe, "allayed Benedict's fear that Church property would dissipate among clerical offspring,"[65] since the children of priests were allowed to inherit Church property.[66] Sipe continues this history:

> The Councils of Limoges and Bourges in 1031 declared that a man could not be ordained to the subdiaconte unless he left his wife or lived with her

with a promise of continence. . . . In 1059, under Pope Nicholas II, a Lateran Synod declared that people could not attend the masses of married priests or receive sacraments from them. . . . Four years later, Pope Alexander II found it necessary to reinforce the decrees of Nicholas' Synod, and in 1074 Gregory VII reinforced them again and suspended from the priesthood the "concubine keepers." . . . In 1123, Pope Callistus II pronounced the marriages of higher clergy invalid, and in 1139 the historic Second Lateran Council under Innocent II declared all marriages of priests to be null and void, and further demanded that existing marriages be severed before a man could be ordained to the priesthood.[67]

One might think all these decrees to be sufficient to affect the behavior of all the clergy, but it took continued threats and instances of excommunication, and Sipe sees a resultant rise in concubinage in the fourteenth and fifteenth centuries.[68] Even the 1545 Council of Trent had to concern itself with the continuing resistance to celibacy.[69]

One of the differences to arise in Christianity during the Reformation was over the celibacy of the clergy. Since the reformers generally rejected the major distinction between clergy and laity found in Catholicism, rules regarding sex and marriage would have to be universal.[70] According to Vern Bullough, neither Luther nor Calvin favored vows of chastity:

Luther felt that the vows of chastity had originated in the belief that divine favor could be won by performing self-imposed disciplines; this in his opinion was a delusion. Along the lines of his basic argument on salvation, continence was as little in our power as were God's other wonders and graces. The essential ingredient for salvation was faith, and not good works, even if chastity could be regarded as a good work. Calvin argued in much the same strain, though as usual he was more cautious than Luther: he made it clear that he disapproved of celibacy vows only when regarded as acts of religious dedication, and which were rashly taken by those who found they could not keep them.[71]

Thus, there was not the degree of divergence between theory and practice in the Protestant religions that there was among the Catholic clergy, a divergence that became the target of satirists and pornographers, to the detriment of the Catholic Church, and that gave importance to the need to check certain varieties of sexually based works of literature.

The Common Person

As already seen, there was a gulf between theory and practice in the requirements of celibacy for the clergy. That was within the ordered structure of the Church. Presumably the differences between theory and practice would be at least as great for the common person. Posner notes that sexual practices were far more liberal than the theory would suggest.[72] The culture against which the Church was set included very old pagan fertility rights. These rites, along with many pre-Christian traditions, were subsumed, and modified to the degree possible, by the Church. David Loth says,

> In France as late as the fifteenth century the ancient rites were so much a part of the casual popular attitude toward sex that the Church reluctantly absorbed some of them. Thus a Feast of Fools was permitted on Epiphany with masking and dancing, singing and fooling, all so Dionysian that bishops admonished the celebrants who felt called upon to copulate to please wait until they got outside the church.[73]

Not all that much seems to have been expected of the ordinary person—not that scripture was not supposed to speak to such people, but the sense of reality among the clergy seemed to be that the common person would not follow scripture. The Church developed a doctrine of "good faith" that provided that priests should not tell their flocks that the sexual practices of the members were sinful, at least if the priest thought that the followers were likely to persist in the practices.[74] The theory behind this doctrine seemed to be that, if the practices were to continue, knowledge of their sinfulness would put the followers in a state of sin that would not be present without that knowledge.[75]

The Church seemed ready to tolerate a significant difference between divine nature and the nature and morality of the ordinary believer. On the other hand, sex was not to be encouraged, even indirectly. In fact, the manuals for priests on conducting confessions showed what Pierre Payer calls a "preoccupation with sex [that was] endemic,"[76] and priests were required to question their penitents so that confessions would be complete and accurate.[77] On the other hand, priests are said to have refrained from reproving their followers too strongly for continuing deeply rooted sexual practices, out of a fear of driving them away from the confessional.[78] Furthermore, according to Posner, priests "were often advised by Church authorities not to interrogate the flock too closely about sexual activity lest the interrogation plant ideas."[79] Not that their flocks needed all that much stimulation of sexual thoughts. As Loth notes, "The Christian ideal of continence so successfully conquered the old pagan fertility ceremonies that we are apt to forget that these still had a great following,"[80] and the old pagan culture of northern and western Europe did continue to have an influence.

Just what practices were sinful, or more accurately how great the sins were, appears from the confessional manuals to have been in some dispute. Although there is indication that simple fornication among the laity was considered by most of the clergy to constitute a mortal sin, that may not have been the universal belief; compared to incest, adultery, and "unnatural sex," some clergy considered fornication to be at most a minor sin and perhaps not sinful at all.[81] On the other hand, even within marriage, it is clear from the confessional manuals that many sexual practices were considered sinful. If a penitent confessed to having had marital sex in an "undue manner," the priest was instructed to ascertain the details. Vaginal intercourse in other than the "usual position" was a minor sin that could be excused because of physical difficulties, but nonvaginal intercourse was a serious sin that could not be justified.[82]

Although the common person may not have been as separate from the animals as the clergy had to be, there were sexual practices that would identify humans with the animals and should be avoided. Most of these followed Jewish law, and Fox explains that in at least one instance a tie between Jewish dietary restrictions and sexual prohibitions was asserted:

> One was an ingenious allegory which seems to have begun with the Christian author of the Epistle of Barnabas (c. 100): why, he asked, did the Mosaic law declare hares, hyenas and weasels to be unclean? They were types of sexual vice, he explained, as their odd habits and details of their rear anatomy proved. . . . Hares, he explained, stood for homosexuals and hyenas for oversexed seducers, while weasels were people who indulged in oral sex.[83]

Another principle based on comparison with the animals was the application of limitations on sex to natural sex, sex aimed at procreation, to bar sex during pregnancy. Such sex was, again in Fox's words, "a habit . . . which placed man even lower than the animals."[84]

With the Reformation there was a change in belief regarding the role of sex. Both Luther and Calvin denied that nonprocreational sex was always sinful. Calvin seems to have been the more conservative of the two, but even he was said to have conceded that God would excuse any sin that might accompany a yielding to lust in marriage, because of the value of holy matrimony.[85] Luther seems to have been less troubled, rejecting St. Jerome's position that even matrimonial sex, when accompanied by strong sexual desire, was sinful.[86]

The Clergy and the Control of Sexual Literature

Although a gap between theory and practice for the ordinary believer might be tolerable, such a gap for the clergy was another matter. As discussed, there was also such a gap between theory and practice for the clergy, but this was far more problematic. The clergy should be closer to God; they were more significant participants in the divine nature. Thus, they should be less animalistic in nature, if they were to have spiritual authority over the masses. They had to be more capable of controlling their sexual appetites. Even if it were, in fact, not the case that they controlled their sexual appetites, it might be possible for the Church to exercise some control over the image of the clergy by placing limits on sexual literature in which the clergy were actors.

According to David Loth, pornography in the Dark Ages "fell from its high estate" of the Greek and Roman era "and for centuries was limited to common jokes and doggerel verse."[87] It often seems to have taken the form of riddles in which the question leads to a seeming sexual conclusion, but the offered answer is far more tame. Sexual material was on its way to becoming obscene. Rather than the Greek celebration of sex, sex was becoming viewed as shameful. The fact that the sexual conduct was only suggested in the riddles and verse is an indication of that movement toward the shame associated with obscenity. By the Middle Ages, doggerel had become the preferred form, and in that era, Loth says that "the shafts of coarse humor were directed chiefly against the clergy, especially wandering friars who begged and stole and lechered their way through most of Europe."[88] Criticism of the Church, including the sexual practices of the clergy, carried over to other work. Loth adds,

> The chief work of England's best satirist of the twelfth century, Nigellus Wireker, was a long poem entitled *Mirror of Fools*. . . . Its hero, Brunellus, was an ass who belonged to a woodcutter but wanted to better himself. The donkey represents the monastic orders, and in his wanderings he displayed the two great sins which were popularly held against the clergy, their greed for property and their pursuit of privilege. But one long section was given over to the sexual vices of monks and nuns.[89]

Interestingly, Loth concludes his section on the pornography of the Middle Ages and the Renaissance by noting that the works were "designed to stimulate healthy laughter, not lecherous desire, to amuse rather than to arouse."[90] This explains the Church's concern over the publication in 1371 of Giovanni Boccaccio's *The Decameron*. The Church was not so much interested in the possibility that the ordinary people would be aroused by what they read in that work. They were instead trying to avoid the laughter and amusement about which Loth spoke, in particular a laughter and amusement at the expense of the clergy.

In the original edition of *The Decameron*, the edition that was placed on the Church's list of banned books, the sexual nature of the clergy was too prominent for the Church, though it is important to note that the sexual content of the book was rather mild. The fourth story of the first day, usually noted as the first with such content, serves as an example. The story concerns a monk who had sexual relations with a woman and was discovered by the Abbot. The monk, knowing of his discovery, puts the Abbot in the position to engage in the same acts, and when he does, the monk is assured of going unpunished. Quotations of the most explicit language of the story show its mildness: The monk was out walking "when his eyes came to rest on a strikingly beautiful girl. . . . No sooner did he see her, than he was fiercely assailed by carnal desire."[91] After talking with the girl and taking her back to his cell, he was "carried away by the vigour of his passion"; he "threw all caution to the winds" and "cavort[ed] with the girl."[92] When the Abbot was alone with the girl in the monk's cell, he saw that "she was a nice, comely wench, and despite his years he was promptly filled with fleshly cravings, no less intense than those his young monk had experienced."[93] When it comes to the Abbot's actual sexual conduct, it is again presented rather mildly:

> He took her in his arms and kissed her a few times, then lowered himself on to the monk's little bed. But out of regard, perhaps, for the weight of his reverend person and the tender age of the girl, and not wishing to do her any injury, he settled down beneath her instead of lying on top, and in this way he sported with her at considerable length.[94]

This would at most barely seem to merit the label "pornography."

In another story—which has been suggested as too licentious to have been fully translated into English, erroneously so thought according to the translator relied on here[95]—the language is a bit more direct. In the tenth story of the fourth day, a young girl named Alibech finds herself, after some journey, in the hut of Rustico, a young religious hermit. Taken with her, he explains the importance of putting the devil back in hell. Asked how to do this, he tells her to copy what he does, as he removes his clothes and sinks to his knees.

In this posture, the girl's beauty was displayed to Rustico in all its glory, and his longings blazed more fiercely than ever, bringing about the resurrection of the flesh. Alibech stared at this in amazement, and said:

"Rustico, what is this thing that I see sticking out in front of you, which I do not possess?"

"Oh, my daughter," said Rustico, "this is the devil I was telling you about. Do you see what he is doing? He's hurting me so much that I can hardly endure it."

"Oh, praise be to God," said the girl, "I can see that I am better off than you are, for I have no such devil to contend with."

"You're right there," said Rustico. "But you have something else instead, that I haven't."

"Oh," said Alibech. "And what's that?"

"You have Hell," said Rustico. "And I honestly believe that God has sent you here for the salvation of my soul, because if this devil continues to plague the life out of me, and if you are prepared to take sufficient pity on me to let me put him back into Hell, you will be giving me marvelous relief, as well as rendering incalculable service and pleasure to God."[96]

The girl agrees, and the holy man takes her to a bed, where he "instruct[s] her in the art of incarcerating that accursed fiend."[97]

Experiencing some pain, the girl says that the devil must be an enemy of God, since he not only plagues humankind but hurts hell when driven back there. Rustico assures her that it will not always be painful and demonstrates that assertion, as they "put him back half a dozen times, curbing his arrogance to such good effect that he was positively glad to keep still for the rest of the day."[98] Over the next several days, the girl comes to enjoy her "religious" exercises, saying, "I can certainly see what those worthy men in Gafsa meant when they said that serving God was so agreeable. . . . To my way of thinking, anyone who devotes his energies to anything but the service of God is a complete blockhead."[99] Eventually wearing Rustico down, she complains that even if his devil has been tamed, her hell needs attention that he is unable to provide.

Nuns fared no better. The first story of the third day concerns a young man who, pretending to be mute and slow-witted, takes on the gardening job at a convent. Two of the young nuns decide that they want to experience sex and that the gardener is the perfect opportunity, since he would be unable to tell anyone. They escort him to a hut, and with the other keeping watch, each has sex with him. They are unable to keep their secret, and soon all eight nuns are enjoying the gardener to the point where he is exhausted. The Abbess later comes across the gardener when he is lying under a tree, tired and exposed. She, too, becomes excited and takes him to her rooms. The gardener, suddenly cured of his muteness, tells the Abbess of the others and that he cannot service all nine constantly. The Abbess's solution is to "divide[] up his various functions among themselves in such a way that he was able to do them all justice."[100]

Other stories are also at the expense of clerics. In the fourth story of the third day, a monk sets out penance for a husband. He is to abstain from sex with his wife for forty days, and he must remain alone and motionless, as if on a cross, all night long for each night of that period. That gives the monk an opportunity to take the husband's place with the wife. In the eighth story of the third day, an Abbot imprisons a husband, making him believe he is in Purgatory, in order to cavort with his wife. In the second story of the fourth day, a friar convinces a woman that the archangel Gabriel is in love with her. He then goes to her regularly in disguise as Gabriel to express that love. And in the second story of the ninth day, an Abbess learns that one of her nuns is with a lover. She throws on what she believes to be her veil to rush to the nun's cell. The veil turns out to be the trousers of the priest the Abbess had in her own bed, and the nun escapes punishment. There are obviously many other stories, and many involve no clerical characters. Neither do any of them seem any more salacious than those discussed.

The objection to the sexual exploits of monks and nuns was not so much a concern over sexual depiction generally; it was a concern over using sexual depiction to bring the clergy down from any participation in divinity to the same level of the animals that was shared by the ordinary person. It is telling that *The Decameron* was not banned when it was published. In fact, the Forbidden List did not exist at the time; it was the later product of the Catholic reaction to the Reformation. Once the list was established, it was not used as a tool to eliminate bawdy or pornographic material. As the UK scholar H. Montgomery Hyde says, "it was only when the bawdy was combined with heresy or a satire or an attack upon the Church . . . that the work was ecclesiastically proscribed or at least not permitted to be read by the faithful until it had been 'expurgated.'"[101] *The Decameron* was indeed later expurgated. A second edition was published in which monks were replaced by conjurors, nuns by ladies of nobility, the abbess by a countess, and the archangel Gabriel by a fairy king.[102] That edition was not forbidden, making clear that the true concern had not been the sexual content of the first edition but the religious status of the actors in that version.

It may be suggested that the invention of the printing press in the mid-fifteenth century lay behind the desire to limit pornographic materials. So long as books were produced as manuscripts, the intensity of the labor and the resultant cost of the product would limit availability and the spread of what might be seen as dangerous ideas. So it is certainly possible that the new availability of widespread circulation played a role in the Church's actions against books such as *The Decameron,* one of the first books to be printed.[103] But the question remains as to just what the dangerous ideas were, and the treatment of the second edition provides the answer to that question. The concern seems not to have been over widespread dissemination of sexual matter generally but over what could now be widespread dissemination of material depicting the clergy as sexually active.

Probably more important than the invention of the printing press was the onset of the Reformation in the sixteenth century. The Reformation was a challenge to the privileged position of the Catholic Church, privileged in the sense of being closer to God. Part of the criticism of the Catholic Church was that the Church was hypocritical, in particular in the difference between its official doctrines on sexual practices and the actual practices of the clergy.[104] The Church's first official attempts at suppressing material were defensive in nature in an attempt to protect the status of members of the clergy as close to God by suppressing material that showed them in a less than divine, more animal, light.

The somewhat minimal concern over the sexual practices of the common people, particularly as compared to concerns over the clergy and sex and closeness to divinity, fits with the era's view of the nature of common people. In Marie of France's collection of the fables of the Middle Ages, as described by Joyce Salisbury,

> the peasants were uniformly shown as stupid. . . . [O]ne of the defining qualities of animals in the Middle Ages was their irrationality. Humans had reason, animals did not. By showing peasants as uniformly stupid and irrational . . . , Marie subtly, yet powerfully, reduced their status to the borders of the bestial.

In addition to rationality, . . . sexuality defines an animal. From the twelfth century onward, peasant sexuality was linked more closely to that of animals than to the more cultured love of the nobility. . . . When . . . [Andrew the Chaplain] considers peasants, . . . he says that peasants cannot really love because they have sex "naturally, like a horse or a mule." Therefore, he, like Marie, reduces peasants as a whole group to a position lower than human by denying them rationality and seeing the proof of that denial in his perception of the nature of their sexuality.[105]

Sex was certainly seen as lowering peasants to a level far below the divine. Given the accepted view of the animal nature of the ordinary person, that might have been tolerable. But the clergy had to be better than that, and to assure that they were seen as better than that, there had to be limits on depictions that showed an animal nature.

This is not to say that there was no concern over the exposure of the growing middle class, the nonnoble, noncleric person with the means to purchase books. Ian Moulton argues that as long as erotic texts circulated only in Latin and were for that reason accessible only to the well educated, there was little concern. It was late-sixteenth-century sales of translations in the London book market to a broader audience that led to concerns among English authorities, although the example cited by Moulton was still on the part of religious authorities.[106] Later in his examination, Moulton notes that this example, the Bishops' Order in 1599, was "an effort to control political discourse" and that "works thought of as ribald or licentious were not differentiated from politically subversive or heretical works but were included in a broad range of material that could seduce the innocent. Erotic writing was clearly seen as having political consequences."[107] These perceived political consequences, not sexual content alone, led to effort to control the material.

There were also other books placed on the Forbidden List that were not as direct an affront to the dignity of the clergy. All the writings of Pietro Aretino were placed on the list in 1558.[108] Aretino's most famous work, the *Sonetti Lussuriosi*, was a set of sixteen erotic poems written to accompany a set of engravings by Marcantonio Raimondi based on drawings by Giulio Romano. The drawings went beyond the simple nude figures that were not uncommon in the era.[109] The drawings and engravings graphically depicted naked couples in a variety of sexual positions.[110] Aretino's addition to the engravings was in the form of sexually explicit dialogs tied to the scenes depicted. In addition to the *Sonetti*, Aretino wrote *Ragionamenti*, a dialog between an older, experienced woman and a younger, somewhat naïve woman that Lynn Hunt says "became the prototype of seventeenth century pornographic prose."[111]

Although the *Sonetti* may not have been the affront to the Church that the *Decameron* had been, it appears that Aretino himself was. The real offense for this "Scourge of Princes" may have been the verses he wrote that satirized as corrupt the Papal Conclave called to select the successor to Pope Leo X.[112] That, in combination with his leadership of a group of younger writers critical of both Italian society and the Catholic Church,[113] may be the best explanation for his inclusion on the List, and in fact all of his works were so included two years after his death.[114] This explanation could be seen as weakened, however, by the fact that the engravings themselves had earlier been suppressed by order of the pope.[115] This potential weakening may itself be unclear, since the drawings by Romano, the basis for the engravings, seem not to have been censored.[116] Furthermore, the works were suppressed by Pope Leo's successor, Pope Clement, whose selection conclave had been criticized. Clement was a strict moralist, as compared to Pope Leo, who had commissioned at least some of the original works.[117]

The work of Rabelais was also suppressed by the French authorities, but again it was not for sexual content. Whatever coarseness *Pantagruel* and *Gargantua* may have contained was not the concern. The placement of the works on the Sorbonne's forbidden list was, once again, because of their lack of respect for the clergy.[118] In one story, a character has a male organ that causes sexual arousal in anyone whom he nears. Although this may be the lead-in to a crude story, the real transgression is that Rabelais has the character, as H. Montgomery Hyde describes it, "enter a theater in which a passion play is in progress, with the result that the performers and spectators alike, angels and devils, men and animals, are so powerfully affected by its presence amongst them that they promptly begin copulating with one another."[119]

For the most part, there was not the level of pornographic depiction in the Christian era up through this time that there had been in the classical era. As art historian Peter Webb puts it, "Eroticism is rare in the art of the Early Christian period and the Middle Ages. Pagan monuments were often overtly sexual, but Christian art shunned the world of physical love and concentrated instead on spiritual upliftment."[120] Webb does note the anomaly of erotic images actually found in Christian churches of the Middle Ages.[121] English and Irish Saxon and Norman churches, for example, contained nude female fertility figures. Webb suggests that these figures were removed from pagan places of worship and incorporated into the churches as a result of a papal directive not to destroy pagan idols. This does not, however, explain the existence of erotic images in later Romanesque and Gothic churches, ranging from nudity to couples engaged in mutual oral intercourse.

Later there was the beginning, outside the churches themselves, of a trend toward the acceptance of pornographic depiction. The Renaissance was the rebirth of classical culture, and it would be natural that that rebirth would include a renewed acceptance of sexual depiction, as found in the often less explicit work of serious artists, as well as the more explicit work of, perhaps, less serious artists. This would explain the role of Romano, Marcantonio, and Aretino in the development of popular pornography. The Italian locus of the Renaissance led to an Italian locus for the production of pornography.

The new Italian pornographic art, however, had little immediate impact on the moral climate of England. Aretino's work was published in London in the late 1500s, but it was published in Italian. It was not until 1658 that an English version appeared.[122] Thus, the illustrations might have been accessible, but the text was less so, until that later date.

The concern in this era over pornography seems to have its roots in the view that sexual activity is degradation and to have focused on the effect of sexual activity on the question of whether humanity is closer to the divine or to the beast. The difference between the reaction to pornography in this era and in the classical era is that, in the earlier era, there was not such a gulf between the gods and the beasts, at least in their sexual appetites. The depiction of human sexuality in the classical era did not degrade because it did not separate human nature from the divine. By contrast, in the early Christian era, sexuality was seen as contrary to the divine nature.[123] Because sexual activity was in the province of the beast, depiction of sexual activity presented a degrading view of humanity, a denial of humans' sharing in any divine nature. Although that might not have raised any official concern when limited to the laity, any such degradation of the holiness of the clergy became a great concern.

It was in the Christian era that pornography became obscene. Pornography could no longer be an unabashed celebration of sex, because sex had become an activity that said something negative about humanity. Pornography became shameful, the hallmark of obscenity, but it was in a sense a limited shamefulness. All sex, since it separated humans from God, could be seen as shameful, and that would speak to sex involving the clergy or the common person. All sexual description and images should then have been seen as degrading, but only those images involving the clergy faced early suppression. The difference seems to be in the low estimation of the common person. A person who was seen as already close to the animals would not really suffer much degradation by any depictions involving sex. There just was not very far to go. The clergy, however, were seen as closer to the divine and had farther to fall by being seen as animal-like. Pornography involving the clergy was more seriously degrading and began to suffer suppression.

The Modern Era

When cutting such wide swaths—thus far roughly a millennium long—through European history, it is difficult to decide when one era has ended and another begun. Some eras may have specific start dates: it seems reasonable, for example, to consider the Reformation to have begun on October 31, 1517, in Wittenberg, Germany, when Martin Luther nailed his Ninety-Five Theses to a church door. Other important eras are more difficult to pin down, and the era for a modern analysis of obscenity is one of that class.

Ian Moulton sees a demarcation for this purpose in the Industrial Revolution or the Enlightenment. He says that "[g]iven the massive social and cultural changes that took place between the seventeenth and nineteenth centuries, it is clear that not only erotic representation but the place of sexuality itself must be vastly different in pre- and postindustrial societies."[1] He finds in that claim a basis to reject the use of the word *pornography* to describe sexual representation prior to the Enlightenment. For him, the word does not apply to "a culture in which . . . technologies of visual reproduction did not exist [and] in which the moral and social ideas surrounding erotic representations were fundamentally different."[2]

Moulton finds all the hallmarks of pornography in the description by Samuel Pepys of his reading of the book *L'ecole des filles*. Pepys's February 9, 1668, diary entry describes his private reading of the book, his arousal, masturbation, and burning of the book so as not to have it in his library. Moulton finds in this solitary action and ensuing shame the precursor of later uses of pornography.[3] In terms of the language used in this book, Moulton is really speaking about obscenity, rather than pornography, which, as we have seen, has a much longer history. Also, Moulton speaks of the shame that marks obscenity.

It seems reasonable in an analysis of both pornography and obscenity to define a start to the modern era as sometime in the late 1600s through the 1700s or even into the 1800s. The Reformation might be considered complete by the time of the Peace of Westphalia in 1648, the treaty ending the religious wars spawned by the Reformation. The Enlightenment was well under way in that era. Indeed, it may be seen as starting earlier. Descartes's publication of the *Discourse on the Method* in 1637 actually occurs somewhat earlier, and Isaac Newton's 1687 publication of *Philosophiæ Naturalis Principia Mathematica* falls within this period. Certainly an earlier start for the Enlightenment could be argued, based on the work of Galileo in the late 1500s and early 1600s or even the work of Copernicus in the early half of the 1500s. The Industrial Revolution comes somewhat later, in the late 1700s and early 1800s.

By the time all these movements were completed or had firmly set in, the modern era may be seen as having arrived. The hegemony of the Catholic Church had ended. Although Europe remained primarily Christian, the Catholic Church's control over sexual materials no longer dominated Europe. The Enlightenment led to a new understanding of nature and the position of man in the natural world. And the Industrial Revolution led to more widespread availability of many goods, including pornographic works. Historian Lynn Hunt suggests that these changes were in fact tied together:

> Pornography came into existence . . . at the same time as—and concomitantly with—the long-term emergence of Western modernity. It has links to most of the major moments in that emergence: the Renaissance, the Scientific Revolution, the Enlightenment and the French Revolution. . . . It was linked to free-thinking and heresy, to science and natural philosophy, and to attacks on absolutist political philosophy.[4]

This emergence with other aspects of modernity does not mean that pornography's arrival was always well received. Peter Wagner notes a general eighteenth-century revival of classical culture that included what he calls a culture of Eros. But, he says,

> The writers and artists who attempted to revive the culture of Eros in the eighteenth century had against themselves a Christian tradition confining sex to marriage while condemning the visual or literary representation of human sexuality. The audience, too, had changed. One of the most interesting phenomena of the reception of erotic books in the eighteenth century is the gradual appearance on the scene of a middle-class readership.[5]

The shame of the earlier Christian era came together with the means to produce pornographic works in volume and at a lower cost. There may have been no greater availability than in the classical era. But in that era, there was no shame in sexual depiction. The new combination of shame and access led to more public concern over the widespread availability of pornography. With shame added to production, there was finally the combination of an industry centered on pornography and reasons to seek to suppress the obscene.

Increasing Availability of Sexual Depictions

Both the growth in availability and popularity and the increase in regulation of obscene materials in England may have had its roots in the Cromwellian period. A tenet of Puritanism was a sense of shame associated with sexual pleasure generally, a sense that has been seen as later developing into the prudery of the Victorian age,[6] an age in which suppression efforts increased greatly. But this sense of shame did not eliminate pornography. Although it did drive pornography underground, the scholar H. Montgomery Hyde says "it flourished exceedingly, and . . . it was the rising middle class in England that was mainly responsible for this changing social attitude."[7]

With the restoration of the monarchy, in 1660, came an increase in the quantity of pornography available in England.[8] Sarah Toulalan notes the "culture of libertinism" in the court of Charles II,[9] perhaps a natural reaction to Puritanism, and the period does coincide with the growth of print generally. Although the availability of sexual material did increase in that period, Toulalan documents the presence of such material prior to the Restoration. This presence was despite the various acts aimed at controlling the press, both before and after the Restoration. Toulalan notes that there was little effort to use the licensing acts to limit sexual material, but as with earlier regulation, the target was material that furthered heretical views or political dissent.[10]

In discussing the nature of the material available before the Restoration, Toulalan notes,

[T]hose few works that were published with explicit pictures illustrating the content of the text appear to have circulated freely. During the 1640s and 1650s a number of texts that purported to reveal the activities of sects such as Adamites and Ranters, and that were illustrated with woodcuts depicting naked men and women (the men frequently with flagrantly displayed erect penises), were printed and circulated apparently without any attempt at either suppression or retribution against the printers and sellers.[11]

Interestingly, however, she says that the images did not explicitly depict intercourse, and when intercourse was suggested by the depictions, there was a lack of nudity.[12]

If explicit depictions of sexual activity were not present in pre-Restoration materials, such content was certainly available after the Restoration. Toulalan provides examples from a 1690 edition of *The Dialogues of Luisa Sigea.* The examples include clear depictions of intercourse, group sexual activity, and mutual oral copulation.[13] Although the examples come from a 1690 edition, she notes the availability of the book in Latin in England at least as early as 1677 and an English translation manuscript in 1676.[14]

Italy had been the center for the production of pornography in the sixteenth century,[15] but the center seemed to shift to France in the seventeenth century, with the best known of the French publications being *L'ecole des filles,* the book that so aroused Pepys, and *L'academie des dames.* The new French works, as shown by Pepys's reading, were available in England by the mid-seventeenth century. Italian works were also available. A translation of an Italian pornographic work, *La retorica delle puttane,* was translated into English as *The Whore's Rhetoric* and was available at least by 1683.[16] A number of these translations were printed through the first half of the eighteenth century by Edmund Curll, who has been called the "father of English pornographic publishing."[17]

There appears to have been a boom industry in the production of pornography in the 1740s. This period saw the publication of what has been described as the "first masterpiece of English pornography," John Cleland's mid-eighteenth-century work *Memoirs of a Woman of Pleasure,* also known as *Fanny Hill.*[18] The book may well have the longest history of case law. Although Cleland was called before the Privy Council but was not punished,[19] efforts to suppress the work stretched to the 1966 U.S. Supreme Court case *Memoirs v. Massachusetts.*[20]

It is, perhaps, not accidental that this pornography boom occurred in the 1740s. As Lynn Hunt notes, the 1740s were also the height of the Enlightenment, with Montesquieu's *L'esprit des lois* and LaMettrie's *L'homme machine* published in the same decade.[21] The understanding of man's place in nature and the acceptance of sexual appetites seem to have been a very important part of the Enlightenment.[22] This new understanding might have been expected to lead to an increase in pornography, which did occur, along with a lessening of any shame, since acceptance of our place in nature would reduce the shame associated with natural activities. That latter expectation of a reduction in shame was not borne out, however, as an increase in obscenity prosecutions followed.

As mentioned, the center of pornographic production had shifted to France in the seventeenth century, but it cannot be said that the genre was originally accepted with open arms. Reportedly, copies of *L'école des filles*, the book with which Samuel Pepys was so taken, were burned in Paris in 1655, and the author was condemned to be hanged.[23] Production of pornography seems to have received additional impetus in the period leading up to the French Revolution. Just as pornography had been used as a form of criticism of the clergy by depicting clergy engaged in the same sort of activities common to the ordinary person, showing a lack of nearness to the divine as well as a hypocritical disconnect between preaching and practice, the weapon of sexual depiction was turned against royalty. Lynn Hunt notes,

> Queen Marie Antoinette was the focus of much of this literature; pornographic pamphlets, couplets and ditties claimed to detail her presumed sexual misdemeanors, questioned the paternity of her children and, in the process, fatally undermined the image of royal authority. If the king could not control his wife or even be sure he was the father of his children, including the heir to the throne, then what was his claim on his subjects' obedience or the future of the dynasty's claim to the throne itself?[24]

Hunt describes one pamphlet, a "very pornographic" essay titled *L'autrichienne en goguettes,* in which Marie Antoinette is "depicted in amorous embrace with the king's brother, the count d'Artois, and with her favorite, the duchesse de Polignac. They are able to begin their orgy as soon as the king passed out after drinking too much champagne."[25]

It was in the French Revolution that Hunt finds the zenith of the political use of pornography, in both the number and the "viciousness" of such works, with about half such material having a political focus, by portraying the nobility as "impotent, riddled with venereal disease and given over to debauchery."[26] Having taken stronger hold in the revolutionary effort, the political focus was dropped in postrevolutionary work, which concentrated on sexuality. The work of French pornographers shifted to the pure depiction of sexual pleasure, marking what Hunt says was the "beginning of truly modern pornography, with its mass-produced text or images devoted to explicit description of sexual organs or activities with the sole aim of producing sexual arousal in the reader or viewer."[27] That new focus also allowed pornography to prosper in France. The attentions of the new authorities in France were not turned to pornography but to counterrevolutionary publications,[28] and the new nonpolitical pornography presumably was not seen as a threat to the new government.

In the era following the French Revolution, a homegrown pornography industry developed in England. The art historian Peter Webb reproduces several prints from the work of Thomas Rowlandson, dating from 1810 to 1820.[29] A similar development took place elsewhere in northern Europe in the same era.[30] On the western side of the Atlantic, the eighteenth century brought with it erotic materials either as imports or as republications of European works. There appears to have been no domestic American pornography, until the 1849 publication of *Venus* in Boston.[31] Even that seems not to have begun any serious development of American pornography. Felice Flanery Lewis says that "[t]he year 1890 roughly marks the beginning of a sexual revolution in the fiction published in the United States and also the beginning of a sustained effort to censor fiction, regardless of its literary quality, through legal actions."[32]

Increasing Regulation of Obscene Materials

It is in this modern era that obscenity regulation became the subject of civil, as opposed to ecclesiastical, law. Until this point, obscenity had been regulated by the Church, and the focus was on blasphemy and other injury to religious interests.[33] As discussed earlier, it was the depiction of clergy involved in sexual situations that drew the concern of religious officials. At some point in the modern era there was a sufficient change in the nature of the concerns that the depiction of sex, divorced from religion, became subject to prosecution.

Just when this shift to civil courts occurred is open to some interpretation. It has been suggested[34] that the earliest example of a pure obscenity case was the 1663 case *The King v. Sir Charles Sedley*.[35] But *Sedley* may be seen as something other than an obscenity case in the current sense; it could well be considered another in the line of blasphemy cases. This is the position taken by Leonard Levy in his historical treatment of blasphemy.[36] Levy notes that, although Sedley also engaged in actions that might be seen as obscene in a more modern sense, he preached blasphemy and abused the scriptures.

It is true that Sedley, a member of Parliament and somewhat notorious reveler, engaged in acts that would have offended for other than religious reasons.[37] He and a group of friends, all rather drunk, were on the balcony of a London inn, where Sedley stripped naked, struck immodest poses, urinated in bottles, and poured the contents on the crowd below, causing a disturbance. Certainly, the combination of the nakedness and immodest poses could be argued to fit with the modern view of obscenity, but the assault on the crowd and the blasphemy involved make questionable the assertion that the case was the first involving pure sexual obscenity. Sedley's conviction was "for shewing himself naked in a balcony, and throwing down bottles (pist in) vi & armis among the people in Covent Garden, contra pacem and to the scandal of the Government."[38] He may have been naked and immodest, but his intent seems not to have been one of appeal to a sexual interest in the crowd but in casting insult (and urine) at them.

A somewhat later case was clearly based on literary obscenity, rather than blasphemy or conduct. That 1708 case, *The Queen v. Read*,[39] is what Leo Alpert takes to be the first true obscenity prosecution.[40] Although Alpert is correct with regard to the target, a sexually explicit book, the *Read* court rejected the bringing of such indictments. The court, in dismissing the indictment, said "[a] crime that shakes religion, as profaneness on the stage, &c. is indictable; but writing an obscene book, as that intitled, *The Fifteen Plagues of a Maidenhead,* is not indictable, but punishable only in the Spiritual Court."[41] Publication of the book was simply not contrary to any law. "[I]t indeed tends to the corruption of good manners, but that is not sufficient . . . to punish."[42] Giving support to the reading of *Sedley* as based on other than the modern form of obscenity, Justice John Powell rejected that case as precedent, finding it distinguishable by the "vi et armis" present there.

A better candidate as the first English case to establish obscene libel as a common-law crime is the 1727 case *Dominus Rex v. Curll*.[43] The book involved, *Venus in the Cloister, or The Nun in Her Smock,* a dialog on lesbian sexuality set in a convent, might lead to the conclusion that the protection of religion was simply being continued. Fred Schauer argues, however, that, despite any religious theme, the fact that the attack was on the Catholic Church in a country in which the protected religion would have been that of the Church of England, speaks against that conclusion.[44] Alpert disagrees, finding the attack on religion still central.[45] Levy also notes that Curll had offended the court and that the offense had led the court to cancel reargument of the case.[46] Presumably, the same offense could have resulted in the failure to distinguish an attack on Catholicism from an attack on the Church of England. Again, the divorce of obscenity from religion may not have been complete. At any rate, Peter Wagner suggests that Curll may well have been surprised by this charge and conviction: "Curll knew exactly how far he could go or how to veil the true nature of his books by inventing pretexts for their publication. . . . *Venus in the Cloister* provided excellent cover in its professed attack on the Roman Catholic Church."[47] This surprise can only have been increased by the fact that the book had previously been published by Henry Rhodes, a man without the enemies or political baggage of Curll.[48]

The years following Curll did little to add to the development of obscenity law, with prosecutions being rare throughout the rest of the eighteenth century.[49] There was, however, the notable prosecution—notable perhaps in its rarity as well as in its motive—of Parliamentarian John Wilkes in the 1760s for his publication of *An Essay on Woman*,[50] a pornographic parody of Alexander Pope's *An Essay on Man*, but Schauer dismisses the importance of the case because of the political motivation for the prosecution.[51] Alpert agrees, noting that the motivation for prosecuting the publication came from Wilkes's publication of another work, a satire that attacked the government for corruption and suggested that King George III was an imbecile and that his mother was involved in an illicit sexual relationship.[52] In Alpert's view, *An Essay on Woman* was simply "an instrument, a strategem [*sic*], and an excuse for hostilities in the guise of a crusade."[53]

Schauer says that it was in the beginning of the nineteenth century that obscene libel came of age and was applied against purely sexual material, material lacking in political or religious concern.[54] In that era, he finds approximately three prosecutions per year, including prosecutions against well-known authors such as Byron and Shelley. Clearly, the first half of the nineteenth century saw obscenity prosecutions become a far more regular event and an event which, despite some lack of definition, was more in keeping with modern views of obscenity. It was the era in which pornography clearly became obscene.

The beginning of the nineteenth century was important in the development of obscenity prosecutions, but it is slightly later that the British legal definition of obscenity developed. In 1868, the Queen's Bench decided *Regina v. Hicklin*,[55] the case that provided that definition. *Hicklin* grew out of the publication of a pamphlet titled *The Confessional Unmasked; Shewing the Depravity of the Roman Priesthood, the Iniquity of the Confessional, and the Questions Put to Females in Confession.* Given the title, it might seem that it was again the protection of religion that was central to the case. That interpretation, as possibly with the *Curll* case, may be seen as less likely because the attack was on the Catholic Church. The development of obscenity law between *Curll* and *Hicklin*, particularly its application to literature that did not attack religion, makes the interpretation even less likely.

Hicklin is important because of the test it sets out for obscenity. The Lord Chief Justice said that "the test of obscenity is this, whether the tendency of the matter charged as obscenity is to deprave and corrupt those whose minds are open to such immoral influences and into whose hands a publication of this sort may fall."[56] It was not the impact on the average person that would determine the obscene nature of a publication. Rather, the material was to be judged based on its impact on the most susceptible person. This is interesting with regard to the thesis of this book: the concern over pornography as commenting on the placement of humans on a scale ranging from God or gods on the one hand and animals on the other. *Hicklin* has particular relevance here, if pornographic materials were seen as obscene not only because they reflect a separation of man from God but also because they contribute to that gap. If so, the weakest of humans would be the most likely to be driven toward the animal side of the divide. Less susceptible persons might well remain in whatever proximity they enjoyed to the divine.

Although there was a case of colonial-era censorship in Massachusetts in 1668[57]—a case that does not seem to have involved a prosecution—the prosecution of obscenity cases in the United States may be seen to have begun with the 1815 decision of the Pennsylvania Supreme Court in *Commonwealth v. Sharpless*.[58] Sharpless was charged with exhibiting

a certain lewd, wicked, scandalous, infamous, and obscene painting, representing a man in an obscene, impudent, and indecent posture with a woman, to the manifest corruption and subversion of youth, and other citizens of the commonwealth, to the evil example of all others in like case offending, and against the peace and dignity of the Commonwealth of Pennsylvania.[59]

The painting was exhibited to a paying public audience.[60] Although Chief Justice Tilghman found no statute barring such an exhibition, he concluded that acts of public indecency may be prosecuted as a corruption of public morality constituting a breach of the peace.[61] Justice Yeates added that acts destructive of morality were punishable under the common law: "The corruption of the public mind in general, and debauching the manners of youth in particular by lewd and obscene pictures exhibited to view, must necessarily be attended with the most injurious consequences, and in such instances courts of justice are, or ought to be, the schools of morals."[62]

The year 1821 saw the Massachusetts case *Commonwealth v. Holmes*.[63] *Holmes* grew out of the publication of a "lewd and obscene print" in John Cleland's aforementioned sexually explicit novel *Memoirs of a Woman of Pleasure*, also known as *Fanny Hill*. Although the court's opinion concerned the lower court's jurisdiction and the sufficiency of the indictment, the opinion seemed to assume that sexual material that is sufficiently offensive may be banned. That year also saw the passage of the first true obscenity law in the United States, in a Vermont statute.[64]

The Supreme Court, in the 1957 case *Roth v. United States,* the case in which the Court recognized the obscenity exception to the First Amendment, cited a number of its own prior cases, dating from 1895, reviewing convictions under federal obscenity law.[65] The *Roth* Court also cataloged twenty federal obscenity laws enacted between 1842 and the time of the decision.[66]

Obscenity law developed slowly through the 1800s. There were few prosecutions prior to the Civil War.[67] After the war, however, prosecutions increased. Most of this increase was due to the efforts of Anthony Comstock, who founded the New York Society for the Suppression of Vice, as a committee of the YMCA in 1872 and as an independent organization in 1873.[68] Other states soon saw the founding of similar organizations, and in 1873 Congress passed the Comstock Act, prohibiting the mailing of obscene materials.[69]

Comstock himself managed to obtain an appointment as a U.S. Post Office special agent and enthusiastically undertook the enforcement of the act. Schauer says, "In the first year after the law's passage, Comstock claimed to have seized 200,000 pictures and photographs; 100,000 books; 5,000 packs of playing cards; and numerous contraceptive devices and allegedly aphrodisiac medicines."[70] Over the course of a career, Comstock claimed he had "convicted persons enough to fill a passenger train of sixty-one coaches, sixty coaches containing sixty passengers each and the sixty-first almost full. I have destroyed 160 tons of obscene literature."[71]

The latter half, or even the latter quarter, of the 1800s saw a significant increase in the prosecution of obscenity both in the United States and in England. This sudden increase, with its focus on sex even without a religious connection, calls for an examination of the impetus for that development.

Why the Increase in Regulation?

The Enlightenment found the place of humanity in the animal kingdom. It would be expected that an acceptance of the animal nature of humans would lessen the shame that had been associated, since the classical era, with pornography. If humans came to be seen as a species of animal, then depictions of humans engaged in animal activities should have been less a cause for shame. Pornography should have been less likely to be considered obscene and subject to prosecution. Why, then, did the law actually go in the opposite direction?

There have been a number of reasons offered to explain this increase that seems contrary to expectation. Richard Posner suggests that English attitudes toward sex turned more conservative in reaction to French liberalization, during a period of conflict between the two countries.[72] It has also been suggested that an increase in the import of French obscene materials after the Napoleonic Wars raised English concerns.[73]

H. Montgomery Hyde finds the first changes in social attitudes toward pornography in a proclamation by King George III in 1787, a proclamation "exhorting the public to 'suppress all loose and licentious prints, books, and publications, dispensing poison to the minds of the young and unwary, and to punish the publishers and the vendors thereof.'"[74] The public answered the call, with William Wilberforce, an Evangelical Member of Parliament, forming the Proclamation Society, and the later founding of the Society for the Suppression of Vice and the Encouragement of Religion, known as the Vice Society.[75] Between 1802 and 1817, the Vice Society successfully prosecuted thirty to forty obscenity cases.[76] With increased importation of pornography from France after the end of the Napoleonic Wars, the Society, perhaps adding a fear of foreign influences to its concerns about vice, stepped up its efforts, raising its total to 159 cases between 1802 and 1857, with convictions in 154 of the cases.[77]

The very fact that so much of the material had come, and was continuing to come, from France may have contributed to the impetus to suppress pornography. The role that pornography had played in the French Revolution and the fear of the social and political disruption inherent in that revolution could have continued an interest in suppression, even after the political focus of such work had faded. Lynn Hunt notices this concern, writing that "the specter of the French Revolution, with its threat of democratization, mass political mobilization through print and social disorder galvanized the trends toward the legal regulation of pornography as a distinct category."[78] Further, Hunt quotes *The Annual Register* of 1798, an annual review of the history, politics, and literature of the preceding year: "The French Revolution illustrated the connection between good morals and the order and peace of society, more than all the eloquences of the pulpit and the disquisitions of moral philosophers had done for many centuries."[79]

Even without the specter of the French Revolution, the 1800s saw a similar growth in obscenity prosecution in the United States. This growth did occur later in that century on the American side of the Atlantic, and it was due in large part to the work, noted earlier, of Anthony Comstock.[80] Even with the influence of Comstock, there must be a reason for the reception his views received, and it seems unlikely that negative feelings toward France, an ally of the United States in the War of 1812, the North American take on the Napoleonic Wars, can provide that reason. The reaction may have been to the import of French postcards,[81] but it seems likely to have been a reaction to the materials rather than the source.

An alternative explanation might come from an argument mentioned by the French philosopher Michel Foucault. It may be that the rise in capitalism and the Industrial Revolution led to sexual repression generally and so, presumably, to the suppression of pornography as well. Sexuality could be seen as incompatible with capitalism and a strong work ethic, because it would serve to dissipate labor capacity.[82] Although Foucault seemingly goes on to reject this argument,[83] it does correspond with the period of growth in obscenity prosecutions. Perhaps more important than any incompatibility with capitalism in the era of the Industrial Revolution is the growth of a literate middle class in that period and the belief that that group would be more susceptible to the impact of pornography than earlier aristocratic consumers were.[84] In addition to the growth of the middle class, books became less expensive and thus more available to the middle and lower classes.[85]

The availability of cheaper books has been noted by a number of scholars as leading to the eventual regulation of obscenity, even if the greatest concerns would have had to come later, as books became even less expensive. Schauer finds the turning point to be earlier, in Gutenberg's 1428 invention of the printing press, which made possible the acquisition of written works by members of all classes.[86] Of course, at that point, the concern was over heresy rather than purely sexual content.

Moulton agrees with Schauer's explanation that it was the printing press that led to increased concern over, and resultant restrictions on, pornographic material. He writes,

In the late sixteenth and early seventeenth centuries erotic poetry in English circulated either in manuscript among a select coterie of readers or in print through the London book market. The latter form of circulation was especially disturbing to contemporary moralists. Printed materials, of course, reached a larger and socially broader audience than texts circulated (however widely) in manuscript. And as the market grew in importance in the later years of the century the regulation of erotic writing in print became a matter of increasing official concern.[87]

He goes on to suggest that the Bishops' Order of 1599 was directed "in part" at erotic books. However, he also notes that that order was aimed at controlling political discourse and that the erotic was simply seen as having political consequences.[88] Thus, erotic material in that era may simply have been caught up in the same concerns over political and religious speech that explains the treatment of earlier sexual content. Indeed, Moulton says that sexual material of that early modern era and the reaction to it had not developed, or at best was in the process of developing, the characteristics that made later eras consider such material obscene.[89]

Finding a basis for the increase in obscenity prosecutions in technological advances may seem plausible, but it is lacking in some regards as an explanation of the changes in societal attitudes. Although books may have become cheaper with the invention of the printing press and movable type and with the later production of works of less quality, prints and sketches did not depend on these advances, and graphic sexual themes in pottery had been popular two thousand years earlier. Sexual material, which would have more impact in these pictorial forms, had long been available to even the illiterate. These technological developments and the increases in literacy do provide a reasonable explanation for the inclusion of textual materials in obscenity statutes that had previously addressed only pictures.[90] It also seems possible that development of the paperback book contributed to concerns, as sexual texts became more available to the masses.

Although offering some explanation, the reliance on technological changes is unsatisfying. It fails to explain the change in focus in obscenity laws from heresy to sex. An explanation that rests not only on increased availability but also on changes in attitudes toward sexual depiction would be an improvement. If that explanation ties together the themes of religion, degradation, and sex, it would also be consistent with the treatment of sexual images across the millennia.

Thus, although printing made pornographic books more available, pornographic pottery had in an earlier era been widespread. The press provided a change in the medium, but that does not seem to be as good an explanation for a change in attitude toward pornography as would be the sort of change in religious view that has explained other differences in views on pornography. Given the earlier religious basis for regulating pornography, an explanation focusing on religion seems preferable to one focusing on technology or literacy. This would be particularly so if something occurred in the era of increased regulation that renewed questions over the relationships among humans, God or the gods, and the animals.

The Evolutionists

An alternative explanation for the increase in regulation of pornography may be found in the changing view on the relationship between humans and the animals. Joyce Salisbury, in her study of animals in the Middle Ages, notes a change in view between the time of St. Augustine and the 1400s. "During that time, thinkers moved from the idea that humans and animals were qualitatively different (Augustine's view) to a notion that we have more in common with the animals than we might like to admit."[91] By the late Middle Ages, "[t]hinkers moved more closely to the Greco-Roman view that saw humans along a continuum with animals, with the potential of lowering themselves to the bestial level by their actions. The view that we can see emerging in the twelfth century dominated Renaissance thought."[92]

The acceptance of humans as part of the animal kingdom could serve to explain the growth of obscene material, particularly in and after the Enlightenment. Finding our place among the animals could have led to a greater acceptance of our animal appetites and an interest in literature exploring those appetites. This change in the view of animals has continued into still more modern times to include humans along with any living macroorganism not seen as a plant. It has been accompanied by increases in the availability of pornographic materials.

The inclusion of humans in the animal kingdom and an understanding of evolution, with its conclusion that we are not only like animals in many ways but are animals that are only more advanced than others, would also have spoken to the status of humans along a divine/animal split. Salisbury says, "This definition of animals (that includes us) means that previous boundaries between humans and animals have disappeared. As James Rachels put it, Darwinism 'undermines the traditional idea that human life has a special, unique worth.'"[93]

The development of obscenity law and the suppression of sexual materials can be seen as a reaction to this placement of humans among the animals and specifically as a reaction to the developing theory of evolution. It is true that Charles Darwin's *Origin of Species* was not published until 1859, and at that point the interest in limiting pornography was already under way, even if the greater growth occurred later in the century. The tie, however, is not weakened by this publication date, because evolution and our place among the animals were both a part of scientific discussion well before 1859.

Carl Linnaeus began the study of taxonomy, the classification of living things, in the middle of the 1700s.[94] Linnaeus placed humans in our own genus, the only living species of the genus homo, but it appears that he did so on other than scientific grounds. He wrote about the decision later:

> I demand of you, and of the whole world, that you show me a generic char-
> acter . . . by which to distinguish between Man and Ape. I myself most
> assuredly know of none. I wish somebody would indicate one to me. But, if
> I had called man an ape, or vice versa, I would have fallen under the ban of
> all the ecclesiastics. It may be that as a naturalist I ought to have done so.[95]

Perhaps the naturalism of the Enlightenment and its recognition of a tie of humanity to the animals would have been acceptable, but a taxonomic tie that put humans in the same genus as any of the animals would, in Linnaeus's view, have been unacceptable. Indeed, even the inclusion of humans and the apes within the same order, Anthropomorpha, met with criticism.[96]

Not only had taxonomic similarities been noted before the beginning of the nineteenth century; there was also early speculation on the origins of animal species. Darwin's own grandfather, Erasmus Darwin, had written a 1794 work titled *Zoonomia, or The Laws of Organic Life*. In that work, he wrote, "when we revolve in our minds the great similarity of structure which obtains in all the warm-blooded animals as well as quadrupeds, birds, amphibious animals as in mankind, would it be too bold to imagine that all warm-blooded animals have arisen from one living filament (archetype, primitive form)?"[97] Thus, though Charles Darwin and Alfred Russell Wallace are credited with explaining the mechanism through which species evolve, earlier scientists had already sug-gested that there were relations between and a common ancestry among spe-cies.[98] Nor was this earlier expression of evolution that of an unknown scien-tist. Erasmus Darwin was of sufficient fame and repute to have been invited to become the physician of King George III, an offer he declined.[99]

Even Erasmus Darwin was not the first to think in evolutionary terms. Georges-Louis Leclerc, comte de Buffon, in his treatise on natural history, a multivolume work written between 1749 and 1789, discussed the origins of similar species from common ancestors, although he did not tie together less similar species.[100] His view was that the current species are the result of degeneration from thirty-eight original forms, a view that seems evolution-ary.[101] The study of fossils in this period also contributed to the recognition that species varied from era to era, although that conclusion met with resis-tance similar to that faced by later evolutionists.[102]

That the theory was sufficiently well advanced in the scientific community in the early 1800s is established by the offering of a counterargument. In 1802, William Paley, a theologian rather than a scientist at Cambridge, presented an analogy still relied on by those who reject evolution in favor of "intelligent design."[103] Paley was the originator of the watchmaker argument, comparing a watch to the human eye. Just as if one found a watch on a beach, one would assume there had been an intelligent designer of the watch, the complexity of the human eye should lead to the same assumption.

So when Darwin began setting out in his notebooks an evolutionary explanation of his observations from the Galapagos in 1837,[104] he was working in a scientific environment in which evolution was fairly widely discussed. What remained was an explanation of how the process worked. Even this issue had been addressed by at least one theory. John Baptiste Pierre Antoine de Monet de Lamarck, beginning in the late 1700s, developed the theory that organisms inherit the acquired characteristics of their ancestors, a theory also espoused by Erasmus Darwin and treated seriously by Charles Darwin.[105]

Although evolutionary thought had been present for some time, the publication of Charles Darwin's *Origin of Species* was a major event. The book was published soon after Darwin and Wallace had read papers setting forth their independently developed theories at a meeting of the Linnaean Society.[106] Both theories announced a mechanism to explain evolution: natural selection, or the survival of the fittest. The difference between the presentations to a scientific society and the publication of Darwin's book was that the book was widely available to the reading public, and the first impression quickly sold out.[107]

The Origin of Species avoided the subject of evolution and humankind. According to Peter Bowler, "Darwin decided not to deal with the emergence of humans in the *Origin*. But he felt it would be dishonorable to conceal his opinions, and he inserted a single sentence at the end hinting that 'light will be thrown on the origin of man and his history.'"[108] The hint seems, at best, rather vague and seems to indicate a concern that his work, if it included humans, would meet with the theological concerns it did, in fact, later face. He also may have been concerned that a negative reception of the idea of human evolution would lead to a broad rejection of his entire theory of evolution.[109]

The idea that humans had a common ancestry with the apes would have raised great concern over the nature of humankind. Again in Bowler's words, "The problem arose from evolution's challenge to the traditional view of the status of humanity's mental and moral qualities. These always had been assigned to the spiritual world as characteristics of the soul, not the body."[110] This tenet that humankind must differ from the apes in a qualitative way was held despite the fact that similarities between humans and apes had been well noted. Darwin had written in his notebooks, "Let man visit orangutan in domestication, hear expressive whine, see its intelligence, then let him dare to boast of his proud preeminence."[111]

This view of the difference between humans and apes may not have applied to Europeans. Bowler says, "Although there was little enthusiasm for the possibility that they themselves might be derived from apes, Europeans were increasingly willing to depict other humans as having apelike features."[112] Darwin himself seemed to accept this view, noting evidence from physical anthropologists that non-European races were more apelike and have smaller brains.[113] He placed the residents of Tierra Del Fuego on the bottom rung of humanity.[114]

Despite Darwin's general avoidance of the topic of human evolution, the religious implications of his theory seemed clear. According to Carl Sagan and his wife and collaborator, Ann Druyan, "His restraint fooled no one. . . . [T]here could be no reconciling *The Origin* with a literal rendition of Genesis."[115] Darwin finally directly addressed the evolution of humans in his 1871 publication *The Descent of Man*. Although that book made an additional contribution to evolutionary theory generally, by recognizing the role that sexual selection could play in evolution, it was the inclusion of humankind within the evolutionary scheme that caused the greatest concern. This was a direct refutation of the biblical account of the creation of humans. It also denied the special status of humankind. As put by James Rachels, a modern scholar of Darwin's philosophical impact, evolution that includes humankind "undermines the traditional idea that human life has a special, unique worth."[116]

Although *The Origin of Species* and *The Descent of Man* had their impacts, Darwin's book that at least should have had the greatest impact was his 1872 work *The Expression of Emotions in Man and Animals*.[117] Peter Bowler says, "Some of those who accepted the basic idea of evolution for the human body nevertheless thought that something quite exceptional must have happened to create the human mind. The critics maximized the gulf between animal and human mental powers and insisted that we had unique faculties that could not be seen as extensions of animal mental powers."[118] It is one thing for humans and some of the animals to have similar skeletal structure. It is quite another for humans and any of the animals to have mental similarities. Darwin's 1872 book directly confronted the belief that, despite any similarities of human and animal physiology, there was something distinctly different about the human psyche that distinguished us from the animals.

Darwin, from his study of the behaviors of humans of a number of "races" and of the apes and monkeys of a number of species, does draw a conclusion that may have been ahead of his time. He notes that the various species of nonhuman primates express feelings in a variety of ways, whereas the differing "races" of humans are rather uniform in their expression of emotions.[119] He sees this observation as "in some degree bearing on the question, whether the so-called races of man should be ranked as distinct species or varieties."[120] This similarity, in his view, "affords a new argument in favor of the several races being descended from a single parent-stock, which must have been almost completely human in structure, and to a large extent in mind, before the period at which the races diverged from each other."[121] Though perhaps short of a recognition of the complete kinship of humanity, it was at least a recognition of the mental similarities of all humans.

It was some of Darwin's other observations that must have seemed more troubling to those who saw a chasm between humans and animals. In his conclusions about laughter, Darwin says that we can be confident in believing that our progenitors laughed as a sign of pleasure or enjoyment, "long before they deserved to be called human," since many varieties of monkey, "when pleased, utter a reiterated sound, clearly analogous to laughter."[122]

Other expressions are more distinctly human, but even this is not due to any categorical differences between human and animal. Instead, the more uniquely human expressions occurred later in the evolutionary process. Darwin says that rage would have been expressed early in our development—that is, in the prehuman stages—through reactions such as reddening of the skin and glaring eyes but not through the frowning that would shade those eyes. "It seems probable that this shading action would not have become habitual until man had assumed a completely upright position, for monkeys do not frown when exposed to a glaring light."[123] Similarly, until humans had evolved to the point of standing upright and fighting with fists or clubs, "the antithetical gesture of shrugging the shoulders, as a sign of impotence or of patience, would not have been developed."[124]

Darwin sees blushing as the most strictly human emotional response, and as a result, evolutionary theory would indicate a late development. "[I]t does not seem possible that any animal, until its mental powers had been developed to an equal or nearly equal degree with those of man, would have closely considered and been sensitive about its own personal appearance. Therefore we may conclude that blushing originated at a very late period in the long line of our descent."[125] Here, we find a reaction that depends on a uniquely human capacity, or at least degree, of self-awareness. Darwin notes that monkeys do not blush but that neither do infants or "idiots."[126] It seems to require a level of brain development that is not only uniquely human but that develops only as a later part of normal human growth and development.

It appears that the existence of blushing in humans had been seen as evidence that humans did not evolve from lower forms of animals. Darwin addresses "[t]he belief that blushing was *specially* designed by the Creator." He says, "Those who believe in design, will find it difficult to account for shyness being the most frequent and efficient of all the causes of blushing, as it makes the blusher to suffer and the beholder uncomfortable, without being of the least service to either of them."[127] Although it is unlikely that those opposed to evolution would have been swayed by this evolution-based argument, framed as it was on characteristics having developed because they contributed to the success of members of the species, it does indicate the importance of issues involving emotion to the debate over evolution.

It is clear that Darwin shook the religious beliefs of his era.[128] In the famous debate on the topic, science was represented by, among others, Thomas Huxley, who had been a public advocate of Darwin's theory. It is hardly accidental that the opposing position was represented by Bishop Samuel Wilberforce, the man who asked Huxley if he claimed descent from an ape on his grandmother's or his grandfather's side.[129] It is also at least an interesting coincidence that Bishop Wilberforce was the son of William Wilberforce, who had played such an important role in the suppression of obscene materials.

What remains to be explained is why the concerns over evolution and its ties of humans to other animals would have focused on sex and would have led to an increase in obscenity prosecutions. Denial of the relationship between human and animal would have focused on asserting differences between humans and the other primates. The primary focus could not be on physical differences but would instead concern behavior, and the behavior of the apes that seems to have been of the greatest concern was sexual.

It was, in fact, in this era that the habits of chimpanzees were becoming known to Europeans and Americans. Thomas Savage and Jeffries Wyman, in 1843–44, published one of the early studies of chimpanzees in the wild. Although their observations led them to conclude that chimpanzees exhibit remarkable intelligence, they also noted that "they are very filthy in their habits."[130] The filthy habits they observed were sexual. Sagan and Druyan say, "Chimpanzees have an obsessive, unself-conscious preoccupation with sex that seems to have been more than Savage could bear. Their zesty promiscuity may include dozens of seemingly indiscriminate heterosexual copulations a day, routine close mutual genital inspections, and what at first looks very much like rampant male homosexuality."[131]

The observation of chimpanzee behavior was, moreover, not available solely to those willing to travel to their natural habitat. Europeans were able to view chimpanzees in zoos, and the animals continued their sexual behavior in that venue. Although some people might have been made uncomfortable by the sexual behavior of any zoo animals, the behavior of chimpanzees was of particular concern. Chimpanzee behavior would have something to say about human nature. Again in the words of Sagan and Druyan, "If, say, ducks or rabbits with a penchant for sexual excess were under review, people would not have been nearly so bothered. But it's impossible to look at a monkey or ape without ruefully recognizing something of ourselves."[132] The religious reaction to Darwin's theory focused on differences between humans and monkeys or apes and included a concern over images or descriptions of humans engaged in the copulations or other sexual activities so common to the chimpanzee.

An Aside on Masturbation

Prohibitions on masturbation are as old as most of the religious regulations of sexual activity and changed at the same time as the religious and other sexuality changes already discussed. In the classical era there seems to have been no real concern about masturbation, matching the generally more open attitude toward sex. The historian Reay Tannahill says, "Masturbation, to the Greeks, was not a vice but a safety valve, and there are numerous literary references to it, especially in Attic comedy."[133] Or as Vern L. Bullough puts it, "Masturbation was regarded as a natural substitute for man lacking opportunity for sexual intercourse, considerable reference to it appearing in the extant literature."[134] The situation seems much the same in the Roman era.[135] With the onset of the Christian era, masturbation became unacceptable along with other forms of nonprocreative sex.

What is interesting in the modern era is the different basis for concern over masturbation that found voice in the beginning of the eighteenth century. The most influential early book may have been one titled *Onania, or The Heinous Sin of Self-Pollution, and All Its Frightful Consequences, Considered,* anonymously published in 1708.[136] Somewhat later, Dr. David Tissot's *L'onanisme, ou dissertation physique sur les maladies produites par la masturbation,* its original 1760 French version or the 1766 English translation, according to Peter Wagner, "became one of the most influential and widely read medical books in the eighteenth and nineteenth centuries."[137] The focus of these works went beyond the effects of masturbation on the immortal soul to include negative impacts on the mind and body.

Tissot believed that any loss of bodily fluids, but especially a loss of semen, contributed to wasting of the body. Masturbation, along with excessive intercourse, would lead to, in Bullough's summation of Tissot,

> (1) cloudiness of ideas and sometimes even madness; (2) a decay of bodily powers, resulting in coughs, fevers, and consumption; (3) acute pains in the head, rheumatic pains, and an aching numbness; (4) pimples of the face, suppurating blisters on the nose, breast, and thighs, and painful itchings; (5) eventual weakness of the power of generation, as indicated by impotence, premature ejaculation, gonorrhea, priapism, and tumors in the bladder; and (6) disordering of the intestines, resulting in constipation, hemorrhoids, and so forth.[138]

Not only males faced these problems. Women were subject to all same problems and additionally would be faced with "hysterical fits, incurable jaundice, violent cramps in the stomach, pains in the nose, ulceration of the matrix, and uterine tremors, which deprived them of decency and reason and lowered them to the level of the most lascivious, vicious brutes."[139]

In a slightly later period, the 1800s, John Harvey Kellogg of the Battle Creek Sanatorium in Michigan added to the negative results of masturbation. He included

> general debility, consumption-like symptoms, premature and defective development, sudden changes in disposition, lassitude, sleeplessness, failure of mental capacity, fickleness, untrustworthiness, love of solitude, bashfulness, unnatural boldness, mock piety, being easily frightened, confusion of ideas, aversion to girls in boys but a decided liking for boys in girls, round shoulders, weak backs and stiffness of joints, paralysis of the lower extremities, unnatural gait, bad position in bed, lack of breast development in females, capricious appetite, fondness for unnatural and hurtful or irritating articles . . . , disgust of simple food, use of tobacco, unnatural paleness, acne or pimples, biting of fingernails, shifty eyes, moist cold hands, palpitation of the heart, hysteria in females, chlorosis or green sickness, epileptic fits, bed-wetting, and the use of obscene words and phrases . . . , urethral irritation, inflammation of the urethra, enlarged prostate, bladder and kidney infection, priapism, piles and prolapsus of the rectum, atrophy of the testes, varicocele, nocturnal emissions, and general exhaustion.[140]

Masturbation had clearly come to be seen as a physically, not just a morally, dangerous activity.

Why the development of a medical concern? Some basis might be found in experience. Promiscuous persons might seem more likely to contract syphilis, and the final stages of syphilis can include insanity.[141] But it seems unlikely that scientists or medical personnel would have believed that all this catalog of results would stem from masturbation. Nonetheless, this belief was widespread and persistent, such that, according to Edgar Gregerson, "half of the 1959 graduates of the Philadelphia medical school believed that mental illness is frequently caused by masturbation, . . . [and] one out of five *faculty* members of that school believed the same thing."[142]

What is perhaps most interesting about this development is that it began in the same era in which Linnaeus developed his taxonomy indicating the close relationship between humans and the other primates. Any similarities in behavior of humans and other primates, as evolutionary theory developed, would have been of concern to those who wanted to maintain a strong distinction between humanity and the animals. People had become familiar with chimpanzees in zoos, and the sexual behavior of those chimpanzees was disturbing. In an era in which people were coming to see the relationship between humans and the primates, that behavior had something to say about humans.

Not only was masturbation and sex generally seen as relating us to the animals, but these activities came to be seen, once the theory of evolution was introduced, as affecting that evolution. A belief developed that masturbation and other sexual habits could be passed on from parent to child. The German psychiatrist Richard von Krafft-Ebing, who wrote the 1886 work *Psychopathia Sexualis,* reported a case of a woman whose regular practice of masturbation seemed to have been passed on to two sons, who began masturbating at an early age.[143] This was part of a general belief that the children of those who engaged in sexual perversions would be born with similarly perverted instincts.[144]

This idea was even more troubling than noting a relationship between humanity and the animals. Some individuals seemed to be lower on the tree of evolution, occupying a similar branch to that of the chimpanzee. Not only that, but in a belief that seems to have been based on the Lamarckian theory of the inheritance of acquired characteristics, excess of sexual activity and masturbation were seen as specifically the sort of characteristics that could be inherited and therefore progressively increase the separation between humans and God from generation to generation.

This sort of concern with regard to degeneration is reflected in a mid-1800s field study of chimpanzees by Thomas Savage and Jeffries Wyman. They reported that the indigenous human population in the area of their study believed in an interesting origin for those creatures. Sagan and Druyan recount: "It is a tradition with the natives generally here, that they were once members of their own tribe: that for their depraved habits they were expelled from all human society, and, that through an obstinate indulgence of their vile propensities, they have degenerated into their present state and organisation."[145] Sex not only served to mark a difference between humans and God, putting us on the animal side of a divine/animal divide; when practiced in excess, it could push us even more to the animal side of that divide.

The tie of all this to pornography seems obvious. Since masturbation and pornography often accompany each other, pornography would have been seen as contributing to whatever evils masturbation was seen as causing. The relationship did not escape Anthony Comstock, the generator of U.S. laws against obscene materials. He found greatest fault with such material in its tendency to cause masturbation.[146] He wrote,

> The boy's mind becomes a sink of corruption and he is a loathing unto himself. In his better moments he wrestles and cries out against this foe, but all in vain; he dare not speak out to his most intimate friend for shame; he dare not go to parent—he almost fears to call upon God. Despair takes possession of his soul as he finds himself losing strength of will—becoming nervous and infirm; he suffers unutterable agony during the hours of the night, and awakes only to carry a burdened heart through all the day.[147]

Although Comstock speaks of a boy in the passage quoted, his concern extended to girls, a fear that masturbation caused debility of physical, psychological, and moral dimension that could even prove fatal.[148]

The Truly Modern Era

The tie between concerns over evolution and concerns over pornography has continued into the current era. Efforts to restrict sexual depiction in even serious works of literature, such as those of James Joyce and D. H. Lawrence,[149] persisted through and to a lesser degree beyond the first half of the twentieth century. Interestingly, it was an era in which states in the United States attempted to prohibit the teaching of evolution.[150]

In the past forty or fifty years, there seems to have been an increase in the tolerance for sexual depictions. This toleration has increased to the point that Cass Sunstein says that, under the constitutional test for obscenity, "most people involved in the production of sexually explicit work have little to fear."[151] The people of most of the American states have, in the past decades, become far more tolerant of pornography. We have come to accept our animal nature, and depictions of humans engaged in activities enjoyed in common with the animals have lost their sting. Although such depictions may still show us as more animal than Godlike, that is something we have come to accept.

Most Americans have also become more accepting of evolution, although a 2008 Gallup poll still showed 44 percent of the American population believing that God created man in our current form, with another 14 percent believing that man has "developed" but with God's guidance.[152] Thus, 56 percent are accepting of our animal past. That does not mean that attempts to prevent evolution from being taught in the schools have disappeared. The striking down, on religious-freedom grounds, of a Louisiana law mandating the teaching of "creation science" whenever evolution is taught[153] was not accepted by those who are troubled by evolution but instead led to a change in label. The foes of evolution became advocates of "intelligent design," offering arguments like those presented by William Paley in 1802.[154] Here, too, the courts, at least initially, have not been receptive to this imposition of what is seen as religious doctrine.[155]

What is perhaps most interesting is the seeming correspondence between those who are troubled by evolution and those who are most concerned over pornography. With the exception of some strong feminists, who are troubled not with sex but with the impact of the most common varieties of pornography on the status of women, those who are most concerned over sexual images are the same group that is still most concerned over evolution. A significant number of those from the conservative, fundamentalist Christian population are still concerned with both topics and what they say about the participation of humanity in the divine, as opposed to animal, nature. But generally, sexual images are no longer seen as degrading in the sense of showing human beings as enjoying less than their proper status. It is not that such images do not depict humans involved in animal acts, but most people are accepting of the animal nature of humans, even if they believe humans enjoy a heightened status due to our mental capacities.

If sexual images are no longer thought to be as degrading as they once were, and if that were all there were to this book, what has been presented so far would amount only to a different take on the history of obscenity. But the relevance of the analysis of obscenity as degradation is what constitutes the subject matter of the second half of the book, in which I argue that hate speech now fills the role once played by pornography. Hate speech can be seen, conceptually if not legally, as the new obscenity. Whereas pornography, at least in the past, may have been seen as depicting humanity in a less than human way, hate speech is now what so depicts its targets. It is hate speech that asserts a lower position in the hierarchy of beings for the groups of persons so attacked. Such speech assigns the target groups to a less-than-human status. Although we may now accept that we are all less than divine, hate speech says that some of us are less than human, and that is degrading speech.

Before proceeding to an examination of hate speech in the context of obscenity, it is useful first to examine the question of whether the changes in attitudes with regard to sex and sexual depiction, as Western civilization went from a polytheistic to a monotheistic religion, were just coincidental. If that were the case, then the thesis that obscenity is based in degradation and that it has been tied to sex because of what sexual depiction said about the place of humans on an animal/divine scale would be weakened. If an examination of other polytheistic and monotheistic cultures shows the same differences in attitudes toward sex and sexual depiction as tied to the relationship between humans, the divine, and the animals, then the thesis is strengthened. For that reason, before going on to the discussion of hate speech, a look at other cultures is warranted.

5

A Look at Other Cultures

The material laid out so far makes a case for the concept of sexual obscenity's being tied to the relationship between humans and God or the gods on the one hand and humans and the animals on the other, but it has done so totally within the context of a Western culture born in Greece and eventually extending to the United States. If the thesis is correct, it should hold true in cultures outside that Eurocentric analysis. This chapter, though necessarily more shallow in its analysis, looks at obscenity in several other cultures. The Hindu culture of precolonial India provides a test for the role of sexual gods, as does a look at China and Japan. Scandinavian countries, though a part of Europe, are somewhat different from the rest of Europe, since the Norse gods remained in ascendancy longer there than the Greek or Roman gods did in the South.

Although the birth of European culture is found in Greece, the birth of the religion that changed that culture and the role and visibility of sex was, of course, not found in Greek culture but in Jewish culture. Although there are Stoic aspects to early Christianity, the religious roots are clearly in the Jewish tradition. An examination of the role of sex in Judaism, then, is appropriate, with a focus not so much on its role in modern Jewish culture but instead on the way sex was treated in early Jewish culture, especially as the religion developed its monotheistic beliefs. At least a brief look at Islam, the third of the great monotheistic religions, is also warranted.

Hinduism in India

The Hindu religion, the major religion of India, is a polytheistic religion. It is said to be the oldest of the great religions still existing in the modern world, and variations in belief developing over such a long period present problems in analyzing the beliefs of the religion. Vern Bullough says, "It has an almost bewildering variety of conflicting schools of philosophy or systems of theology. . . . Interpretation is also difficult because unlike Christianity or Islam it has no particular individual whom it regards as its chief founder or guide."[1] There is, nonetheless, a body of legends of the Hindu gods that speaks to the thesis of this book.

The gods of the Hindu religion present a somewhat complex picture.[2] In the first place, the statement that the religion is polytheistic might be debated. It is suggested that the proper characterization of the Hindu religion is "monotheistic polytheism,"[3] which involves a multitude of gods that are actually manifestations of a single god. These multiple gods do not have any independent existence, as the Greek gods did, but are dependent in their existence on a single Supreme Being. Although that might at first seem odd to Western eyes, the approach may not be that different from the Catholic view of the Trinity. Catholics certainly believe in the existence of a single God, but there are different aspects of that God in God the Father, God the Son, and the Holy Ghost or Holy Spirit.

Putting the monotheistic assertion aside, there are three major gods, Lord Brahma, Lord Vishnu, and Lord Shiva. Brahma may be seen as the leading god or at least as the first member of the Hindu trinity. Brahma is the creator of the universe and of all the creatures that inhabit the universe.[4] Although Brahma may be the leading god, he is not the most honored in India. This would seem rather odd, except for the belief that Brahma, Vishnu, and Shiva are all manifestations of the same Supreme Being. In that context, which manifestation is most honored seems less important. Since Brahma is the manifestation that created the universe, and that job is done, Brahma seems less important than the other manifestations.

There is another aspect to the importance of Brahma, one that speaks to the thesis of this book and also serves to distinguish the Hindu trinity from the Catholic Trinity. In the Catholic Trinity, none of the three aspects has a sexual nature. That is not true of Brahma. Brahma's first creation was a woman named Shatarupa, who was to assist him in creating the universe, but Brahma became infatuated with her. Brahma's gaze followed her wherever she went, and her attempts to escape that gaze caused Brahma to grow extra heads to see her wherever she went. Some sources say that Shatarupa kept changing her form, becoming every creature on earth in an effort to avoid Brahma; he, however, changed his form to the male version of each of her forms, leading to the creation of every animal community.[5] This part of the story again speaks to the sexual nature of Lord Brahma and ties that sexual nature to the existence of all the creatures of the earth.

Shatarupa is also called Saraswati, *Shatarupa* meaning "she of the hundred forms," and *Saraswati* meaning "speech."[6] Saraswati is also said to be the consort of Brahma and to be the goddess of knowledge or knowledge itself. The relationship between Brahma and Saraswati may also be considered incestuous, since she is said to have been his daughter.[7] On the other hand, Saraswati may be seen as an aspect of the Supreme Being focused on learning and knowledge,[8] and the relationship was then not between father and daughter but between two aspects of the same Supreme Being.

The second of the Hindu trinity is Vishnu, the god charged with the preservation and protection of the universe created by Brahma. Vishnu returns to the world from time to time to restore the balance between good and evil.[9] He has been reincarnated nine times so far, with some of these incarnations of particular interest. After three incarnations as a fish, a turtle, and a pig or boar, the fourth[10] or in some accounts fifth[11] incarnation is as a man with the head of a lion. This man-lion, Narasimha, is the sort of god-as-man and god-as-animal mix found in the Greek legends, a mix that defies the divine/animal divide in the Christian religion. There was a particular purpose to this incarnation that explains the mix. It was to save a potential victim from an evil king who had been assured by Brahma that he could not be killed by god, man, or beast, either inside or outside his palace and in either day or night.[12] Vishnu, by being both man and beast, and still a god, attacks and kills the king at dusk and at a pillar to the palace.[13] Despite the purpose of the mix, it is an interesting analog to the Greek myths.

The later incarnations of Vishnu are as men. One is as Rama, who is said to have embodied righteousness, to have been a great warrior, and to have been the ideal man. Rama was a king, and his story involves his rescuing his wife, Sita, from a demon king. Since Vishnu had both his own consort, Lakshmi,[14] and, as his incarnation Rama, a wife in Sita, that adds an additional level to the sexual activities of the Hindu gods. But Sita can be equated with Lakshmi,[15] with Sita being an incarnation of Lakshmi, paralleling the incarnation of Vishnu as Rama. In fact, Lakshmi is said to appear with Vishnu in each of Vishnu's incarnations.[16]

Another incarnation of Vishnu is Krishna, a very popular incarnation considered by some schools as having all the attributes of divinity.[17] Krishna had a favorite childhood friend, Radha, who did not become a legal consort.[18] Nonetheless, Radha is said to have been Krishna's beloved, and the two are the theme of much of the poetry and many of the cults of India.[19] Interestingly, Radha appears not to have been an incarnation of Lakshmi, since she is said sometimes to be considered an aspect of Shiva.[20] Krishna is also said to have been addicted to women.[21] He is said to have had 16,108 wives, with each bearing ten sons and a daughter.[22]

As indicated, Vishnu's consort is Lakshmi, the goddess of fortune and of beauty.[23] She is also said to be the goddess of wealth and purity.[24] As the goddess of beauty, she is also the mother of Kama, or lust.[25] There does not seem to be much focus on any sexual side of Lakshmi, but she is worshiped to bring fortune, virtue, and bravery.[26]

The third of the Hindu trinity is Shiva. While Brahma created the universe, and Vishnu is the preserver, Shiva is the destroyer of the universe. Shiva may have the most sexual nature of the three.[27] He is sometimes represented as a linga, a phallic statue, representing power and masculinity. Hindus believe the linga represents the seed or creative force of the universe, and worshipers celebrate a festival in which the linga is bathed in water, milk, and honey.[28]

Not surprisingly, Shiva too has a consort, Devi, the mother-goddess.[29] Devi has taken a number of forms. A significant one is Kali, the goddess of death. She is also the wife of Shiva in two forms: she is Sati, the faithful goddess of marital fidelity,[30] and she is Parvati, a goddess who is Shiva's "eternal wife."[31] The tie between Parvati and Shiva is so strong that Shiva is sometimes depicted as half man and half woman, one half showing him and the other showing Parvati, and when they are not depicted sharing the same body, they are almost always depicted together.[32]

All three of the major Hindu gods, then, have their sexual side. Although none matches the promiscuous nature of Zeus, save perhaps Vishnu's incarnation as Krishna, they are all sufficiently sexual that the sexual nature of humanity does not distinguish humans from the gods. Thus, as with the Greeks, we would expect that in Hindu culture sexual depiction would not be a source of shame and pornography would not be considered obscene and subject to limitation.

There is another similarity of Hinduism to Greek and Roman mythology. The Greek legends include individuals who are half man and half god, those who are half man and half animal, and those who are half god and half animal. The incarnations of Vishnu include the god as a fish, a turtle, and a boar, as well as men. Also included is the half-man and half-lion incarnation. Beyond Vishnu's incarnations, there are minor gods that show this same mixture of man, god, and animal. Hanuman is described as a "monkey-headed demigod"[33] who serves as Rama's envoy. He is depicted as having a human body, with the head of a monkey.[34] A second example is Ganesh, or Ganapati. Ganesh is a god with the head of an elephant and the body of a large-bellied human, but with four arms.[35] In India too, then, there are combinations of god, animal, and, at least in form, human.[36] There are not clear lines to be drawn between the three, and depictions would not be the source of shame by putting humans on the animal side of a divine/animal split. For these reasons, we would expect that the rest of the Indian culture would be more like the Greek and Roman cultures than like the later Christian culture.

The art of precolonial India reflects this polytheism of sexually active gods, to the degree that art historian Peter Webb says, "That sexual force, or libido, is the basic driving energy of mankind, is a belief which lies behind practically all the imagery we find in Indian art."[37] Sex was divine and certainly no occasion for guilt. Temples were adorned with numerous carvings of couples engaged in sexual acts and commonly contained sculptures of beautiful women in sexually evocative poses, and most contained a phallic icon as a focus for worship.[38] The excitement the sculptures may have aroused in men could be spent on temple women. According to Webb, the temple women's "official function was to dance in front of the sacred *lingam* three times a day. Their other duties involved sexual activities; they were literally married to the god, and so intercourse with them assimilated the pilgrim and the god. Thus, they were sacred prostitutes, as honourably considered as their counterparts in Ancient Greece."[39] They were also said to be very gymnastic and often to entertain more than one male partner.[40] The temple of Samanatha was said to have had five hundred dancing girls so engaged.[41]

Webb provides photos to justify his claims of temple carvings depicting orgies, and he describes in some detail one thirteenth-century temple that demonstrates this "high peak of artistic ability":

Perhaps the greatest of all is the partly ruined Temple of Love or Black Pagoda at Konorak. . . . The whole of this fantastic building is covered with erotic sculptures depicting soldiers with lion headdresses and Brahmins with turbans engaged in an endless variety of sexual activities with the heavenly *apsarases*. These women are also shown coupled with animals, a perfectly acceptable idea since the Hindu belief was that the goddess had to be fertilized by all the beasts in order to produce the various species of the animal kingdom.[42]

The sexual content of the temple carvings was matched by the content of the literature and the two-dimensional arts. The *Kama Sutra*, if not the first sex manual, is certainly a very early one. It is said to be reflective of sexual attitudes in the fourth century.[43] It is not salacious but instructive, recognizing sex as an extremely important activity that had to be performed in accord with definite rules and rituals.[44] Among its sixty-four ways to make love, it appears that some would take a good bit of practice and athletic ability.

Webb also provides photos of album miniatures detailing varieties of sexual intercourse. Although many depictions are of ordinary couples, others depict Krishna as a blue human male making love to Radha, a girl who represents humanity and the world.[45] Other manuals are said to contain from 84 to 729 sexual variations, some not being capable of performance by a single couple and some dependent on, as Bullough says, "physical peculiarities of the individual or of the genitalia."[46]

As Bullough says, "With the examples of the Gods before them, the Hindus could give much freer reign to feelings of sensuality and sexuality than the Christians of the West."[47] In ordinary life, sex was not regarded as at all sinful. Again in the words of Bullough, "Hinduism welcomed sex. Unlike Christianity marriage was never regarded as a condition inferior to virginity, nor was there any notion of sex being impure."[48] Although chastity was expected of unmarried daughters, it lasted only until marriage. Women needed to marry and, once married, were believed to be the more sexual of the partners.[49] Bullough says, "It was the belief that without sexual enjoyment a woman would pine and ache. But love was not only a tonic for woman, it also had noble meaning since it filled her whole being, made her steadfast and faithful, and as it grew ever deeper, it strongly mingled with the altruistic."[50] The greatest joy was to be found within marriage, and adultery and prostitution would result in the loss of caste.[51]

That is not to say that prostitution did not exist. There were the sacred prostitutes, but there were secular prostitutes as well. Bullough finds a parallel between the Greek and Hindu practice of early marriage for girls and the development of a courtesan class in both cultures. The necessity of marriage to the well-being of a Hindu girl led to early marriage, and the large differences in age between husband and wife led, as with the Greeks, to husbands seeking companionship, sexual and otherwise, with women of more culture and sophistication, a class similar to the Greek hetaerae.[52] Less cultured prostitutes were also in demand, and the institution was accepted openly and with tolerance.[53]

Epitomizing this link between a religion of a multitude of sexual gods and earthly art and sexual practice is the discipline of tantric sex. Peter Webb says, "Tantracism . . . holds that sexual activities constitute a way of inflating one's inner sexual energy which can then be used for religious purposes. Tantra is a cult of ecstasy, focused on a vision of cosmic sexuality, sex as philosophy and philosophy as sex. It is a special yoga, and requires careful preparation."[54] It is clear that within this discipline, sex, though pleasurable, is serious and very religious. Hindu culture, then, provides another example of a culture in which a religion of sexually active gods is matched by an acceptance of sexual depictions in the arts and in sexual activity in real life. Sex and its depictions do not debase humanity. They are instead seen as a route to the divine and to congress with the gods themselves. Depictions, including temple carvings, may have been pornographic, but in Hindu culture there was not the shame that would make them obscene.

China and Japan

The difficulty in looking at Chinese religion and its impact on society is that there is a conflict between major early schools of thought in China. Confucianism and Taoism both came into existence in the first millennium BCE, and there was further complication as Buddhism came into China in the first few centuries CE. Between the earlier schools, Confucianism seems the more conservative in sexual matters, and there has been tension with Taoism over the centuries. For Confucians women were inferior, and premarital chastity was of the greatest importance, whereas for the Taoists woman was venerated as closer to nature.[55] Bullough describes the balance produced between the two views:

> These seemingly contradictory attitudes were reconciled in Chinese society by following the Confucian ideal regarding the social position of the two sexes, but their sexual relations were governed by Taoist ideology. Outside the bedchamber the wife was usually little more than an indispensable but emotionally negligible member of the household; inside the bedroom she was the guardian of the mysteries of life and of sex.[56]

Buddhism complicated the situation still further with a view that women and men are equals.[57]

This bifurcated view of women may have made natural the development of multiple marriage and a culture of concubines and prostitution. If the wife is an emotionally negligible member of the household, there is no reason why her position in the household has to be unique when it comes to the household role or to sex. As a result, Chinese men were polygamous, having both secondary wives, who were subordinate to the primary wife, and concubines.[58]

There was also prostitution within commercial brothels, fully tolerated by Chinese society and religion. Prostitution was encouraged by Confucian and Taoist ideas on sex, and Buddhism did not alter this view.[59] It seems that sex was to be encouraged, and this led to the development of a large sex industry.

Sex was seen as playing a major role in the health of the individual. As explained by Bullough,

> Sexual intercourse was thought to have a twofold aim. . . . Primarily the purpose of the sexual act was to bring about conception. . . . The sexual act was also vital to strengthen man's vitality through absorbing woman's *yin* essence, and at the same time giving woman physical benefit by stirring her latent *yin* nature. . . . [A] man's semen was his most precious possession, the source not only of his health but of his life; every emission of semen diminished his vital forces unless it was accompanied by the acquisition of an equivalent amount of *yin* essence from the woman, which all women possessed in unlimited supply. Men only received this *yin* essence from women during their orgasm, they should therefore strive to give women complete satisfaction every time they performed the sexual act. The man, however, should control his passion so that he reached orgasm only occasionally, in order to build up his *yang* for use when there was a chance for pregnancy.[60]

In another explanation, this one provided by Peter Webb, it is said that "[t]he stimulation of sexual intercourse could cause the man's *yang* to travel up his spinal column to his head, along with the woman's captured *yin*. . . . The more *yin* and *yang* a man could store in his head, the nearer he would be to immortality."[61]

Webb, in his examination of the exotic arts in China, also notes the difference between Confucianism and Taoism. He says that although China's official religion since the second century BCE has been Confucianism, most of the people have actually been Taoists.[62] Webb points out that Confucius never declared sex wrongful or associated guilt with sex but was "a deeply religious man with puritanical leanings . . . [who] disapproved of frivolity, whether in sexual relations or in erotic pictures."[63] With Confucianism as the official religion, it is not surprising that there were various periods of censorship of the erotic arts through China's history.

The periods of censorship did leave some works intact or partially intact. Webb says that the oldest of the Taoist books on sex remain in textual form but that their illustrations were destroyed.[64] He does discuss works left from the sixteenth and seventeenth centuries, the Ming period. There is a set of watercolors from that period depicting sexual intercourse in a variety of positions, including on furniture specifically designed for that use.[65] Another set of seventeenth-century illustrations "shows a man and a woman performing amazing feats of copulation on the back of a rather startled horse going at full gallop."[66] Webb also provides photos of eighteenth- and nineteenth-century erotic prints and plaques that are rather explicit in their depictions of the sexual act.[67]

Just how tied Chinese sexual morality and art may have been to the gods or God is again confused by the combination of religions. It does seem that the sexual adventurousness of the Chinese has been inspired by Taoism, and the urge to censor may have been inspired by Confucian views on frivolity, but Confucius and Lao Tzu were not gods. Chinese religious thought and Chinese philosophy have been, as a result, somewhat conflated. This view of a Chinese philosophy/religion with no gods is, however, disputed. The anthropologist George Ryley Scott notes that the Chinese have always worshiped a multitude of deities.[68] He finds an extensive pantheon of Chinese gods, most of which he characterizes as phallic, along with a fertility goddess.[69] If so, the Taoist approach to sex would parallel the lives of these gods in the way found among the Hindus and in ancient Greece and Rome.

This confusion among religious traditions is paralleled by some confusion in the acceptance of sexual depiction. The pantheon of gods noted by Scott, with their fertility aspects, would suggest an acceptance of sexual imagery, and there is indeed such an acceptance in some periods and among some people. The later religious beliefs, though not monotheistic in the Western sense, seem somewhat less accepting, with periods of censorship. These later religious beliefs, however, lacked the single Western God, who would be nonsexual. Sex and sexual depiction would not drive a wedge between humans and any divine figure. Even if sexual depictions were limited as a result of an attitude similar to the Stoics, there would not be the sense of shame that met sexual depictions in Christian Europe.

Turning to Japan, we find what may be a stronger case for the relationship between a sexually active polytheism and an open acceptance of sex and its depictions among the people. The Shinto religion was phallic in nature, with what Webb calls an "August Celestial Pillar . . . known as the Phallus of Heaven, and giant phalluses . . . carried in Shinto processions, exactly as in the cult of Dionysius in Ancient Greece and Rome."[70] There was a phallic deity, who would be invoked by courtesans.[71] The creation myth was also sexual, with Izangi, "The Inviting Male," and Izanami, "The Inviting Female," creating the land, erecting the already mentioned August Celestial Pillar, and, through their sexual communion, thereby creating humans.[72] Put somewhat differently, by Scott,

According to another legend, the creative deity was called *Kunitokodachi No Mikoto*. The story runs that the god *Izanagi No Mikoto* and the goddess *Izanami No Mikoto*, both phallic deities, watched two wagtails engaged in amorous adventure. As a result of this occurrence and of subsequent experiments on their own account, they invented the art of sexual intercourse, and from their own union there sprang into existence the mountains, the rivers, the trees, the beasts, the fishes, and, more importantly, the other deities and mankind.[73]

The erotic arts in Japan are interesting, and different from that in other cultures, in that there is little nudity. Webb says that "the Japanese have little interest in the nude, and couples engaged in sexual intercourse are rarely depicted without at least a little clothing."[74] He suggests that this has nothing to do with any shame associated with nudity. Rather, nudity was natural and commonplace in communal baths, while clothing may be sexually stimulating.[75]

The lack of nudity did not mean a lack of erotic art in Japan, however. Webb discusses Japanese "pillow books" that were intended as sex manuals, dating from the 1200s, and he provides photos of prints from the 1700s.[76] He also discusses *shunga*, which he describes as nonromanticized and nonreligious depictions that were "truly sex pictures." "They concentrate on showing the pleasure that results from sexual union, and they imply that this is one of man's greatest pleasures."[77] A number of these prints from the eighteenth and early nineteenth centuries, all of which are very explicit and some of which are fairly imaginative, are reproduced in his book.[78]

The Danish scholar Poul Gerhard's work makes many of the same points as Webb's. Summing up the difference between Japan and Christian Europe, he says, "Pornographic art in Japan had free and unlimited possibilities, whilst the gloomy sexual anxiety of Europe repressed the open, scientific and esthetic treatment of the subject."[79] Gerhard distinguishes between bridal books and pillow books: "From the early Middle Ages in Japan it has been the practice to impart a good sexual education. The young marriageable girl was given a so-called bridal-book. In this work she was able to see, in pictures and text, what was to go on, and she was thus able to gather a great deal of knowledge about eroticism."[80] He describes pillow books, rather than as being educational, as serving the purpose of being erotically stimulating.[81] Again, the photos Gerhard provides show an explicitness and imagination that are part of a sexually open culture.[82]

Both Webb and Gerhard tie this art to the role of sex in Japanese society. Sex was to be enjoyed whenever possible, and the role of women was to satisfy men. As Gerhard puts it, "The role of woman has been, from the oldest times, to satisfy and refresh the man. Her ability to do this was proportional with her happiness and harmony in life."[83] That explains the openness of the instructive erotic arts. It also draws some parallel with the classical era. Gerhard argues that Japanese women may have been quite similar to the women of classical Greece or Rome, with the major difference being that we know more of the Japanese women, because the culture continued to exist into more modern times.[84]

Any match between classical and Japanese culture in the attitude toward sex is carried over to the attitude toward prostitution, although the Japanese view may have been even more liberal. Scott, writing in the early 1940s, says, "There is little or no sense of shame attached to the profession by the public generally and, therefore, by the practitioners themselves. They look upon the adoption of the life of a joy-girl for a period of years, as little different from that of any other profession."[85] If Scott is correct, that seems even more accepting of prostitution than in Greece, where prostitutes and hetaerae formed classes that were accepted and even honored, but prostitution among citizens would not have been so accepted.

An interesting additional class of women attending to the needs of men also developed in Japan. The geisha provides companionship but is not the sex worker that the prostitute is. Scott says that sex for a geisha is not out of the question but distinguishes the two callings as follows:

The truest thing that can be said in comparing the geisha with the prostitute is that while, by the very nature of her profession, the prostitute must have sexual relations with a miscellany of men; the geisha *can* pursue her calling without including in it any such relationships. Whether or not she does indulge in fornication as a side-line is entirely her own affair.[86]

The geisha seems to be of a type different from the hetaera. She has the culture of the hetaera, without the seemingly necessary sex role of the hetaera. She also seems to represent less of a long-term relationship, but again the geisha is far different from filling the short-term role of the prostitute in most other cultures.

Webb does note a period of censorship in Japanese erotic art, including in a 1722 government edict. It is interesting that he labels the government's attempt to limit these depictions as Confucian.[87] Thus, the same conflict between Confucianism and Taoism in China seems to have carried over to become a Confucianism/Shintoism conflict in Japan. And perhaps the claim that the Confucian concern in China was based on a shunning of frivolity rather than a negative view of sex would carry over to this censorship in Japan as well.

The cases of China and Japan seem to reinforce the differences in the treatment of sex and sexual images in cultures with a multitude of sexually active gods compared to cultures with a single, nonsexual God. The gods, being sexually active and having that activity play a role in creation, engage in the same acts as people and animals. People, then, by engaging in sex or in allowing depictions of people engaged in sex, do not separate themselves from the divine and put themselves in the same camp as the animals. People, along with the gods and animals, are engaged in natural and enjoyable activities, and with no shame associated with those activities, the depictions of human sexuality can be open. Pornography would not evoke the sense of shame that turns it into obscenity, which again is tied to the relationship among humans, the gods, and the animals.

Scandinavia

An analysis of the sex laws of the Scandinavian countries in the medieval era adds an interesting aspect to this examination. The Scandinavian countries are both European and Christian, so it might seem likely that the treatment of sex would correspond to that in other European countries of the era. Christianity, however, came later to Scandinavia than to the south of Europe, and that may make a difference. There is also variation from country to country within Scandinavia, perhaps due simply to regional cultural differences but also seemingly dependent on when the laws were compiled in relation to the coming of Christianity in those countries.[88] The laws of Iceland and Norway on the subject date from the first half of the 1100s, whereas those of Denmark and Sweden come from the 1200s.[89] Although the coming of Christianity in the eleventh century predates all four sets of laws, Christianity was more firmly established by the time Denmark and Sweden developed their laws. Until that time, the Norse gods would have been, as with the Greeks and the Romans, the models of behavior.

Compared to the Greek myths, there is a dearth of Norse mythology. The classical scholar Edith Hamilton suggests that the mythology of northern Europe, of England and Germany as well as Scandinavia, was largely destroyed as a part of the Christianization of the region. She counts the still extant *Beowulf,* the *Nibelungenlied,* and a small number of Icelandic Eddas as the only sources.[90] Cambridge don Raymond Page notes the same scarcity, while also pointing out issues regarding the particular lack of primary sources. He notes that the Vikings were illiterate, except for some inscriptions, and recorded little in the way of beliefs and myths. Our knowledge of the culture, he says, comes from outside Scandinavia if it is from the Viking age or, if it comes from within Scandinavia, it is from the post-Viking period.[91] He, too, notes the influence of Christianity and the unsympathetic view of Norse mythology that would be present in outside recordings of then-contemporary culture, as well as a lack of accuracy and a Christian influence that would have affected later recording of myth within Scandinavia.[92]

The picture that does remain from Norse mythology shows a far different religious culture from the Greeks and Romans. Although the Norse gods do have their sexual side, they are not the ribald characters found in Greek myth. They are a rather somber sort. Hamilton describes Asgard, the home of the Norse gods, as unlike any other heaven:

> No radiancy of joy is in it, no assurance of bliss. It is a grave and solemn place, over which hangs the threat of an inevitable doom. The gods know that a day will come when they will be destroyed. Sometime they will meet their enemies and go down beneath them to defeat and death. Asgard will fall in ruins. The cause the forces of good are fighting to defend against the forces of evil is hopeless. Nevertheless, the gods will fight for it to the end.[93]

The chief god, Odin, does not seem to have had the sexual appetites of Zeus.[94] He was, however, married to the goddess Frigga, and they had offspring, among them the god Balder, who was married to Nanna, and Thor, who was married to Sif. Odin also had a child named Vali, born of a union between Odin and Rind, the daughter of a human king.[95] Given the existence of these relationships and children, it seems that there would have been a sexual side to Odin and the rest, but it is not emphasized to anything approaching the degree present for the Greek gods. Odin was attended by a group of maidens, the Valkyries, but their role was also not sexual. They waited on Odin, but their main task was to go to battlefields and decide who would win and who would die, carrying the brave back to Valhalla.

There was also a goddess of love and beauty, Freya or Freyja, but even her role is tied to battle. Only half of those slain in battle went to Valhalla; the rest belonged to Freya and went to live with her. Freya and her twin brother,

Freyr, were said to have come from the old gods, the Vanir gods of nature and fertility, to join the new gods, the Aesir.[96] Freya was the goddess of lust, as well as of love, and there is a story about her that has a sexual content. It is said that she wore the necklace of the Brisings, made by four dwarfs, and she had to have sex with all four to obtain the necklace.[97] Although that upset Odin, it seems not so much because of the fact that there had been sex involved, since that may not have been uncommon for Freya. Instead his displeasure seems to have come from the fact that the relations had been with dwarfs, a group seemingly disliked by the gods.[98]

There is also a story of the creation of classes of humans that seemingly involved sexual relations between a god and humans or proto-humans. The god Rig, who appears to be the god Heimdall in disguise, is said to have visited Midgard, the world of humans, and to have fathered the three castes of humans.[99] Rig visited an old couple and spent the night sleeping between the man and woman. Nine months later a child was born, an ugly child whose descendants became the slave caste. Rig then visited a younger couple and stayed several nights, again sleeping between them. Again, nine months later a child was born. The offspring of that child became the peasant farmer caste. Repeating the sequence with a still younger couple led to a child who began the caste of humans who could ride, hunt, and fight. Thus, at least insofar as this story implies, the very existence of humans, or of the varieties of humans, is the result of sexual interaction between a god and the ancestors of humanity.[100]

The Nordic gods were also married and had children. They engaged in sexual relations among themselves, as well as with humans and dwarfs. They were not the sort of sexual ascetics that should lead to a sexually repressed culture of followers. The practice of the Nordic peoples matched the practices of other people with a similar multitude of gods. A monk writing in the mid-eleventh century, describing a major temple in Sweden spoke of an image of Freyr, who provides mankind with sensuous pleasure, with a mighty phallus.[101] At the temple in Uppsala, worshipers sang obscene songs, and there were dramatic acts performed that may have included ritual copulation.[102] The goddess Freyja is said to have survived into the thirteenth century.[103] Given her reputation for promiscuity, this influence on the people continued into an era far closer to the present.

If the theory is valid that the sexuality of the gods or nonsexuality of God sets the standard for human behavior and the depiction of sexual images, it would be expected that the attitudes to both would have been more liberal later in Scandinavia than elsewhere in Europe. Indeed, we might expect them to be more liberal in the medieval era in those Nordic countries to which Christianity came later. A survey of medieval law in the area bears out those expectations. In Iceland the clergy rejected celibacy, and adultery among the laity was not considered adequate grounds for a divorce.[104] In Denmark and Sweden, adultery by a wife was severely punished, whereas adultery by the husband was not punishable.[105] In all the Scandinavian countries, fornication was seen only as an act affecting the determination of the woman's marriage and was not strongly punished.[106]

Jenny Jochens's work also supports this point. She examines the sex and sexuality of the Norse world in the medieval era through the Icelandic sagas.[107] Assuming that the sagas provide an accurate view, the old Norse world had the perhaps expected mix of sexuality and violence. She says that "Icelandic young men . . . pass[ed] through a violent phase when they were involved with the other sex. . . . [M]en regularly acquired women through capture, retaining some as wives and mistresses."[108] She concludes that sex was available not only through marriage but through extramarital outlets as well, including the services of female slaves and servants.

The difference between attitudes in Scandinavia and in the rest of Europe may be seen to come down to the present day. Summing up the Scandinavian approach, Grethe Jacobsen says, "These different attitudes toward irregular sex and illegitimacy have had a long career. . . . Icelandic society . . . shows a general acceptance of non-marital sex. Only in the more isolated parts of Norway did one find the same pattern, until the last two to three decades when all the Scandinavian countries became famous (or infamous) for their liberal attitudes toward sexual irregularities."[109] This assessment is echoed by Cathy Jorgensen Itnyre with regard to Iceland. She notes a "smorgasbord of sexual practices" known to medieval Icelandic people, and she goes on to say, "Much has been made of the late conversion of Icelanders to Christianity: can it be that the sexual habits of the pre-Christian era lingered on?"[110]

It is at least arguable that the emergence of a more open sexuality in the Scandinavian countries, before any similar emergence in the rest of the West, was the result of a shorter period of dormancy for that open sexuality. The Norse gods were with the Scandinavian people long after the Greek and Roman gods were gone. The sexual attitudes present with such a sexual, polytheistic group were submerged for a shorter period by the more restrictive attitudes that accompanied a religion focused on a single nonsexual God. Scandinavia's more liberal sexual attitudes included an acceptance of pornography as nondegrading and nonobscene, as shown by a greater and earlier acceptance of pornography there than elsewhere in modern Europe.

Judaism

David Loth says that the "Biblical Jews regulated sex more rigidly than any other people who have left so great an impression on other societies. They detailed just what sexual activities were permitted, where and when and with whom. . . . Our moral attitudes toward sex derive more from them . . . than from Greece."[111] Whereas the Greeks concentrated on who could be a sexual partner, the details of how and when sex was permitted were spelled out for the Jewish people. It is true that there was sexual content to their writing, including in the Old Testament of the Bible, but the graphic, pictorial aspects found in Greece and Rome are lacking. This seems to match the expectations for a monotheistic culture, but the development of these views is interesting and strengthens the tie between a culture's views on sex and the variety of its religion.

Louis Epstein traces the development of sex laws in Judaism.[112] He notes a code of sexual morality in the Bible's earliest sections, a simple code setting out rules on marriage and adultery and forbidding, among other things, rape and male homosexual acts.[113] He finds a lack of preaching on sexual matters in what he calls the preexilic period and suggests that sexual immorality had not become a problem, with behavior controlled by simple aversion to certain acts and a feeling that nakedness was shameful and humiliating.[114]

It was the development of commerce and city life in the seventh century BCE that led to moral laxity and then to restrictions on the movement of women and the eventual development of a degree of asceticism.[115] Although some asceticism may have lasted into the Talmudic era, certainly not all sex was unacceptable, and sex within marriage was seen as sustaining the species, the Hebrew people, and the family.

The view of nakedness as shameful seemed to live on, although Epstein says it was not as a matter of sexual modesty.[116] Given this view of nakedness as shameful rather than erotic, it is perhaps unsurprising that there is not a chapter on Jewish pornography or erotic arts in books discussing the topic in other ancient cultures.[117] The old Assyrian practice of women being veiled in public also entered Jewish culture, although Epstein suggests that it was done as a mark of distinction and luxury, rather than out of modesty.[118]

Prostitution existed in early Jewish culture. Epstein says that there were instances of sacred prostitution, both in the sense of women and men attached to a temple providing sex to worshipers as a sort of temple rite and in the sense of engaging in more ordinary prostitution, with the gain going to the temple.[119] Epstein considers these forms of prostitution to have been imported into Judea, but nonsecular prostitution he sees as homegrown, with both long-term and momentary relationships.[120]

What is interesting in this role of sex in Jewish culture is the suggestion that limitations were adopted as a part of separating that monotheistic culture from the polytheistic religions of the region. Peter Webb spends some time talking about the religions and erotic arts of Mesopotamia and the Syria-Palestine region. He begins that effort with the rise of the Sumerian civilization in the fourth millennium BCE as the basis for the religions of the Babylonians and the Assyrians. He finds sexual content in the Mesopotamian myths. In one, the god of rain rapes the grain goddess, producing the moon god, and in another, fresh water springs from the phallus of the god Enki, who impregnates a number of vegetarian goddesses.[121] Thus, life-sustaining water actively impregnates the grain, or a sexual organ provides the necessary water for agriculture and is sexually involved with the goddesses of the crops.

There was also a goddess of female sexuality, and of fertility, who had a consort who was her husband, lover, and son. Part of the worship of this goddess involved sacred prostitution. As it carried into Babylon, according to Webb, "every Babylonian woman had a religious duty to prostitute herself, at least once, to a stranger within the temple precincts as an offering to Ishtar. Professional 'hierodules, votaries with duties of sacred prostitution,' ministered in temples."[122] Not surprisingly, there is a body of Mesopotamian erotic art. Webb recounts five-thousand-year-old images of a naked woman pictured with a bull, fully frontal nude images of Ishtar and her votaries, partially clothed images of Ishtar with her skirt raised to reveal her genitals, and reliefs depicting sexual intercourse, sometimes between a sacred prostitute and more than one male.[123]

The culture of Mesopotamia carries over to the Canaanites, or Phoenicians of the Syria-Palestine region. The most powerful god, Baal, has the attributes of a bull. There is a Canaanite-Phoenician terra-cotta figure of a bull with an erect human penis and testicles between its horns, and, again according to Webb, Baal "copulates with a heifer, an aspect of his mate and sister-protector, the young warrior-goddess Anath."[124] Again, not surprisingly, sacred prostitution was a part of this fertility-based cult.

This was the background out of which the Jewish religion grew. As David Biale explains,

> The religion of ancient Israel is frequently seen as a refutation of the fertility cults of the Canaanites and other peoples who lived in the area that became the land of Israel. Fertility rites are thought to be particularly char-

acteristic of polytheists, who are said to engage in wild sexual orgies that will incite the gods and goddesses to copulate, which, in turn, is meant to bring fertility to the worshipers and their land.[125]

Whereas a polytheistic, fertility-based cult may have allowed, or even required, a role for sacred prostitution, there was no need for such an institution in monotheistic Judaism. Epstein says that it is because of the connection between prostitution and the idolatry of the Canaanites that the Bible prohibits both prostitution in connection with the temple or priesthood and providing the proceeds from prostitution as an offering.[126] As the Jewish people moved away from the Canaanites, prostitution generally became proscribed, with the penalty being death in some circumstances and flagellation under others.[127] Although Judaism did not develop a similar legal bar to fornication, a moral standard against pre- or extramarital relations did develop, with community watchfulness of the young serving that end.[128]

Within marriage, there was a far more liberal attitude toward sex in Jewish culture than in Christian culture. There was, according to Talmudic writers, a sexual obligation to marriage, with details set out as to the required minimal amount of intercourse, varying from occupation to occupation. The sexual obligation, though it might also increase the fertility of the group, was not centered on that fertility; that is, unlike in the Christian Church, in Judaism sex served a pleasure role separate from reproduction, and it need not end at the end of one's fertile period.[129] That is not to say that all acts that could be considered sexual were accepted. For example, vaginal intercourse was considered the only proper sexual outlet.[130]

As the Jewish people moved into different parts of Europe, some regional differences seemed to develop. Among the Ashkenazic Jews of France, Germany, and eastern Europe, Biale notes a normative preoccupation among the rabbis with sexual temptation outside marriage and an acceptance of marital sexual satisfaction as a deterrent to such temptation.[131] Among the Sephardic Jews in southern France and Spain, Biale finds a culture that was more affected by Muslim and Christian neighbors than were the Ashkenazic Jews, resulting in a dramatically different culture.[132] He finds a difference between popular Jewish culture in these southern regions and rabbinic normative teachings, to the point of suggesting sexually dissolute lives among the Jewish population there and noting that any rejection of sexual pleasure by these Jews was in conflict with a larger regional culture that affirmed it.[133]

Among the Kabbalistic writers of thirteenth-century Spain, Biale finds "an astonishing positive attitude toward sexuality in traditional Judaism."[134]

Again in Biale's words, "As opposed to many medieval Christian writers who believed that the Holy Spirit could not be present while human beings were engaged in carnal intercourse, the Kabbalists—and medieval Judaism in general—held the very opposite: intercourse between man and wife brings the Shekhinah, the divine presence, into the conjugal bed."[135] This view, together with a Kabbalistic belief that sex should take place on the Sabbath, reflects a view very different from that of Christian teachings.

There was a major difference in the teachings of Judaism and Christianity regarding sex within marriage. Although both traditions recognized the role of sex in procreation, the attitude among Jewish religious leaders seems to have been much more positive than for Christian leaders. As opposed to a negative activity even within marriage, although necessary both for procreation and for the avoidance of temptation, in the Jewish tradition sex within marriage was wholly positive.

The example of Judaism adds to the analysis in two ways. First, as one of the other great monotheistic religions, it provides additional evidence that in such religions, with a necessarily nonsexual God, there are more likely to be restrictions on sex and on depictions of sexuality. These separate us from God, and they may be seen as debasing humanity. The second addition is the examination of the genesis of this sort of prohibition. In the development of the Jewish religion, we see its limitations on sex as a seemingly consciously adopted method of distinguishing the religion from the polytheistic and more sexually centered religions of the region. Thus, a changing view on sex is not only a difference but a founding difference, as religion moves from the polytheistic to the monotheistic.

Of even more interest than any similarity between Judaism and Christianity with regard to sex are the differences. Judaism is simply more accepting of sex than Christianity is. Sex is a positive, rather than the necessarily tolerated negative of the Christian Church. Given that both religions are monotheistic, there should be, under the arguments presented here, a more negative attitude in Judaism as well. But there seems to be a ready explanation for this difference, one that also still explains the similarities.

As to the similarities—the lack of ritual sex and public art depicting sexuality and the greater containment of sex to marriage—these may be explained by the difference between monotheism and the polytheistic Greeks, Romans, and Norse. When Christians and Jews were sexually active, they were not emulating God. Sex served to distinguish them from God and spoke to their animal nature. To that degree, we would expect that the attitudes toward sex in Judaism and Christianity should be the same.

The differences can be explained, within the context of the general approach argued for here, by the central figures of the religions. Although God may be central to both, there is a difference between Jesus Christ, on the one hand, and the major figures of Jewish tradition. On the Christian side, God became man through the person of Christ. There was then an earthly example of the behavior of God, and that behavior was seen as nonsexual. Christian leaders, in modeling their behavior on that of God, had not only a heaven-dwelling and less knowable God but had an earthly example to demonstrate the behavior of God, and that behavior was believed to be nonsexual.

The Jews had the same heaven-dwelling God, but the earthly leaders of the religion and nation were completely human. Furthermore, their lives were not celibate. Abraham, the patriarch not only of the Jews but of all three of the monotheistic religions, was married to Sarah, but when Sarah was infertile, Abraham had a child by Sarah's servant Hagar. It is through that child, Ishmael, that Abraham is the patriarch of the Islamic religion. Later, after Sarah was well beyond normal childbearing age, Abraham also had a child with her. It is through Isaac that Abraham is the patriarch of the Jews. Isaac, too, was married, in his case to two sisters, Leah and Rachel.

The great king of Israel, David, not only was married twice, but his second wife, Bathsheba, had an adulterous relationship with him while she was the wife of Uriah, one of David's generals. Although David was not God, he was an important leader and hardly an example of sexual purity. His sins do bring on negative consequences, so God cannot be said to have endorsed his actions, but again, he was a Jewish hero and a far different example than Christ.

Moses was married to Zipporah, but his relationship raises an interesting parallel to the Christian position on clerical celibacy. It has been argued that Moses's siblings, Aaron and Miriam, criticized Moses for failing in his sexual duty to Zipporah. It is suggested that Moses took a vow of celibacy as the person through whom God spoke. As explained by David Biale, "If the male Israelites were required to refrain from sexual intercourse for three days at Mount Sinai, then the one who was to be in constant communication with God must surely do so permanently."[136] The dispute, as Biale sees it, was over the relationship between sexuality and prophecy. He draws further support from Rabbi Nehemiah's story of Noah, who though commanded to be celibate on the ark, remained celibate after the flood and received a divine revelation. Here, too, abstinence is connected to communication with God. As Biale says, "Rabbi Nehemiah appears to teach that there is a higher level of holiness, such as that practiced by Moses, that requires abstinence."[137]

If Biale is correct, there is a relationship between holiness and abstinence for the Jews as well as for Christians, but it is much more limited in application. Whereas for Christians the presumed closeness of the clergy to God and the earthly example of Christ required clerical celibacy, rabbis could follow general Jewish law requiring procreation. Only those who were prophets, and thus in direct communication with God, would be limited. That restriction would not apply to the ordinary rabbi. As Biale says, "The rabbis clearly did not see Moses or Noah as models for subsequent holy behavior, especially since they believed that prophecy no longer existed in their time."[138]

Islam

The non-Muslim, influenced perhaps by the traditional modesty of Muslim women, might well be surprised by the description of Islam as a "sex-positive religion."[139] The description might also be seen as a problem for the arguments in this book, since Islam is a monotheistic religion, growing out of the same roots as Judaism and Christianity. Nonetheless, support for the claim is provided by H. R. P. Dickson, a 1930s Western observer of Arab customs. Even though those customs may not be identical to those of other Islamic peoples, Dickson says it is

> no exaggeration to say that sexual intercourse is loved by the ordinary Arab above all pleasures in the world. It is the one great pleasure common to rich and poor alike, and the one moment of forgetfulness in his daily round of troubles that Badawin or townsmen can enjoy. Men and women equally love the act, which is said to keep men young.[140]

So although Islamic public art may not have matched that of the Greeks or Romans, the attitude toward sexuality was a far cry from that of early Christianity, and although Dickson's observation may have been from a later era, this attitude seems to have been one of long standing.

The modesty that may influence non-Muslims' perception of Islam is firmly established and finds a basis in the Koran.[141] Nudity was discouraged, and, as Bullough says, "Men were . . . not to look at strange women, except in the face, which was veiled, the hand or the foot."[142] It can hardly be surprising, then, that the public art of Islam lacked the widespread overt sexuality of at least some of the art of the Greeks and Romans.

Modesty, however, is not the same as prudery. Intercourse was seen as a good, indeed, as a religious deed. Men were encouraged to marry, and not for the early Christian reason of providing a way to avoid sin. Rather than as second best to chastity, marriage was seen as a great good, and sex was a positive part of marriage. People were expected to confine their sex to marriage, and premarital and extramarital sex were seen as sinful,[143] with both fornication and adultery seen as abominations.[144] That may not have been very restrictive for men, since multiple wives were allowed; there could be short-term marriages, at least in early Islam, seemingly as a carryover from prior Arabic culture; and a man could have relations with slaves as concubines.[145] Within marriage, there seemed to be little interest in regulating sexual activity. Bullough says that most commentators on Islam hold that there are no forbidden sexual positions, encompassing the acceptance of oral and anal intercourse, and he says that "Muslims accept and tolerate many sexual activities that the West has traditionally condemned."[146]

The lack of public erotic art, by the standards of the classical era, does not mean that all such art did not exist. Peter Webb says that "the Arab world has produced an enormous amount of erotic poetry and also, as far as we can tell from the few surviving examples, a great deal of erotic art of a high standard."[147] The fact that the erotic art of which Webb writes did not, in large part, survive may speak to later periods of puritanism, but Webb also suggests that "the inherent dislike of many Moslems for representational art has told against sexually explicit pictures."[148]

Webb does provide an example of erotic art from an Islamic culture. His book reproduces a plate from an Islamic treatise that depicts graphically a lesbian scene.[149] The scene includes a depiction of the female genitalia and the use of an artificial male organ attached to a bowlike device that could be used to provide movement. What the existence of this plate may say about Islamic erotic art in general may be open to some question. The image is of Mogul origin from the seventeenth century, and any influence that Indian/Hindu culture may have had would have to be accounted for, before attributing this variety of erotic art to Islamic culture as a whole. Webb, however, does cite to other examples, known only from their descriptions, drawn from what are now Afghanistan and Iraq. He also notes the existence of sex manuals containing erotic art that were popular into the modern era. One of them, Sheikh Nefzawi's *The Perfumed Garden*, Webb calls "the Islamic counterpart of the *Kama Sutra*."[150]

Again, the difference between Islam and Christianity, despite both being monotheistic religions, may be in the status and perceived behavior of the central earthly figures for the two religions, a difference similar to that suggested between Judaism and Christianity. The central figure of Christianity was a divine figure made human. This earthly existence provided a role model for divine behavior in an earthly context. The accepted sexual abstinence of Jesus could further the view that sex separated humans from God, distinguishing Christianity from a Greek or Roman view that human sexuality was an analog to the divine sexuality of the gods. Muhammad, though the greatest of prophets, was not seen as God made human. The earthly behavior of Muhammad would not then establish a mark for the divine, although that behavior might well be seen as a standard for the very holy, even if not divine, person.

In fact, there is an indication that the God of Islam, while the same God as that of Judaism and Christianity, may have been perceived somewhat differently. The Koranic version of the creation of humans is not from dust but from a combination of dust, congealed blood, and, importantly, semen.[151] As Bullough says, "With the recognition that God had semen, Islam could easily regard sex as a good."[152]

There is a further difference, and one that also may be drawn between Islam and Judaism, in that Muhammad himself was far from abstinent. Muhammad "has often appeared to prudish Western observers as the incarnation of sensuality and sexuality,"[153] although it is suggested that his legendary virility may be the result of an Arabic folklore that featured male virility.[154] Nonetheless, there seems to be no question that Muhammad regarded sexual intercourse as one of life's joys.[155] He was sufficiently opposed to celibacy to have said that marriage was a duty for all those who were so capable.[156]

Islamic, as well as Jewish, culture did not find shame in sex. The major figures of both religions had a sexual side, so engaging in sex did not separate the believer from the leader or leaders. There was also no God made human, and made celibate, to provide an example that might make sex shameful. There also seems, however, not to have been the pornography of Greece or Rome in either culture. One explanation may be cultural roots that limited or proscribed nudity. Perhaps more important, however, is that monotheistic Islam and Judaism did not celebrate sex in the way that Greece, Rome, India, and the precursor cultures of the Middle East did. Without fertility cults and myths in which sex among gods was ubiquitous and even led to the creation of humanity, sex might be natural, but it was not a cause of public celebration. Thus, even if the attitude toward pornography in Islam and Judaism might not be the shame of Christianity, there was a more limited reception than in the polytheistic cultures.

6

What about Hate Speech?

Now that we have examined the concept of obscenity, what should that tell us about hate speech? Before turning to that question, it should be noted that one does not have to accept the argument as developed so far to find the remaining material relevant. That is, one may conclude that obscenity is only about sexual depiction and has nothing to do with degradation. If so, the move from the regulation of obscenity to the regulation of hate speech may not seem justified. After all, although hate speech is degrading, it need not be sexual in its nature. Nonetheless, obscenity, even if it is solely about sex, is regulated because it is seen as offensive. Society's interest in regulating hate speech also grows out of a sense of offensiveness. So even if obscenity is about sex and hate speech is about degradation, both are forms of offensive speech, and to a great degree obscenity law is the law of offense.

If one does accept the argument so far, the transition is more obvious. Sexual depictions were seen as degrading in some eras and not in others. In the eras in which such depictions were seen as degrading, they were regulated. Society in the current era may not see sexual images as degrading, although that attitude is clearly not universal. Most people do currently recognize hate speech as being degrading, although again the attitude may not be universal. If hate speech is the current form of degrading speech, then past experience with the regulation of degrading speech would be valuable in examining how to regulate hate speech. The law of obscenity could then provide guidance to any efforts in that direction. The process of developing hate speech regulation can be facilitated by the lessons learned in the development of obscenity law.

How degradation is conceptualized in obscenity law can help in examining the factors that may make speech about race, gender, or sexual orientation degrading and thus create instances of hate speech. The role of statutes and community standards and the possibility of some speech's having sufficient value as to be nonsanctionable, despite any seemingly degrading nature, may also carry over from obscenity law. Before turning to the adaptation of obscenity law, however, it is worth examining the current status of hate speech in the law of the United States and other countries.

Hate Speech as Obscenity?

I am not suggesting that obscenity, properly understood, includes hate speech, although I have argued elsewhere that the concept of obscenity has been unreasonably limited to sexual depiction.[1] In an examination of drama in the Greek and Roman eras, I compared the treatment of sex with the treatment of violence in the classical era, arguing that what made a depiction obscene was a focus on the physical nature of the acts depicted. Whereas a depiction of sexual acts might be in the context of a story focused on an emotional relationship and therefore not be considered obscene, a depiction that focused on nothing but the physical aspect of the relationship might be considered obscene. I argued that the same could be true of violence: the depiction of an act of violence that presented only the physical aspects and did not treat the victim as a full person could be considered obscene. In both cases, it is ignoring the higher-order aspects of humanity that make for obscenity. Similarly, hate speech may be seen as focusing solely on physical characteristics and ignoring the humanity of the speech's target.

Although the philosophical arguments offered to include violence within the concept of obscenity might also apply to hate speech, the history regarding depictions of violence is not matched in the treatment of hate speech. It seems unlikely that there were eras in the past in which hate speech was restricted to the degree that depictions of violence were. Hate speech is probably as old as the recognition of differences among peoples. The Greeks considered non-Greek speakers to be barbarians. The English and the French through much of the past millennium would not have had kind things to say about each other. Wars of one nation against another, be it France and Germany or China and Japan, were not just nation against nation but ethnic group against ethnic group. Hate speech seems a natural part of these ethnic conflicts.

Legal history with regard to hate speech also does not match the treatment of depictions of violence. It is really only in very recent times that attempts have been made to limit such speech. There is, however, one early American case that has some relevance. On December 8, 1807, John Knowles displayed a sign at a street corner in New Haven, Connecticut. The sign was a picture on canvas of a "horrid and unnatural monster"[2] with a legend below it saying, "This astonishing Monster to be seen here." The "monster" is described in the court's opinion:

> And the head of said *monster,* represented by said picture, resembles that of an *African,* but the features of the face are indistinct: there are apertures for eyes, but no eyes; his chin projects considerably, and the ears are placed unnaturally back, on or near the neck; its fore legs, by said picture, are here represented to lie on its breast, nearly in the manner of human arms; its skin is smooth, without hair, and of a dark, tawny, or copper colour.

After placing the picture on the corner, Knowles carried into a nearby public house the "monster" described, exhibited him or her to the people and collected money from the viewers.

Knowles was charged, based on the exhibition, and was fined sixty dollars. The conviction was upheld on first appeal, but when the case reached the state's highest court, that court searched for a basis for conviction. Knowles's attorney argued that, though the information for the charge claimed a violation of a statute, stating an offense *contra formam statuti,* the only statute cited by the prosecutor was one for the suppression of mountebanks.[3] That statute stated,

> That no mountebank, tumbler, rope-dance, master of puppet-shows, or other person or persons, shall exhibit, or cause to be exhibited, on any public stage or place whatsoever, within this state, any games, tricks, plays, shows, tumbling, ropedancing, puppet-shows, or feats of uncommon dexterity or agility of body, or offer, vend or otherwise dispose of on any such stage or place, to any persons so collected together, any drugs or medicines recommended to be useful in various disorders.[4]

In the view of Knowles's attorney, and the view accepted by the court, Knowles's activities did not fit the statutory terms. He was not himself a mountebank, tumbler, ropedancer, or master of puppet shows, although he could certainly have been an "other person." He was also not exhibiting any of the things listed in the statute, unless the display was considered a "show." The court found this word too vague to be a basis for criminal prosecution, accepting the appellant's arguments that in the prosecution's broad application, it would apply to a farmer exhibiting a large ox or the curator of a museum or a scientist showing meteor fragments. That, the court said, could not have been the intent of the legislature.

The prosecution also contended that the exhibition was a violation of the common law, arguing that "[w]hatever is against good morals; whatever strongly affects the feelings of mankind, and gives them offence, is punishable at common law."[5] The defense countered by arguing that it was not so under English common law and that, even if the conduct was immoral in its tendencies, it was still not punishable by the courts—a reasonable position, given the fact that obscenity was only beginning to develop as a criminal category. The court held that a show that "outrages decency, shocks humanity, or is contrary to good morals" is punishable at common law, but it also held that the information charging the offense had to state with particularity the nature of the "indecency, barbarity or immorality," so that the court could make its own determination. The description in the information was not sufficient. Since the charge was unsupported by the statute and the common-law application was too vague, the conviction was reversed.[6]

The defense raised another issue that is of interest here, although the court showed no concern with it. The issue was whether this sort of display was immoral. The "monster" was a production of nature, so what of other such productions? The defense argued, "A young lady was lately seen in our principal towns without hands or feet. No one thought this exhibition criminal, or in the least degree immoral. This lady, to be sure, was *handsome*; but can the beauty or deformity of the object make any difference as to the point under consideration?"[7] But perhaps it can.

It would not actually be beauty that would distinguish the woman without hands or feet from the "horrible monster." It might, instead, be the treatment of the latter as a monster. The argument by Knowles's attorney does not indicate the context in which the earlier woman appeared in the streets. Certainly, there could not be any immoral exhibition in a woman with a physical disability simply being out in public. If, in addition, she presented a lecture on coping with life with such a deformity, that too would seem unobjectionable. Even having her demonstrate how she accomplished ordinary tasks would be informative and hardly immoral. In short, any situation in which the woman was treated as a human being might be distinguishable from the treatment in Knowles's case.

The objection to the exhibition in *Knowles*, and perhaps the distinction between it and the woman described by the defense, is that a human being was exhibited as something less than human. It was not a case of a person with a disability being shown as a person coping with that disability. It was the display of a "horrible monster," the display of a human being as something less than human. That is a degradation of humanity. It, like the display of sexuality to the early Christians, was a removal of a human being to a lower level. The treatment of the man was not only a removal of a human from the divine toward the animal, along with the rest of humanity; it was a removal of that person from the class of humanity toward the class of animals.

Knowles' case was one of the cases relied on by the U.S. Supreme Court in its 1957 decision in *Roth v. United States*.[8] The Court in *Roth* recognized the obscenity exception to the free expression provisions of the First Amendment. It justified that exception, in major part, on a series of old statutes and cases from the colonial era and from the early days of the republic. Knowles' case was cited as a case from the era of the Bill of Rights demonstrating that obscenity was unprotected by the First Amendment.[9] But note that there seems to have been nothing at all sexual about the exhibition in that case. The effect of the display seems not to have been one of eroticism but of horror or disgust. If it was to be an obscenity case, obscenity had to be about more than just sex. It had to be about degradation of humanity. Whereas in some eras that degradation might have been the result of sexual display, the prosecution, jury, and lower-court judges had a broader view of what constitutes obscenity. Although the state supreme court reversed the conviction, it did not do so in a way that refuted that view. The justices had difficulty with the statute and with the vagueness of the information. Had they thought that only sexual content was limited by the statute, they could have said so and reversed the conviction more easily.[10] This appears to be at least one indication of a view in U.S. law that obscenity is all about the degradation of humanity or a portion of humanity, a view that could also speak to the degradation of humanity through hate speech.

Thus, a case might be made for including hate speech within the legal concept of obscenity. Obscenity law would then clearly apply to hate speech. The argument for this inclusion, though, seems weaker than that for the inclusion of violence, and with the exception of one federal district court,[11] the U.S. courts have not accepted the stronger argument for the inclusion of violence in the concept of obscenity. The inclusion of hate speech within the obscenity exception to the First Amendment, then, seems even more unlikely. That does not mean that the argument could not be offered, but it counsels in favor of considering other routes to the regulation of hate speech.

The International View on Hate Speech

The United States is fairly well isolated from much of the world in its toleration of hate speech. Strong interpretations of the First Amendment by U.S. courts have protected hate speech, even seeing it as a form of political speech.[12] The United States has, as a result, become the home of hate speech websites that were driven out of Europe. The position of the international community is shown by the adoption of international agreements directed at limiting hate speech. The General Assembly of the United Nations, in December 1966, adopted the International Covenant on Civil and Political Rights.[13] Article 19 of the Covenant provides for the protection of the freedom of expression, with Section 2 providing, "Everyone shall have the right to freedom of expression; this right shall include freedom to seek, receive and impart information and ideas of all kinds, regardless of frontiers, either orally, in writing or in print, in the form of art, or through any other media of his choice."[14] But despite this recognition of the right of expression, the following article, Article 20, provides that "any advocacy of national, racial or religious hatred that constitutes incitement to discrimination, hostility or violence shall be prohibited by law."[15]

The Covenant is not the only United Nations action directed toward hate speech. In March of the same year as the Covenant, the United Nations opened for signature the International Convention on the Elimination of All Forms of Racial Discrimination.[16] Article 4 of the Convention provides,

States Parties condemn all propaganda and all organizations which are based on ideas or theories of superiority of one race or group of persons of one colour or ethnic origin, or which attempt to justify or promote racial hatred and discrimination in any form, and undertake to adopt immediate and positive measures designed to eradicate all incitement to, or acts of, such discrimination and, to this end, with due regard for the principles embodied in the Universal Declaration of Human Rights and the rights expressly set forth in article 5 of this Convention, *inter alia*:

(a) Shall declare an offence punishable by law all dissemination of ideas based on racial superiority or hatred, incitement to racial discrimination, as well as all acts of violence or incitement to such acts against any race or group of persons of another colour or ethnic origin, and also the provision of any assistance to racist activities, including the financing thereof;

(b) Shall declare illegal and prohibit organizations, and also organized and all other propaganda activities, which promote and incite racial discrimination, and shall recognize the participation in such organizations or activities as an offence punishable by law;

(c) Shall not permit public authorities or public institutions, national or local, to promote or incite racial discrimination.[17]

Articles 6 and 7 of the Convention go on to require states to provide effective protection against racial discrimination and to take effective measures to combat prejudices and promote understanding and tolerance.

The European Community has also taken action on hate speech. In 1997, the Committee of Ministers of the Council of Europe, noting the resurgence of racism, xenophobia, and anti-Semitism but also recognizing the importance of the freedom of expression, recommended that governments of member states move to combat hate speech.[18] That general statement was followed, six years later, by a protocol aimed at the dissemination of racism through computer systems.[19] The protocol requires that "[e]ach Party shall adopt such legislative and other measures as may be necessary to establish as criminal offenses under its domestic law, when committed intentionally and without right, the following conduct: distributing or otherwise making available, racist and xenophobic material to the public through a computer system."[20] The protocol does not require actual criminalization of such material by countries whose domestic law will not allow such action or if a country provides other effective remedies.[21]

There is also case law in other countries accepting statutory limits on hate speech. The few examples to follow are far from exhaustive with regard either to the totality of cases or to the range of countries permitting such limits.[22] Beginning with a close neighbor of the United States, Canadian law contains prohibitions on hate speech. The seminal case on this issue, a 1990 decision by the Supreme Court of Canada, is *Regina v. Keegstra.*[23] James Keegstra was a high school teacher in Alberta. In his teaching he described Jewish people as treacherous, subversive, sadistic, money loving, power hungry, and child killers. He also said in his classes that Jewish people were out to destroy Christianity and were "responsible for depressions, anarchy, chaos, wars and revolution." He further claimed that the Holocaust had been created by Jews to gain sympathy and that, whereas Christians are honest, Jews are deceptive, secretive, and inherently evil. Not only did he deliver these anti-Semitic comments in class, but students' grades would suffer if their own comments in class and on exams were not in conformance with Keegstra's views.

Not surprisingly, Keegstra lost his job. Perhaps most surprising, at least to an American audience, is that he was charged with a criminal violation.

His comments had run afoul of a statute prohibiting the "willful promotion of hatred" toward any group defined by color, race, religion, or ethnic origin. Although such comments were permitted in private conversation, Keegstra's public comments violated the law. Keegstra was convicted, and his appeal eventually reached the Supreme Court of Canada on the issue of whether the conviction violated his free expression rights.

The Canadian Charter of Rights and Freedoms does provide for the protection of free expression. Section 2 of the Charter provides, "Everyone has the following fundamental freedoms: a) freedom of conscience and religion; b) freedom of thought, belief, opinion and expression, including freedom of the press and other media of communication; c) freedom of peaceful assembly; and d) freedom of association." The provision seems to contain everything contained in the First Amendment to the U.S. Constitution and sounds very protective of free expression.

The Canadian Charter, however, also makes explicit that the freedoms and rights it protects are not absolutely protected. Section 1 of the Charter provides, "The *Canadian Charter of Rights and Freedoms* guarantees the rights and freedoms set out in it subject only to such reasonable limits prescribed by law as can be demonstrably justified in a free and democratic society." Accepting that Keegstra's speech was a form of expression covered by Section 2 and that the limits on his expression had been "prescribed by law," the issue for the Court was whether the limitation was reasonable and could be justified in a free and democratic society.

In answering those questions, the Court used the test it had developed in 1986 in *Regina v. Oakes*.[24] That test first asks whether the limitation addresses a pressing and substantial concern in a free and democratic society. In that regard, the Court found that a sufficiently substantial presence of hate propaganda in Canada was of concern and that this hate propaganda had a significant negative impact on its target groups and created discord in society. The Court, noting that Canada is a nation that prides itself on tolerance, human dignity, and respect for diverse groups, found the concern addressed to be sufficiently pressing and substantial.

The second step in the *Oakes* test is an examination of proportionality. This test goes beyond looking at what values a statute furthers and looks also at the damage the limitation of the statute may do to the protections of Section 2. That is, to what degree does the limitation harm the principles that justify free expression? In examining that question, the Court noted that the core value behind the protection of freedom of expression is the protection of the search for truth and the common good. In that regard, the Court said, "There is very little chance that statements intended to promote hatred against an identifiable group are true, or that their vision of society will lead to a better world. To portray such statements as crucial to truth and the betterment of the political and social milieu is therefore misguided."[25]

The Court also addressed the role of free expression in individual self-fulfillment. While the Court recognized that the statute in question could interfere with the self-fulfillment of those for whom a part of that fulfillment included the uttering of racist sentiments, it also recognized that such content itself affected the self-fulfillment of its targets.

Turning to the importance of free expression to the political process, the Court recognized that protection of free expression helped assure that all can participate in the political process. The Court also noted, however, that hate speech can also undermine that participation value:

> [E]xpression can work to undermine our commitment to democracy where employed to propagate ideas anathemic to democratic values. Hate propaganda works in just such a way, arguing as it does for a society in which the democratic process is subverted and individuals are denied respect and dignity simply because of racial or religious characteristics. This brand of expressive activity is thus wholly inimical to the democratic aspirations of the free expression guarantee.[26]

The suppression of hate speech was seen as the best way to encourage the protection of the values that motivate free expression.

That was not the end of the *Oakes* proportionality analysis. The Court also had to consider whether the limitation is rationally connected to the objective and whether the impairment of the Charter of Rights and Freedoms is minimal and justifiable. Given what the Court had already said about hate speech, it is unsurprising that the limitation at issue passed these tests. The purpose of the legislation was valid, and the means chosen were rational. Nor was the statute seen as being overbroad or vague. The impact was minimized by restricting punishment to public speech that is "the most severe and deeply felt form of opprobrium"[27] and thereby addressing a category of speech "only tenuously connected with the values underlying the guarantee of freedom of speech."[28]

The United Kingdom also limits hate speech. The Race Relations Act, passed in 1965, "made it a crime to utter in public or to publish words 'which are threatening, abusive or insulting' and which are intended to incite hatred on the basis of race, colour or national origin."[29] The British experience does point out the fact that hate speech prohibitions can limit the expression of minorities as well as members of the majority. A number of convictions under the Race Relations Act were against leaders of the Black Liberation Movement.[30]

The British, of course, do not have a written constitution, and their courts have accepted parliamentary supremacy and have been reluctant to declare invalid acts of Parliament. The lack of textual guarantees of individual rights has, to a degree, been changed by the Human Rights Act of 1998.[31] The act was intended to provide textual inclusion in British law of the European Convention for the Protection of Human Rights and Fundamental Freedoms.[32] Even if textual guarantees were to make the British courts more likely to enforce individual freedoms, Article 10 of the European Convention, the article that guarantees freedom of expression, includes its own limitations. Article 10, in Section 1, provides, "Everyone has the right to freedom of expression. This right shall include freedom to hold opinions and to receive and impart information and ideas without interference by public authority and regardless of frontiers. This article shall not prevent States from requiring the licensing of broadcasting, television or cinema enterprises." Section 2, however, provides,

> The exercise of these freedoms, since it carries with it duties and responsibilities, may be subject to such formalities, conditions, restrictions or penalties as are prescribed by law and are necessary in a democratic society, in the interests of national security, territorial integrity or public safety, for the prevention of disorder or crime, for the protection of health or morals, for the protection of the reputation or rights of others, for preventing the disclosure of information received in confidence, or for maintaining the authority and impartiality of the judiciary.

Given the willingness and ability of other member states to place limits on hate speech, the Human Rights Act will have no impact on the Race Relations Act.

Another interesting take on the relationship between free expression and limitations on hate speech is found in the German legal system.[33] Article 5(1) provides, in seemingly clear terms, that "[e]very person shall have the right freely to express and disseminate his opinions in speech, writing, and pictures and to inform himself without hindrance from generally accessible sources. Freedom of the press and freedom of reporting by means of broadcasts and films shall be guaranteed. There shall be no censorship."[34] But, as in other countries with a seemingly clear grant of expression rights, other provisions limit those rights. Within Article 5, Section 2 provides, "These rights shall find their limits in the provisions of general laws, in provisions for the protection of young persons, and in the right to personal honor."

Perhaps the most important, and rather regularly invoked, provision limiting expression is Article 1(1), which provides, "Human dignity shall be inviolable. To respect and protect it shall be the duty of all state authority." The German Basic Law is seen as setting up a hierarchy of values. Ronald Krotoszynski says, "free speech simply is not the most important constitutional value in the German legal order; instead, pursuant to the first clause of the Basic Law, human dignity holds this position. Article 1 of the Basic Law 'is both "the supreme constitutional principle" and a fundamental right.' Accordingly, when cases present facts in which human dignity and free speech collide, free speech usually must give way."[35] Much of the impetus for this enshrinement of dignity comes from Germany's experience with its Nazi era and the Holocaust. Thus, again in Krotoszynski's words, "German law . . . generally prohibits political speech that endorses or supports Nationalist Socialist ideologies. The best way to lose a free speech claim is to embrace anti-democratic values or anti-Semitic ideologies."[36] The expression of anti-Semitic sentiments does not merit protection, and neo-Nazi parties are banned.[37]

Concern over anti-Semitism and the Nazis extends to prohibitions on Holocaust denial and Nazi paraphernalia. The 1994 *Auschwitz Lie* case[38] was the result of a rally planned by the National Democratic Party in Munich that was to feature David Irving, a revisionist historian and Holocaust denier. The government required that the party take steps to assure that the Holocaust not be denied, even to the extent of stopping the rally. When the requirements were appealed, the Federal Constitutional Court concluded that there had not been a violation of Article 5's protection of the expression of opinion. The Court distinguished between an opinion, which states the individual's subjective relationship to a statement and is not amenable to proof of truth or falsity, and factual assertions, which claim an objective relationship between reality and the statement. False statements and incorrect information do not merit protection, particularly when they injure dignity.

The most interesting case involving Nazi symbols demonstrates not only that such symbols are banned but also that the Federal Constitutional Court is capable of drawing lines in applying this ban. In the 1990 *Nazi Symbols* case,[39] the Court overturned a conviction for using Nazi symbols. The use had been in the context of T-shirts which were clearly satirical, rather than being supportive of Nazi principles. One shirt, the "European Tour" shirt, had the image and name of Hitler, the dates 1939 and 1945, an outline of Europe, and a list of European nations. Most of the nations were those that had been invaded by Germany, but the list also included England and Crete, each with a line through the country's name and the notation "Cancelled." The second shirt also had an image of Hitler, this time with a yo-yo, and the legend "European Yo-Yo Champion, 1939–1945." The Court recognized that the shirts were not intended to further Nazi principles and anti-Semitism and that they were satirical and should be protected as art. On the other hand, where there is an intent to further Nazism, limitations persist. Again according to Krotoszynski, "One cannot legally sell copies of *Mein Kampf* either in Germany or to Germans, . . . and Web sites featuring prohibited political ideas give rise to criminal prosecutions. The . . . campaign against German language neo-Nazi Web sites continues into the present."[40]

Germany is not the only European country taking the dignity-over-expression approach. Alexander Tsesis says, "the Austrian Penal Code places a greater emphasis on the dignity rights of the targets than the rights of intimidating hate speakers. Section 283 of the Austrian Penal Code makes it an offence to incite hostilities against religious, racial, ethnic, or national groups and to violate 'their human dignity' through slander."[41] Indeed, the willingness to limit hate speech has grown far beyond Canada and the European countries already mentioned. According to Tsesis, "Countries that have enacted laws penalizing the dissemination of hate speech include Austria, Belgium, Brazil, Canada, Cyprus, England, France, Germany, India, Israel, Italy, Netherlands, and Switzerland."[42]

In some cases, European countries have been willing to tackle the issue of hate speech originating outside their borders and found only virtually in their own countries. Spain has required its Internet service providers to block websites that would violate Spanish laws on hate speech.[43] France has gone even further, finding a U.S. content provider liable for violating French law linked to hate speech. Yahoo! is a U.S. company with its principal physical location in the United States. In addition to its main website, www.yahoo.com, the company maintains websites specific to a number of countries including France. The case grew out of the auction service that Yahoo! provides. There were goods offered on that service that violate French law—approximately one thousand items that were characterized as related to Nazis and the Third Reich. Since these items were available to residents of France, either through the yahoo.com website or the French site yahoo.fr, the French court concluded that Yahoo! was in violation of French law prohibiting the exhibition and sale of Nazi propaganda and artifacts.

The court ordered Yahoo! to deny residents of France access to these materials. Although Yahoo! seemed capable of complying with the order for its French website, it claimed it was impossible to keep French residents from accessing the material on its main website. The French court was unimpressed and ordered Yahoo! to comply under penalty of one hundred thousand francs per day. It also said that the penalties would be assessed against Yahoo!, not against Yahoo! France. That was, of course, not the end of the case. Since Yahoo! is a U.S. company, it went to U.S. federal court seeking a declaratory judgment that the penalties assessed could not be enforced by U.S. courts. The U.S. district court recognized that France has a right to enforce its law within its territory, but it concluded that the First Amendment would prohibit U.S. enforcement of any penalties. Although the case was later dismissed by the Ninth Circuit, over jurisdictional issues, the First Amendment arguments were not refuted.[44]

It should be clear from the foregoing that most of the rest of the world has become intolerant of hate speech. Having seen the impact of such speech directed by the Nazis at the Jewish population of Europe, most of the world is unwilling to let that happen again. Hate speech restrictions will remain in force and will have to be interpreted; that is, courts will have to consider just what speech constitutes hate speech. Most of the cases, thus far, have been of the easy, "I know it when I see it or hear it" variety. Nonetheless, at least one court, the lower court in the German *Nazi Symbols* case, saw it when it was not really there.

If these cases are to persist, and if more difficult cases come to the courts, some analysis of what makes the speech hate speech would be useful. The German and Austrian references to dignity indicate again the usefulness of obscenity analysis. If the concern is human dignity, and if the hallmark of obscenity has been the degradation of humanity, the function of hate speech to degrade people to a subhuman level shows its similarity to obscenity. The law of obscenity is the law of degrading images, and experience developed for considering such images that were sexually based can be useful in analyzing speech and images that are nonsexually degrading.

U.S. Acceptance of the International View

Turning to the situation in the United States, it has been suggested that American courts could learn something from the experience of other countries. Richard Delgado,[45] Kathleen Mahoney,[46] Mari Matsuda,[47] and Michel Rosenfeld[48] have all argued that the limitations on hate speech found in so many fully functioning democracies should lead to the conclusion that the United States could impose limits on hate speech without any danger of falling into totalitarianism. These scholars see hate speech limitations as compatible with free expression, at least as compatible with the sort of free expression necessary to the maintenance of a democracy.

Not everyone has jumped on this sort of "but all the democracies are doing it" bandwagon. Krotoszynski finds at least the German experience to fall short in providing a model:

> [T]he German approach seems to fail in several key respects. The Basic Law has criminalized speech advocating the overthrow of the existing constitutional order; nevertheless, citizens have continued to join organizations having this objective. Over fifty years of censorship have failed to get the job done. Reports of anti-Semitism and acts of violence against ethnic minorities in Germany continue to abound. . . . The use of a speech ban as a means of eradicating bad ideas has, as an empirical matter, simply failed to work.[49]

If the test of efficacy is the complete elimination of anti-Semitism and acts of violence against minorities, then clearly the German approach has been unsuccessful. But if the test is simply a reduction of anti-Semitism and ethnic violence, then the continued existence of these sorts of acts does not demonstrate failure. What would be required for empirical proof is a comparison between the state of affairs with the speech restrictions and the state of affairs without the speech restrictions. The best control, the best comparative sample without the speech restrictions, is the Germany of the 1930s. Although there were clearly other factors at work in that era, the speech of the Nazis led to more horrific anti-Semitism and acts of violence against ethnic minorities than are present today. So perhaps Germany is not such a bad model for other democracies, and even if Germany is not the model, there are other democracies with limits on hate speech that could serve that role.

At one point in the not too distant past, the United States might have been seen as following what is now the view taken by much of the rest of the world. In 1952, the U.S. Supreme Court decided *Beauharnais v. Illinois*,[50] a case that considered an Illinois statute providing,

> It shall be unlawful for any person, firm or corporation to manufacture, sell, or offer for sale, advertise or publish, present or exhibit in any public place in this state any lithograph, moving picture, play, drama or sketch, which publication or exhibition portrays depravity, criminality, unchastity, or lack of virtue of a class of citizens, of any race, color, creed or religion

which said publication or exhibition exposes the citizens of any race, color, creed or religion to contempt, derision, or obloquy or which is productive of breach of the peace or riots.[51]

There is at least some similarity between this statute and the provisions found in later international conventions, covenants, and protocols.

The hate speech nature of Beauharnais's conduct can be seen in the description of his actions. He had distributed a leaflet calling for "'One million self respecting white people in Chicago to unite . . .' with the statement added that 'If persuasion and the need to prevent the white race from becoming mongrelized by the negro will not unite us, then the aggressions . . . rapes, robberies, knives, guns and marijuana of the negro, surely will.'"[52] The Illinois Supreme Court characterized the statute as aimed only at speech "liable to cause violence and disorder," and the U.S. Supreme Court accepted that construction, saying that it "paraphrases the traditional justification for punishing libels criminally, namely their 'tendency to cause breach of the peace.'"[53] Whatever may have been the concerns over breaches of the peace, the statutory language and the defendant's actions leading to the charges match the sort of speech now classified as hate speech.

Beauharnais appealed his conviction, claiming that his expression was protected by the First Amendment, but the Court rejected his arguments. The Court found no difficulty in concluding that statements such as those made by Beauharnais—that is, assertions of criminality—would be libelous when aimed at an individual. The fact that the assertions were aimed instead at a group made no difference. The Court said, "if an utterance directed at an individual may be the object of criminal sanctions, we cannot deny to a State power to punish the same utterance directed at a defined group, unless we can say that this is a wilful and purposeless restriction unrelated to the peace and well-being of the State."[54] It is true that there was a potential for breach of the peace in *Beauharnais,* and the statements asserted criminality, rather than simple inferiority, but if this case were still good law, the case might be seen as an acceptance of limitations on hate speech.[55]

A number of cases call into question the continued vitality of *Beauharnais.* The first is from a lower federal appellate court, but it too was an Illinois case and shows the change in attitude in a period of just over twenty-five years. *Collin v. Smith,*[56] a 1978 case, grew out of a planned demonstration by the National Socialist Party of America, a Nazi organization, in the Village of Skokie, Illinois. Skokie had a significant Jewish population, including several thousand survivors of the Holocaust. The village believed that the display of swastikas and military uniforms reminiscent of the Nazis would be traumatic to that population. The village tried to apply to the demonstration its "racial slur" ordinance, barring material that incites racial or religious hatred.

The court held that the village's attempt to protect its residents was unconstitutional. Rather than coming down on the side of a group being subjected to hate speech, the court could not distinguish between the infliction of psychic trauma, on one hand, and other invitations to dispute or the inducement of unrest, on the other, which it found to be within the "high purposes" of the First Amendment. Dismissing the impact on residents of the village, the court said that those who would be offended could simply avoid the Village Hall for the half hour on a Sunday afternoon for which the demonstration was planned.

At the U.S. Supreme Court level, there are two cases involving cross burning that call *Beauharnais* further into question. The 1992 case *R.A.V. v. St. Paul*[57] concerned a group of teenagers who had fashioned a crude cross, which they burned in the fenced yard of an African American family. They were charged under the city's Bias-Motivated Crime Ordinance, which made it a misdemeanor to place an object, specifically including a burning cross or a Nazi swastika, on public or private property "which one knows or has reasonable grounds to know arouses anger, alarm or resentment in others on the basis of race, color, creed, religion or gender."[58]

Even accepting the Minnesota Supreme Court's construction of the ordinance as applying only to fighting words, the U.S. Supreme Court still held the ordinance to be a violation of the First Amendment. As the Court saw it, denying the use of fighting words to those who would express racist sentiments, while not limiting those who would advocate toleration and equality, was unacceptable. "St. Paul has no . . . authority to license one side of a debate to fight freestyle, while requiring the other to follow Marquis of Queensbury Rules."[59]

The second case is the 2003 case *Virginia v. Black*.[60] It was actually the consolidation of two cases, both involving cross burning, one at a rally by the Ku Klux Klan and the other at the residence of an African American. The defendants were charged under a Virginia statute making it a felony to burn a cross with the intent of intimidating a person or group of people. The Court, on the grounds that the First Amendment does not protect the uttering of a "true threat," held that that portion of the statute was constitutional. The statute, however, also contained a provision that the burning of a cross was itself prima facie evidence of the intent to intimidate. That provision was held unconstitutional. Without the requirement that the jury actually find an intent to intimidate, the Court was concerned that a cross burner who lacked the intent to intimidate would be punished for what the Court characterized as core political speech. Thus, cross burning, which must be considered to be among the worst varieties of racist expression, was granted the protection of the First Amendment, so long as there was no proof of an intent to intimidate.[61]

There is one additional case that should be mentioned here. That 1942 case, *Chaplinsky v. New Hampshire*,[62] recognizes a First Amendment exception for fighting words. Words which "by their very utterance inflict injury or tend to incite an immediate breach of the peace"[63] are not protected by the First Amendment. Some hate speech may, then, be proscribable. The publication of a racist tract or a racist speech delivered to a like-minded audience might not constitute fighting words. The New Hampshire court, however, said that its statute reached

> what men of common intelligence would understand would be words likely to cause an average addressee to fight. . . . The statute, as construed, does no more than prohibit the face-to-face words plainly likely to cause a breach of the peace by the addressee, words whose speaking constitute a breach of the peace by the speaker—including "classical fighting words," words in current use less "classical" but equally likely to cause violence, and other disorderly words, including profanity, obscenity and threats.[64]

Certainly, some racist invective, in a face-to-face situation, would have to constitute fighting words.

So could the U.S. Supreme Court ever come to the position that hate speech is unprotected expression? It is true that *Beauharnais* has never been overturned, but what of the later cases that seem so inconsistent with *Beauharnais*? One might try to argue that *Black* was more about a statute that contained an element for which the burden of proof was shifted to the defendant. Intent to intimidate was an element in the statute, but the prosecutor did not have to prove that element. The cross-burning act itself provided prima facie proof of the intent. A presumption of criminal intent might simply be unacceptable. However, the concern expressed by the Court that, without proof of intent to intimidate, protected political speech could be the basis for prosecution seems to lead in a different direction. It is not just that political speech might *unintentionally* come within the scope of the statute. The problem seems to be in the inclusion, intentional or unintentional, of political speech within the statutory prohibition.

One might also attempt to read the comment in *R.A.V.* regarding requiring one side to adhere to the Marquis de Queensbury rules, while allowing the other side to fight freestyle, as still allowing restrictions on hate speech, so long as the restrictions are placed on both sides of a debate. That, too, seems a stretch. The St. Paul ordinance addressed material that causes anger, alarm, or resentment on the basis of race, color, creed, religion, or gender. It did not specify minority races and seems to have limited minorities and nonminorities equally in their use of hate speech.

It must be recognized that for the United States to accept bans on hate speech it would, in fact, be a change in the law. It is a change, however, that must be considered. The United States, rather than being the beacon of free expression it would like to consider itself, is in danger of becoming a pariah nation that is the home to hatemongers. A 2007 article in the *Chicago Tribune* reports, "Hundreds of foreign-language Web sites . . . are using U.S. servers to dodge laws abroad that prohibit Holocaust denial or racist and anti-Semitic speech. Run by hosts in the United States, they thrive out of the reach of prosecutors in Europe, Canada and elsewhere."[65] In particular, Polish authorities have been especially concerned with the website Redwatch, which is hosted in the United States but in the Polish language. Blacklisting of individuals on that site has led to fire bombings and a stabbing.[66] The rest of the world finds it odd that the United States cannot shut down such sites; a UK target of Redwatch expressed disbelief over that inability in a country that does manage to shut down pedophile sites.[67]

So how much of a change would it be? Though significant in impact, it might be minor in theory, and *Chaplinsky* might provide the basis. Most use of racist invective would, in a face-to-face situation, constitute fighting words. The average target would take the words as an invitation to fisticuffs; that is, they are words that "men of common intelligence would understand would be words likely to cause an average addressee to fight."[68] Application to sexist speech raises an interesting issue. If racial minorities are to be protected against racist speech, at least in face-to-face situations, should women not receive the same protection, even if it is assumed that women are less likely to be provoked to physical assault? That is, if women are less likely to respond to insulting, abusive speech with violence, do women deserve less protection? If avoiding a breach of the peace is all that the fighting-words doctrine is about, that would seem to be the case, but making the target pay such a price for having a better demeanor seems unreasonable.

The real difficulty in applying the fighting-words doctrine to much of what constitutes hate speech is the frequent lack of a face-to-face confrontation. Hate websites confront their targets but not in a face-to-face manner. Indeed, in many cases a U.S. hate site confronts its targets an ocean away. In this regard, it is important to note that the *Chaplinsky* Court's definition of hate speech was in the form of a disjunction, in which there are two distinct alternative conditions that lead to speech's not being constitutionally protected. The Court said that words which "by their very utterance inflict injury or tend to incite an immediate breach of the peace" are not protected by the First Amendment.[69] If the Court really meant this definition as a disjunction, then the tendency to incite an immediate breach of the peace is not a requirement, and that seems to be the part of the definition that requires the face-to-face setting. The other disjunct, words which "by their very utterance inflict injury," does not require such close proximity. It is true that such utterances in a face-to-face setting may be seen as more insulting or abusive in the fact that the speaker is willing to make such comments directly to the target. But hate speech that is delivered in other than a face-to-face setting may still by its very utterance inflict injury.

It is true that the *Chaplinsky* Court did go on to quote the New Hampshire court as saying that the statute reached only face-to-face confrontations likely to cause a breach of the peace. But if that understanding was not necessary to its decision, then the face-to-face condition would not be required. This should not be taken as an argument that there is not really any change in U.S. law required to bar hate speech. The general understanding of the fighting-words doctrine does seem to rest on the face-to-face aspect of such confrontations. My argument here simply presents a way in which the fighting-words exception could be changed to reach hate speech in a way that would have at least some consistency with Supreme Court precedent.

There would still be *R.A.V.* to contend with, but the Court there did not say that no distinction can be drawn within the category of fighting words. It did say that, despite regular claims that fighting words are not protected by the First Amendment, free expression provisions are not completely irrelevant. Although distinctions between classes of fighting words cannot be drawn along lines that are themselves illegitimate distinctions, some lines can be drawn. The most fighting of fighting words could be singled out for prohibition. Perhaps epithets based on one's race, sex, or sexual orientation should be considered just that—the most fighting of fighting words. They are words directed at the core of one's identity. They are directed not at what one has done or has chosen but at what one is. That makes them a good candidate for special consideration.

It is hard to say if the Court will ever come to see the harm in hate speech to a degree that it is willing to allow proscriptions, but if it does, then the United States, too, will need a framework for the analysis of hate speech. Again, obscenity, as the law of offense, as the law of degradation, seems a good candidate.

Hate Speech in the Employment Context

Even without a change in the law of hate speech, there are situations in which hate speech may lead to negative consequences for the speaker. As a result of the Civil Rights Act of 1964,[70] workers in the United States are entitled to employment that is free from discrimination on the basis of race, color, religion, sex, or national origin. That includes the right not to be subjected to a hostile environment, and sufficiently pervasive racist or sexist speech may constitute such an environment. In the 1986 case *Meritor Savings Bank, FSB v. Vinson*,[71] the court said that the statutory phrase prohibiting discrimination in the "terms, conditions, or privileges of employment" showed that Congress intended "to strike at the entire spectrum of disparate treatment of men and women,"[72] and that included prohibiting the subjection of workers to a hostile or abusive environment.

It is true that the Court did say in *Meritor* that the simple utterance of an epithet that was offensive to its target might be insufficient to find a violation of the Civil Rights Act, but the Court also said that such use of epithets is a violation if it is "sufficiently severe or pervasive to alter the conditions of the victim's employment and create an abusive working environment."[73] Later, in the 1993 case *Harris v. Forklift Systems*,[74] the Court reaffirmed the *Meritor* standard for a violation when a workplace is sufficiently permeated with "discriminatory intimidation, ridicule, and insult."

The *Harris* Court saw itself as taking "a middle path between making actionable any conduct that is merely offensive and requiring the conduct to cause a tangible psychological injury."[75] The Court provided a test or, perhaps, a standard:

> Conduct that is not severe or pervasive enough to create an objectively hostile or abusive work environment—an environment that a reasonable person would find hostile or abusive—is beyond Title VII's purview. Likewise, if the victim does not subjectively perceive the environment to be abusive, the conduct has not actually altered the conditions of the victim's employment, and there is no Title VII violation.[76]

The Court provided further guidance regarding what constitutes an injury sufficient to find a violation of the Civil Rights Act.

> Title VII comes into play before the harassing conduct leads to a nervous breakdown. A discriminatorily abusive work environment, even one that does not seriously affect employees' psychological well-being, can and often will detract from employees' job performance, discourage employees from remaining on the job, or keep them from advancing in their careers. Moreover, even without regard to these tangible effects, the very fact that the discriminatory conduct was so severe or pervasive that it created a work environment abusive to employees because of their race, gender, religion, or national origin offends Title VII's broad rule of workplace equality.[77]

Although both *Meritor* and *Harris* involved women as complainants, it is obvious from a number of cases that derogatory comments based on race and religion are to be treated in the same way as sexist comments.[78] Although the federal statute does not include sexual orientation, in any state with an antidiscrimination statute including sexual orientation, similar results may hold.

It should be noted that it is the employer who can be found liable for the racist or sexist remarks of employees when a fellow employee is targeted. It is the employer who is prohibited from "requiring people to work in a discriminatorily hostile or abusive environment."[79] When the abuser is the complaining employee's supervisor, the liability seems easily justified through a theory of vicarious liability. In 1998, the Supreme Court so held in *Burlington Industries, Inc. v. Ellerth*,[80] but the Court also allowed a defense in cases when no tangible employment action was taken and the basis of the complaint is one of hostile environment. "The defense comprises two necessary elements: (a) that the employer exercised reasonable care to prevent and correct promptly any sexually harassing behavior, and (b) that the plaintiff employee unreasonably failed to take advantage of any preventive or corrective opportunities provided by the employer or to avoid harm otherwise."[81]

Lower courts have also held employers liable for a hostile environment created by a coworker without supervisory authority over the complainant. In such cases, liability has been found only when the employer "knew or should have known of the harassment in question and failed to take prompt remedial action."[82]

The point of all this is that employers have an incentive to prevent hate speech in their facilities. If such speech reaches the level of producing a hostile environment, and the employer has not taken reasonable steps to prevent such abuse, in particular known verbal abuse, it will be liable to the target of the invective. Any reasonable employer, learning of instances of hate speech, will take disciplinary action against the speaker. In the case of a private employer in an employment-at-will situation, this could include discharge. Even if cause were to be required, subjecting the employer to potential liability might be seen as providing such cause.

It should also be noted that public employers face similar liability. The Civil Rights Act, in defining the persons to whom the act is addressed, includes governments and governmental agencies, although the United States itself and certain organizations sufficiently closely related to the United States are not included.[83] It might be thought that a government employer would be unable to discipline its employees for speech, because of First Amendment limits. Public employees could, however, face similar discipline on the theory that racist comments are a discriminatory action, rather than pure speech, or because public employers are not faced with the same sort of First Amendment restrictions when limiting the speech of their employees as they are when regulating the general population.[84]

Since discipline in the employment context may be based on hate speech, this provides another context in which the analysis of what constitutes such speech may be important. Here, too, it is important to understand what it is that makes certain speech offensive. And here again, obscenity, as the law of offense, can provide some insight.

Sexist and Homophobic Speech

The examples of international agreements do not reach to sexist speech. Perhaps this is the result of history, in that the Holocaust was directed primarily at an ethnic and religious group, and there is not an analogous history of such widespread hatred based on gender. Nonetheless, there is clearly a great deal of speech that expresses, if not hate, at least derision and degradation, and certain aspects of the definitions presented in international agreements seem to reach this sort of speech.

As discussed in the next chapter, the International Convention on the Elimination of All Forms of Racial Discrimination addresses "propaganda . . . based on ideas or theories of superiority of one race or group of persons of one colour or ethnic origin."[85] The 1997 recommendation by the Committee of Ministers of the Council of Europe on hate speech included in its definition "forms of expression . . . which spread . . . hatred . . . expressed by . . . discrimination and hostility against minorities."[86] Lastly, in a European protocol aimed at racism spread by computer, the speech targeted was that which "advocates, promotes, or incites . . . discrimination."[87] It is true that I have selectively chosen to quote language from all the definitions in a way that deemphasizes hate and focuses on the ban on speech that encourages discrimination or perhaps hostility, but it is clear that at least some of what is included in the definitions could reach the sort of sexist speech that expresses inferiority or superiority or encourages discrimination. Thus, although the international agreements do not reach sexist speech,[88] the same sorts of concerns about harmful speech have been included in those agreements addressing racial hatred. Should international sentiment turn to include bans on sexist speech, there is a template for defining the speech to be included.

There are also present inclusions in law of the sexist variety of hate speech. The cases under the Civil Rights Act discussed earlier were not only concerned with race. Many of the discrimination cases under the act have been based on gender, and clearly strongly sexist speech could constitute a hostile environment for which an employer would be liable. Thus, employers have incentive to take action against not only employees who utter racist speech but also those who express sexist sentiments.

Homophobic speech is also not included in the definitions provided in international agreement. History does not provide the difference here. Homosexuals were also targeted in the Holocaust, and hate speech so directed seems to raise historical concerns similar to those raised by racist speech. The same sort of look at the definitions of hate speech shows that they could easily be adapted to homophobic speech, and there would not need to be the deemphasis of hate aspects, since homophobic speech often seems based on hatred as well as an expression of inferiority.

Given what seems to be a growing recognition of the rights of homosexuals and the growing acceptance of homosexuals as another minority, it may just be a matter of time before statutes also address homophobic speech. Indeed, as demonstrated by the Massachusetts and New Jersey statutes at issue in 1995 in *Hurley v. Irish-American Gay, Lesbian and Bisexual Group of Boston*[89] and in 2000 in *Boy Scouts of America v. Dale*,[90] there are a number of states with antidiscrimination statutes that include discrimination based on sexual orientation. At least in those states, homophobic speech in the workplace could lead to an employment sanction. Furthermore, at least one country has included speech aimed at homosexuals in its hate speech statute. The Norwegian penal code, Article 135a, in translation provides,

Any person shall be liable to fines or imprisonment for a term not exceeding two years who by any utterance or other communication, including the use of symbols, made publicly or otherwise disseminated among the public threatens, insult, or subjects to hatred, persecution or contempt any person or group of persons because of their creed, race, colour, or national or ethnic origin. The same applies to any such offensive conduct towards a person or a group because of their homosexual bent, life-style or inclination.[91]

Thus, homophobic speech has been added to other forms of hate speech in Norway's prohibition, and given changing attitudes regarding homosexuality, the addition may well spread to other statutory and international provisions.

Much of the rest of the world has come to believe that hate speech, at least on the basis of race or ethnicity, should be regulated. There may be a growing belief that hate speech on the basis of gender or sexual orientation should be similarly treated. The experience with Nazi Germany has demonstrated the effects that sufficiently degrading speech may have. If a group of people is spoken of as less than fully human, it certainly becomes easier to treat those people in an inhumane way. The conclusion of other countries has been that the costs to free expression are worth the benefits of barring speech that degrades people, not on the basis of what they have done but on the basis of who they are, to a subhuman level.

The position of U.S. law has not followed the international example. Free expression has enjoyed far stronger protection in the United States, and the result has been an acceptance, at least legally, of speech that degrades others on the basis of their core characteristics. Even in the United States, however, such speech is not always fully protected, as the employment cases show.

If speech such as hate speech is to be in any degree unprotected, an analysis is required as to just what constitutes hate speech. If, as I have argued, hate speech is objectionable because it degrades humanity to the subhuman level in the same way that pornography was once seen as placing humans on the animal side of a divine/animal split, the sense of degradation captured in obscenity laws must be adapted to capture the variety of degradation that is present in utterances of hate speech. It is to that task that the next chapter turns.

7

Using Obscenity Doctrine to Address Hate Speech

The Miller Test for Obscenity

The current U.S. test for obscenity was set forth by the Supreme Court in the 1973 case *Miller v. California*.[1] There the Court noted that it had already recognized a legitimate state interest in prohibiting the distribution or exhibition of obscene material when there was a significant danger of offense to unwilling recipients or exposure to children.[2] In *Miller* the Court set about defining such obscene material.[3] In determining whether material depicting or describing sexual conduct is obscene, the Court said that

> [t]he basic guidelines for the trier of fact must be: (a) whether "the average person, applying contemporary community standards" would find that the work, taken as a whole, appeals to the prurient interest, (b) whether the work depicts or describes, in a patently offensive way, sexual conduct specifically defined by the applicable state law, and (c) whether the work, taken as a whole, lacks serious literary, artistic, political, or scientific value.[4]

The Court explained its reliance on community standards, noting that the nation is simply too diverse for the Court to expect that a single formulation could be set forth for all fifty states. A single national standard was therefore unworkable. Furthermore, the Court said that different localities should be able to set their own levels of protection. "It is neither realistic nor constitutionally sound to read the First Amendment as requiring that the people of Maine or Mississippi accept public depiction of conduct found tolerable in Las Vegas, or New York City. People in different States vary in their tastes and attitudes, and this diversity is not to be strangled by the absolutism of imposed uniformity."[5]

The third prong of the *Miller* test required more explanation, an explanation it received in 1987 in *Pope v. Illinois*.[6] The issue there was whether the standards of the community were to be used in evaluating whether the work at issue had serious literary, artistic, political, or scientific value. The Court noted that *Miller* had said that "[t]he First Amendment protects works which, taken as a whole, have serious literary, artistic, political, or scientific value, regardless of whether the government or a majority of the people approve of the ideas these works represent."[7] Expanding on that idea, the *Pope* Court said,

> Just as the ideas a work represents need not obtain majority approval to merit protection, neither, insofar as the First Amendment is concerned, does the value of the work vary from community to community based on the degree of local acceptance it has won. The proper inquiry is not whether an ordinary member of any given community would find serious literary, artistic, political, or scientific value in allegedly obscene material, but whether a reasonable person would find such value in the material, taken as a whole.[8]

Thus, even if only a minority of a particular population believes a work to have serious value, the work may still be protected.[9]

The *Miller* test, even with its refinement in *Pope,* has not been without its critics. The critics have taken two tacks. One is the position that the First Amendment should be more broadly interpreted and should protect even depictions of obscenity that meet the *Miller* test. The other is that the test is hopelessly flawed. Although there are many academic commentators who could be cited for either position, the two views can also be found in dissenting opinions in the central Supreme Court cases.

The first position, that explicit, offensive depictions of sexual acts should be protected, had in 1957 already found voice in *Roth v. United States*,[10] the case that originally recognized the obscenity exception. The majority in *Roth,* with Justice Brennan writing, said that the Court's opinions had always assumed that obscene material was not included within the constitutional protections of expression.[11] The Court pointed to law in ten of the fourteen states that had ratified the Constitution by 1792 to show that not all expression was protected at the time.[12] More specifically, the Court also said that there was evidence that, by the time of the adoption of the First Amendment, obscene material was unprotected.[13] The Court went on to say that the protection of expression was intended to protect the "unfettered interchange of ideas for the bringing about of political and social changes desired by the people," the "advancement of truth, science, morality, and arts," and "[a]ll ideas having even the slightest redeeming social importance," but obscenity lacked any importance.[14]

Justice Douglas wrote a dissent in *Roth* in which Justice Black joined. He stated his objection in his opening sentence: "When we sustain these convictions, we make the legality of a publication turn on the purity of thought which a book or tract instills in the mind of the reader. I do not think we can approve that standard and be faithful to the command of the First Amendment."[15] In his view, punishment because of the thoughts one provokes, rather than for "overt acts" or "antisocial behavior," could not "be squared with [the Court's] decisions under the First Amendment."[16] Although that statement may fail to recognize the overt act of distribution or the view that such distribution might be considered antisocial behavior, Justice Douglas does make clear that an act consisting of the expression of ideas should not be punishable:

> To allow the State to step in and punish mere speech or publication that the judge or the jury thinks has an undesirable impact on thoughts but that is not shown to be a part of unlawful action is drastically to curtail the First Amendment. . . . If we were certain that impurity of sexual thoughts impelled to action, we would be on less dangerous ground in punishing the distributors of this sex literature. But it is by no means clear that obscene literature, as so defined, is a significant factor in influencing substantial deviations from the community standards.[17]

If any such impact is not clearly demonstrated, Justice Douglas said that the Court should come down on the side of free expression.

The test in *Roth* did not significantly change the situation. It left the censor, judge and jury, in what Justice Douglas saw as too strong a position to exercise arbitrary power:

> Any test that turns on what is offensive to the community's standards is too loose, too capricious, too destructive of freedom of expression to be squared with the First Amendment. Under that test, juries can censor, suppress, and punish what they don't like, provided the matter relates to "sexual impurity" or has a tendency "to excite lustful thoughts." This is community censorship in one of its worst forms. It creates a regime where in the battle between the literati and the Philistines, the Philistines are certain

to win. If experience in this field teaches anything, it is that "censorship of obscenity has almost always been both irrational and indiscriminate." The test adopted here accentuates that trend.[18]

The First Amendment's guarantee of free expression, in Justice Douglas's view, protects protest even against the prevailing moral code, a position which is, of course, true but does not necessarily defeat obscenity laws any more than the right to protest against a system of private property would limit the ability to enforce laws against property crime. That is, there is a difference between the right to protest against the law and a right to violate that law.

As mentioned earlier, Justice Brennan wrote the Court's opinion in *Roth*, recognizing the obscenity exception to the First Amendment. By the time of the *Miller* decision, however, he had second thoughts that reflect the other major criticism of the exception. Justice Brennan's explanation of his concerns is not found in *Miller*, in which he wrote only a short dissent, in which Justices Stewart and Marshall joined. Instead, it is found in his dissent in a case decided the same day in 1973 as *Miller*, *Paris Adult Theatre I v. Slaton*.[19] There, joined by the same two justices, Brennan argued that experience with obscenity cases since *Roth* showed the unworkability of the *Roth* test and of the tests succeeding *Roth*, as well as the *Miller* test adopted that day. Although the Court had recognized two levels of sexual expression, one of which was obscene and outside the protection of the First Amendment, that was still "a long and painful step from agreement on a workable definition of the term."[20] The tests, in his view, simply had fallen short:

[A]fter 16 years of experimentation and debate I am reluctantly forced to the conclusion that none of the available formulas, including the one announced today, can reduce the vagueness to a tolerable level while at the same time striking an acceptable balance between the protections of the First and Fourteenth Amendments, on the one hand, and on the other the asserted state interest in regulating the dissemination of certain sexually oriented materials. Any effort to draw a constitutionally acceptable boundary on state power must resort to such indefinite concepts as "prurient interest," "patent offensiveness," "serious literary value," and the like. The meaning of these concepts necessarily varies with the experience, outlook, and even idiosyncrasies of the person defining them. Although we have assumed that obscenity does exist and that we "know it when [we] see it," we are manifestly unable to describe it in advance except by reference to concepts so elusive that they fail to distinguish clearly between protected and unprotected speech.[21]

Justice Brennan was concerned that a vague statute does not provide adequate notice as to what material is acceptable and what it is criminal to distribute. "The resulting level of uncertainty is utterly intolerable, not alone because it makes 'bookselling . . . a hazardous profession,' but as well because it invites arbitrary and erratic enforcement of the law."[22] In addition to the problem of fair notice, Justice Brennan said that vagueness may inhibit even protected speech on the part of one unwilling to chance a violation of the law. He concluded,

> Our experience since *Roth* requires us not only to abandon the effort to pick out obscene material on a case-by-case basis, but also to reconsider a fundamental postulate of *Roth*: that there exists a definable class of sexually oriented expression that may be totally suppressed by the Federal and State Governments. Assuming that such a class of expression does in fact exist, I am forced to conclude that the concept of "obscenity" cannot be defined with sufficient specificity and clarity to provide fair notice to persons who create and distribute sexually oriented materials, to prevent substantial erosion of protected speech as a byproduct of the attempt to suppress unprotected speech, and to avoid very costly institutional harms.[23]

Interestingly, Brennan did allow that the state's interests may sometimes be sufficient to require toleration of these deficits in the obscenity test. The state has an interest in protecting children and nonconsenting adults from exposure to obscene material that "may stand on a different footing from the other asserted state interests."[24] In language that seems far more appropriate for hate speech than for obscenity, he wrote, "It may well be, as one commentator has argued, that 'exposure to [erotic material] is for some persons an intense emotional experience. A communication of this nature, imposed upon a person contrary to his wishes, has all the characteristics of a physical assault. . . . [And it] constitutes an invasion of his privacy.'"[25] Exposure to hate speech, particularly as the target, would also have to be an "intense emotional experience" with "all the characteristics of a physical assault." If Justice Brennan could see that as grounds for limits on obscenity's being thrust on a person, it seems that the same should be true of hate speech. Furthermore, additional interests he recognized in shielding children seem to carry over to any considerations on limiting hate speech in that special context.

Some of the criticism of the *Miller* test is unavoidable, if expression is ever to be subjected to limits. Language is too nuanced to allow precise definition of that which goes beyond the pale. This is true not only in obscenity but in other contexts as well. For example, King Henry VIII's question, "Will no one rid me of this meddlesome priest?" was not a direct solicitation of murder but seemed to get the message across, while maintaining deniability. Even with pictures or film attached, the nature and impact of the expression may be open to interpretation. Offense may be difficult to define, prurience difficult to delimit.

These problems may speak against hate speech regulation, but if we conclude that it is necessary to regulate hate speech, then the issue here is one of how to define unacceptable hate speech. The *Miller* test, since it is a test for speech that is offensive—and it has been argued here that it is offensive because it is degrading—would, despite any unavoidable shortcomings, be a good starting point in developing a test aimed at hate speech.

Before turning to that task, I must offer one last word on differentiating the criticism of obscenity regulation from any similar effort directed at hate speech. The argument that obscenity regulation is aimed at enforcing a morality that is not shared by all does not carry over particularly well. It is far more plausible to argue that sexual images do no harm and are limited just because people think they should not be available in their communities. Obscenity, if it is still seen as degrading by some people, speaks of humanity generally. It says something of the nature of all of us with regard to our place in the animal kingdom. It does not single any of us out for particular attention.[26] It speaks to the nature of humanity generally.

Hate speech does not speak to all of us. It singles out a particular group, on the basis of race, gender, sexual orientation, or some other characteristic, and degrades that group. The offense is not based in a belief that we should all somehow be above the activities depicted, again an idea not all that widely shared for sex anymore. It, instead, has identifiable victims, and wanting to protect those victims is a different interest than simply being concerned with the depiction of humanity generally.

Furthermore, obscenity is not, or at least may not be, thrust on an unwilling public. Although such material may find its way into the hands of the young or the unwilling recipient, the unwilling recipient can simply cast it aside, and special precautions can be taken to protect the young.[27] But the Court has gone beyond that and allowed the prosecution of obscenity even when it is shown only to consenting adults,[28] when it is certainly not thrust onto an unwilling audience.

Much of the harm in hate speech comes from its being so thrust onto unwilling recipients. It is the racist invective hurled at a member of an ethnic or racial minority that causes the psychic, and even physiological, damage. There is no consent to receive that speech, and society's interest in shielding this victim is stronger than shielding from obscenity the willing viewer. It is true that there has, historically, been danger in the expression of hate speech delivered to a crowd of willing recipients, as in Munich rallies in the 1930s. Limits on that sort of speech to a crowd that may well not include the intended targets raises additional First Amendment issues, since it is concerned with the possibility of inciting the crowd to act on the racist sentiments expressed. Again, that touches on the subject of the preceding chapter, but the difference in impact on a particular subpopulation, as opposed to the universal sentiment in obscenity, may serve here as well to distinguish the criticism of obscenity legislation from hate speech regulation.

If the *Miller* test is to serve in the area of hate speech, it will need to be adapted to that purpose. It is to that task that I now turn, taking on the three prongs of that test one at a time.

Adapting the Miller Test to Hate Speech
Appeal to the Prurient Interest

When *Roth* defined obscenity in terms of an appeal to the prurient interest, it provided a definition of the word *prurient* as "material having a tendency to incite lustful thoughts."[29] The Court went on to provide a definition from *Webster's*, defining *prurient* as "[i]tching; longing; uneasy with desire or longing; of persons, having itching, morbid, or lascivious longings; of desire, curiosity, or propensity, lewd" and defining *prurience* as the "[q]uality of being prurient; lascivious desire or thought."[30] Lastly, in its attempt to provide clarity, the Court said it did not see any significant difference between the definition of obscenity to be found in the case law and the Model Penal Code definition: "A thing is obscene if, considered as a whole, its predominant appeal is to prurient interest, i.e., a shameful or morbid interest in nudity, sex, or excretion, and if it goes substantially beyond customary limits of candor in description or representation of such matters."[31]

All this, somehow, seems unhelpful. An interest in sex, and for that matter in nudity, seems very common and is seemingly healthy. We would not have survived as a species without such an interest. And a great many things may incite lustful thoughts. It is only that which arouses the "shameful or morbid" interest, presumably rather than the normal and healthy interest, that the Model Penal Code takes to be obscene, when it also goes beyond customary levels of candor. This part of the definition may be the most useful, but it requires an examination of what makes some representations appeal to a morbid or shameful interest.

The shamefulness of obscenity has been much of the focus of this book thus far. It is that sort of image that degrades humanity, moves us to a lower level. At an earlier time, in most of the Christian era, that may have included a wide range of sexual image, whereas in the classical era, sex did not have any such impact. If we have come to accept ourselves as nondivine, as animals, and to accept our sexual nature as not making us less human, then what now serves to distinguish some sexual images as degrading, that is, as appealing to a shameful or morbid interest?

Here, an examination of the etymology of the word *obscene* might be useful. Since the Court has spoken in terms of a shameful or morbid interest in sex, it would be helpful to understand how the concept of obscenity ties into this idea of shame, and the origin of the word may be somewhat explanatory. There seem to be competing derivations offered by those who have looked for an origin. One suggested derivation is from *ob caenum,* meaning "on account of filth" or simply "filth."[32] The other is from *ab scaena* or "off the stage," meaning that which has been barred from the stage.[33]

If the derivation of *obscene* relates to filth, it remains to be considered what makes some depictions of sex "filthy" and others acceptable. Harry Clor offers a suggested definition of *obscenity* that contains the distinction required. He argues that obscenity is "a degradation of the human dimensions of life to a sub-human or merely physical level."[34] Clor uses an example that lacks direct relevance here but is, nonetheless, enlightening. He considers a passage from Joseph Heller's novel *Catch-22* in which the character Yossarian encounters a wounded friend, who is disemboweled but still alive. Seeing his friend in this state, Yossarian concludes that "man is garbage."[35] The conclusion seems to be that the human body, viewed as purely physical and lacking the human spirit, is garbage. This, for Clor, is obscenity: "Obscene literature may be defined as that literature which presents, graphically and in detail, a degrading picture of human life and invites the reader or viewer, not to contemplate that picture, but to wallow in it."[36]

Clor's insights are useful. In his view of obscenity, it is the dimension of the human spirit that distinguishes a romantic film, even if it involves explicit sex, from an obscene film. An obscene film reduces people to filth or garbage and does so by denying the human spirit. It is not the sex itself that makes the film obscene; it is the focus solely on the physical aspects of sex that makes for obscenity. In the process the characters, in a sense, lose their character and are reduced to the subhuman, the merely physical, or in Yossarian's word, garbage.

Clor actually also takes on the "off the stage" derivation and explains its application in a way that also has some relevance. He says "obscenity consists in making public that which is private; it consists in an intrusion upon intimate physical processes and acts or physical-emotional states."[37] He argues that the two definitions are related, in that "when the intimacies of life are exposed to public view their human value may be depreciated."[38] Once again, it is the portrayal of the individual as purely physical that not only treats the person as garbage or filth but is that which we remove from the stage of our own lives and do not display to those not directly involved. In Clor's words, "The element of obscenity . . . consists in one's being 'too close' to other persons performing intimate physical acts."[39]

We withhold from one another's view acts that are governed by animal urges rather than the human spirit or at least acts for which the observer can only experience the subhuman or animalistic aspects. Clor says,

> There are certain bodily acts which will tend to arouse disgust in an observer who is not involved in the act and is not, at the time, subject to its urgencies. What the observer sees is a human being governed by physiological urges and functions. Now, to the participants, the act . . . can have important personal and supra-biological meanings. But the outside observer cannot share the experience of these meanings; what he sees is simply the biological process.[40]

In relation to the usual targets of obscenity restrictions, Clor's view explains the private nature of sex, along with the privacy usually surrounding excretory activities. In the physical urges of lust and in the need to eliminate, humans are governed by subhuman, animalistic urges. It is the reduction of humans to the subhuman, to garbage or to filth, that leads to barring such activities from open view. Again in Clor's words, "obscene literature is that literature which invites and stimulates the reader to adopt the obscene posture toward human existence—to engage in the reduction of man's values, functions, and ends to the animal or subhuman level."[41]

In this view, what makes some depictions of sex obscene is that they degrade those involved to the animal or subhuman level. This fits well with the discussion of obscenity in the first half of this book. It is in cultures in which sex may be seen as lowering the status of humans to that of being less than divine that there are laws prohibiting obscenity. Even in later periods, such as in the Victorian era, in which humanity's place among the animals may have been accepted, the position that man was merely an animal was unacceptable to some people and may have led to further limits on sexual depiction.

It seems that it is this degradation that is seen as shameful or morbid. It is the degrading aspect of some depictions of sex, sex without the human dimensions of a romantic encounter, that make for an appeal to the shameful or morbid interest in sex that constitutes a prurient interest. When sexual images have the effect of lowering the status of humans to the subhuman, they become obscene.

What better analogy to hate speech? The entire purpose of hate speech seems to be to degrade. The person hurling racial epithets is asserting the inferiority of his or her target. The assertion is not simply that the speaker is better than the individual target in some way. It is instead the claim that members of the target's race, gender, sexual orientation, or other class are, as a class, inferior to the class to which the speaker belongs. It is an assertion that the class being targeted is less human than the class of the speaker. That is a degradation that is just as shameful or morbid as any sexual depiction that is seen as denying the humanity of the participants.

That, then, should be the hallmark of the sort of speech that is to be proscribed, either in any potential criminal statute or in any less significant context, such as discipline for speech by employees. The appeal to the prurient interest of obscenity law should become an appeal to a degrading view of the racial, gender, or sexual orientation targeted—the claim that certain groups are less fully human than others, are subhuman and closer to the animals. That is utter degradation in a far stronger way than is a depiction that appeals to the prurient interest in sex and that says something about the nature of all of us. The purveyor of the sexual image, to the degree that any such images are still seen as degrading, degrades us all,[42] including him- or herself. The utterer of hate speech attempts selectively to degrade a subpopulation, while leaving his or her own group in a superior position.

There is another interesting comparison. The prurient appeal of sexual material is visceral. It is an appeal to the endocrine system, rather than an appeal to intellect. Much the same may be said of hate speech. Its impact on the target is likely to be visceral, rather than intellectual. Indeed, that would be the basis for the negative physical effects noted by some commentators on hate speech.[43] It also seems to reflect a visceral dislike on the part of the speaker. It is certainly not an intellectual affirmation but seems, instead, to be the manifestation of an inner anger, bias, or, perhaps, fear.

Patent Offensiveness and Statutory Definition

The second prong of the *Miller* test requires that material be patently offensive under contemporary community standards and be adequately defined by statute. The offensiveness requirement should carry over to hate speech, and it seems that a jury would be similarly qualified to determine whether specific hate speech was so offensive as they would be for sexual material. Greater adaption may be required to provide statutory definitions for hate speech.

There have been definitions of hate speech provided in international agreements that can provide guidance here. One of the first potential definitions may be found in the December 1966 adoption by the General Assembly of the United Nations of the International Covenant on Civil and Political Rights.[44] That document, in Article 19, recognizes the freedom of expression.[45] But the very next article limits that right, providing, "Any advocacy of national, racial or religious hatred that constitutes incitement to discrimination, hostility or violence shall be prohibited by law."[46]

The United Nations had in fact, in March 1966, also opened for signature the International Convention on the Elimination of All Forms of Racial Discrimination.[47] Although it did not specifically provide a definition, Article 4 of the Convention indicates that the Convention intends to reach "all propaganda and all organizations which are based on ideas or theories of superiority of one race or group of persons of one colour or ethnic origin, or which attempt to justify or promote racial hatred and discrimination in any form, . . . ideas based on racial superiority or hatred, incitement to racial discrimination, as well as all acts of violence or incitement to such acts against any race or group of persons of another colour or ethnic origin."[48]

Another definition may be found in a 1997 recommendation by the Committee of Ministers of the Council of Europe regarding hate speech. In recommending a number of steps for member nations, the Committee also provided a definition: "'hate speech' shall be understood as covering all forms of expression which spread, incite, promote or justify racial hatred, xenophobia, anti-Semitism or other forms of hatred based on intolerance, including: intolerance expressed by aggressive nationalism and ethnocentrism, discrimination and hostility against minorities, migrants and people of immigrant origin."[49]

Still another definition was provided six years later, in a protocol directed at the dissemination of racism through computer systems.[50] The definition given for racist and xenophobic material is similar to that found in the recommendation of the Committee of Ministers of the Council of Europe. It includes "any written material, any image or any other representation of ideas or theories, which advocates, promotes or incites hatred, discrimination or violence, against any individual or group of individuals, based on race, colour, descent or national or ethnic origin, as well as religion if used as a pretext for any of these factors."[51] The definitions offered in international agreements and covenants seem more than adequate to identify the material being addressed in those instruments. Similar definitions should serve to provide notice to potential speakers as to what is prohibited in any potential bans on hate speech within the United States, and they may easily be adapted to address speech that serves to degrade on the basis of sex or sexual orientation.

The standard statutory definition of obscenity in U.S. state statutes relies on language such as "offensive representations or descriptions of ultimate sexual acts, normal or perverted, actual or simulated."[52] Some statutes go on to add an explanation that such acts may "includ[e] sexual intercourse, sodomy, and sexual bestiality"[53] or that "'[u]ltimate sexual acts' means sexual intercourse, anal or otherwise, fellatio, cunnilingus or sodomy."[54] Few have the specificity of Michigan's definition of ultimate sexual acts as "sexual intercourse, fellatio, cunnilingus, anal intercourse, or any other intrusion, however slight, of any part of a person's body or of any object into the genital or anal openings of another person's body, or depictions or descriptions of sexual bestiality, sadomasochism, masturbation, or excretory functions."[55] Although the more specific statutes may be more descriptive than the definitions in international agreements, the acceptability of the more general definitions of obscenity should indicate the acceptability of the no less specific definitions found in the covenants and agreements.

It should be noted that some statutes add other acts of which the sufficiently offensive depiction would be obscene, including, for example, "[p]atently offensive representations or descriptions of masturbation, excretory functions, sadism, masochism, lewd exhibition of the genitals, the male or female genitals in a state of sexual stimulation or arousal, or covered male genitals in a discernibly turgid state."[56] This addition does little to add specificity for at least two reasons. First, when other acts are added to the definition, they are added as an alternative, so that any concerns over vagueness that may result from the "ultimate sexual acts" language at least remains for that disjunct. Second, adding language such as "lewd exhibition of the genitals" has its own interpretational difficulties.

The point here is that language may, as the critics of obscenity law argue, lack the specificity to make absolutely clear what is covered under an obscenity statute. The courts have been, however, willing to live with some level of uncertainty in the obscenity context. Should hate speech ever be banned, the same should hold for the definitions of such speech, since the clarity seems to be at least as good in those definitions as it is for obscenity.

It is also important to note that in situations other than criminal prosecutions, the Supreme Court has been far less demanding regarding the clarity of the rules involved. An example can be found in the 1986 case *Bethel School District v. Fraser.*[57] That case involved a high school disciplinary code. Fraser, a student, made a nominating speech in a school assembly, proposing another student for a position in student government. The speech was aptly described as an extended sexual metaphor, and the student faced punishment. Although the case is better known for its ruling on the First Amendment in the school context,[58] there was also a discussion of the requirements of due process in such settings.

Fraser claimed that he had no way of knowing that his speech would be taken to be a violation of the disciplinary code's provision barring obscene language and that such a situation was a violation of his due process rights. Putting aside the fact that two teachers, who had seen the speech he intended to deliver, had told him it would lead to trouble, the Court addressed the general merits of due process arguments in this context:

> We have recognized that "maintaining security and order in the schools requires a certain degree of flexibility in school disciplinary procedures, and we have respected the value of preserving the informality of the student-teacher relationship." Given the school's need to be able to impose disciplinary sanctions for a wide range of unanticipated conduct disruptive of the educational process, the school disciplinary rules need not be as detailed as a criminal code which imposes criminal sanctions. Two days' suspension from school does not rise to the level of a penal sanction calling for the full panoply of procedural due process protections applicable to a criminal prosecution.[59]

Before *Fraser,* the Court had in 1974 already come to a similar conclusion regarding due process in the employment context. In *Arnett v. Kennedy*[60] a nonprobationary civil service employee had been discharged for having made recklessly false defamatory statements about fellow employees of the Office of Equal Opportunity. He appealed his termination on a number of grounds, including that the standards for discharge of nonprobationary employees denied such employees due process by not being sufficiently specific as to potential grounds for firing.

The regulations allowed discharge for "such cause as will promote the efficiency of the service," and the Court had to consider the sufficiency of that standard. In that regard the Court concluded that "the standard of 'cause' set forth in the Lloyd–La Follette Act as a limitation on the Government's authority to discharge federal employees is constitutionally sufficient against the charges both of overbreadth and of vagueness."[61]

This result was also based on the sort of action that was taken, a discharge rather than a criminal charge. The Court added,

Congress sought to lay down an admittedly general standard, not for the purpose of defining criminal conduct, but in order to give myriad different federal employees performing widely disparate tasks a common standard of job protection. We do not believe that Congress was confined to the choice of enacting a detailed code of employee conduct, or else granting no job protection at all.[62]

The relevance of this position to hate speech is strong, because the decision to discharge in *Arnett* was based on speech, as would be any action involving hate speech. When it came to decisions based on speech, the Court said, "Because of the infinite variety of factual situations in which public statements by Government employees might reasonably justify dismissal for 'cause,' we conclude that the Act describes, as explicitly as is required, the employee conduct which is ground for removal."[63]

From the case law on obscenity, assuming that is to be a source of guidance, it is clear that the level of specificity in a law, regulation, or workplace rule can vary with the nature or the action. A criminal charge, if one were ever to be allowed under U.S. law for hate speech, requires the greatest clarity. But it seems that the definitions provided in international agreements have a specificity that matches that of obscenity laws, and they should suffice for hate speech. School and workplace regulations would require less specific definition. In any case, there would also be a requirement of offensiveness. In any criminal case, a patent offensiveness under community standards seems indicated by the obscenity cases. The degree of offensiveness and the arena in which it is tested might vary when the sanctions are noncriminal. This aspect of formulating hate speech law is taken up again in the context of the examples presented in the following chapter.

Lack of Serious Value

There may be some argument for eliminating the third *Miller* require-ment, the provision that material that, taken as a whole, has serious literary, artistic, political, or scientific value not be considered obscene and be pro-tected expression. That was the position taken by the Court in establishing that child pornography falls outside the protections of the First Amendment. In 1982 in *New York v. Ferber,*[64] the Court upheld, as against a First Amend-ment challenge, a statute banning the distribution of child pornography that did not contain an exception for material with serious value.

The Court allowed the prohibition because of the harm caused to children in the production of such material, both in the sexual abuse of the child in the performance of the acts filmed and in the permanent record of the abuse in the form of the continuing existence of the film. The prohibition could reach distribution of such material, because the distribution provided the market that drove production and because distribution, unlike production, was of a more public nature, providing the opportunity for the government to reach the abusive material.

Turning to the lack of protection for child pornography with serious value, the Court, in explaining why the *Miller* standard did not meet the state's needs in protecting children, said, "a work which, taken on the whole, contains serious literary, artistic, political, or scientific value may neverthe-less embody the hardest core of child pornography. 'It is irrelevant to the child [who has been abused] whether or not the material . . . has a literary, artistic, political or social value.'"[65] Despite this language, the Court might be viewed as not abandoning completely the serious-value provision. The statute at issue in *Ferber* did not contain such protection, and the Court's analysis on the lack of a serious-value provision was a consideration of overbreadth, that is, whether there would be significant instances of protected speech likely to fall within the scope of the prohibition. Only that situation would allow a facial challenge to the statute; otherwise, the issue could be raised in a case directly presenting material with serious value. The Court concluded,

> Applying these principles, we hold that [the statute] is not substantially overbroad. We consider this the paradigmatic case of a state statute whose legitimate reach dwarfs its arguably impermissible applications. New York, as we have held, may constitutionally prohibit dissemination of material specified in [the statute]. While the reach of the statute is directed at the hard core of child pornography, the Court of Appeals was understandably

concerned that some protected expression, ranging from medical text-books to pictorials in the National Geographic would fall prey to the stat-ute. How often, if ever, it may be necessary to employ children to engage in conduct clearly within the reach of [the statute] in order to produce edu-cational, medical, or artistic works cannot be known with certainty. Yet we seriously doubt, and it has not been suggested, that these arguably imper-missible applications of the statute amount to more than a tiny fraction of the materials within the statute's reach.[66]

Thus, it might be arguable that serious value need not protect what would otherwise be hate speech, a statute need not contain an exception for such speech, and that serious value could be argued in individual cases. The better approach, even with *Ferber,* however, is to include such an exception. Even if the Court would allow child pornography with serious value to be pro-hibitable, the harm done to children in the production of such material is of a different character and degree compared to the harm done to the target of hate speech. For one thing, the need to protect children may be of a higher order. More important, the harm from hate speech is in the message; the harm from child pornography is in the production.

Perhaps more on point is the pornography ordinance adopted by India-napolis in 1984. The ordinance prohibited distributing pornography, defining pornography as sexual images combined with depictions of women as enjoy-ing pain, assault, humiliation, or certain other forms of degradation, and the ordinance did use the word "degradation."[67] The ordinance contained a num-ber of prohibitions, making it illegal to traffic in pornography, so defined, to coerce anyone into performing in pornographic works, or to force pornog-raphy on anyone. Also prohibited was assault on any person "in a way that is directly caused by specific pornography."[68] Additionally, anyone injured by someone who had read or seen a pornographic work was provided a cause of action against the producer or distributor of that work, and any woman generally aggrieved by trafficking in pornography was given the right to file a city equal-opportunity complaint "as a woman acting against the subordina-tion of women."[69]

The ordinance seems to have been aimed at degrading expression, although the inclusion of women presented in postures of display[70] may have gone beyond what would necessarily be considered by most people to be degrading. There was no requirement that the images appeal to the prurient interest, as is required for obscenity prosecutions. There is also no require-ment of prurience in the suggested approach to hate speech herein, but there is offered a substitute directed at the same concerns addressed by the prurience requirement. Although the Indianapolis ordinance may have also been aimed at degradation, the specific requirement of a prurience-like factor here, in the appeal to a degrading view of the target, may serve to distinguish the two efforts.

Of more relevance to the specific issue in this section, the ordinance lacked a savings clause for material that, taken as a whole, has serious literary, artistic, political, or scientific value. That failure was not accidental. The ordinance drew on the work of Catharine MacKinnon and author and feminist activist Andrea Dworkin, and MacKinnon had earlier written "if a woman is subjected, why should it matter that the work has other value?"[71] The subjection, the harm done to women, as seen by the school of feminism behind the ordinance, was that pornography influences attitudes and needs to be addressed to change the way both men and women are socialized.

The concerns over pornography motivating the ordinance were not the usual moral concerns, although the goals certainly had their own moral dimension. The concern was the harm done to women. Pornography was seen as both a symptom and a cause of gender inequality and as defining of reality. Pornography, according to MacKinnon, "institutionalizes the sexuality of male supremacy, fusing the eroticization of dominance and submission with the social construction of male and female. . . . Men treat women as who they see women as being. Pornography constructs who that is."[72] Pornography is seen as raising a civil rights issue and as the cause of discrimination and sexual harassment. Again in MacKinnon's view, pornography increases the acceptance of aggression against women, reduces the desire of both men and women to have female children, and fosters views of male domination.[73]

The life of the Indianapolis ordinance was rather short. It was declared unconstitutional in *American Booksellers Association v. Hudnut*.[74] The court found fault with the ordinance because of its discrimination on the basis of the content of the speech involved, and the failure to protect material with serious value played a role in that assessment: "Speech treating women in the approved way—in sexual encounters 'premised on equality' . . . is lawful no matter how sexually explicit. Speech treating women in the disapproved way—as submissive in matters sexual or as enjoying humiliation—is unlawful no matter how significant the literary, artistic, or political qualities of the work taken as a whole."[75] The court found an unconstitutional flaw in the ordinance's viewpoint discrimination. The court pointed out that, just as the First Amendment protects speech by the Nazis or the Ku Klux Klan, it also protects using nonobscene sexual images to express views feminists might find deeply troubling.[76] In the court's view, the lack of content neutrality was fatal. "This is thought control. It establishes an 'approved' view of women, of how they may react to sexual encounters, of how the sexes may relate to each other. Those who espouse the approved view may use sexual images; those who do not, may not."[77]

Of course, the thesis of this part of this book depends on hate speech's being regulable, either internationally, generally in the United States, or in noncriminal situations in the United States. In those situations, the analogy to the speech of the Nazis or of the Ku Klux Klan loses force. If such speech may be banned, then the expression targeted by the ordinance might also be banned. Nonetheless, the lack of protection for speech with serious value, whether offered by Nazis, the Ku Klux Klan, or pornographers, raises concerns regarding the impact on political speech, which requires protection under the First Amendment.

One last point from *Hudnut* deserves mention. The defenders of the ordinance had maintained that because pornography is, in a sense, "unanswerable," the "marketplace of ideas" theory of the First Amendment does not apply.[78] The court's response to that argument was that the likelihood that the truth would win out was not necessary for the invocation of First Amendment protection:

> A power to limit speech on the ground that truth has not yet prevailed and is not likely to prevail implies the power to declare truth. At some point the government must be able to say (as Indianapolis has said): "We know what the truth is, yet a free exchange of speech has not driven out falsity, so that we must now prohibit falsity."[79]

In the court's view, this went beyond the power the state may exercise. The state may not determine what the truth is and limit the expression of those who disagree.

The best approach seems to be to follow at least that part of the *Hudnut* position that addressed serious value and to protect expression with serious value from being considered hate speech. A book such as *The Bell Curve*,[80] whatever one may think of its conclusions and methodology,[81] does seem to be an attempt to present a view on a serious topic. There is a difference between arguing that there are differences in mean intelligence among racial or ethnic groups and yelling at someone, "You're just a stupid [insert a racist, sexist, or homophobic label]." The first is a statement about means on intelligence scales, and given the standard deviations among any population, individual differences will be far greater than any difference in means. Thus, the conclusion, even if accepted, says little to nothing about any individual member of any group. On the other hand, the "you're just a stupid ——" seems to be an application of a believed universal inferiority in the target group.

The claim of a difference in means has as its most significant implication the possibility that a lack of representation in some positions may not be because of discrimination but instead be because of differences in abilities. This conclusion can certainly be rejected, and even if there is any difference in means, a history of discrimination may overwhelm that difference as an explanation for underrepresentation. The point is not that the conclusion is by any means correct but that it is seemingly intended as a serious contribution. It is again of a different nature than the insult that assumes all members of the target group are somehow inferior.

This position is, at any rate, the view of at least one federal court. In a decision to be discussed in the next chapter, a campus speech code was struck down because, at least in part, it would have applied to a claim in a serious discussion than men and women may have different academic talents.[82] Although some people may be willing to assert that a particular position cannot be correct, when the position is put forward, the claim that the best remedy for bad speech is good speech is apt.[83] The government, and for that matter the university, should not declare orthodoxy, even on issues of race, ethnicity, gender, and sexual orientation, and declare other views unacceptable.

It might also be the case that at least most instances in which speech would be saved from condemnation because of serious value might well have fallen outside the scope of punishable speech on other grounds. For instance, most speech with serious value would probably not be offered with the intent to degrade the targeted individual or group. Nonetheless, some people may see a book such as *The Bell Curve* in that light. Furthermore, that book in suggesting the inferiority of a racial class seems to fit the definitions taken from United Nations and European sources, and most people may find it offensive, so protecting work with serious value remains an important consideration.

State of Mind

The Supreme Court, in the 1974 case *Hamling v. United States*,[84] discussed the mental state required for a person to be guilty of a violation of obscenity laws. The defendants in the case sought to make a profit from the *Presidential Report of the Commission on Obscenity and Pornography* by issuing a version of the report containing photographic representations to illustrate the report's contents and mailing an advertisement for the illustrated report. They were found guilty of mailing obscene material with regard to the advertisement, which contained a collage of photos from the illustrated report. The photos seem, from the Court's description, to have been strongly sexual, containing depictions of ultimate sexual acts of all variety, heterosexual and homosexual, as well as bestiality.

Despite the hard-core nature of the material, the defendants claimed that their conviction was flawed because the government was required to prove that they knew the materials to be obscene. The statute on which the conviction was based did say that "'[w]hoever knowingly uses the mails for the mailing . . . of anything declared by this section . . . to be nonmailable . . .' is guilty of the proscribed offense."[85] The defense's position regarding this statute was that it required that the government prove the defendant's knowledge of both the content of the material and the obscene nature of that material.

The Court rejected that position regarding the "knowingly" language, while still maintaining a requirement for a scienter, or knowing, element in the crime:

> It is constitutionally sufficient that the prosecution show that a defendant had knowledge of the contents of the materials he distributed, and that he knew the character and nature of the materials. To require proof of a defendant's knowledge of the legal status of the materials would permit the defendant to avoid prosecution by simply claiming that he had not brushed up on the law. Such a formulation of the scienter requirement is required neither by the language of [the statute] nor by the Constitution.[86]

Thus, the defendant must have known of the sexual nature of the material but does not have to have been aware that the jury would find the materials to be obscene. The Court was untroubled by the effect that understanding would have on decisions to publish: "Whenever the law draws a line there will be cases very near each other on opposite sides. The precise course of the line may be uncertain, but no one can come near it without knowing that he does so, if he thinks, and if he does so it is familiar to the criminal law to make him take the risk."[87] Whereas the person who mails material not knowing the content is not in violation of the law, a person who sends sexual material through the mail, knowing it to be such, simply bears the risk that it will be held to be obscene.

More recently, in 1994, the Court, in *United States v. X-Citement Video, Inc.*,[88] showed how strong the scienter requirement is in reading a statute in a somewhat unnatural way to avoid what it said would otherwise be a constitutional flaw. The statute was the Protection of Children against Sexual Exploitation Act of 1977,[89] which provides punishment for

(a) Any person who—
(1) knowingly transports or ships in interstate or foreign commerce by any means including by computer or mails, any visual depiction, if—
    (A) the producing of such visual depiction involves the use of a minor engaging in sexually explicit conduct; and
    (B) such visual depiction is of such conduct;
(2) knowingly receives, or distributes, any visual depiction that has been mailed, or has been shipped or transported in interstate or foreign commerce, or which contains materials which have been mailed or so shipped or transported, by any means including by computer, or knowingly reproduces any visual depiction for distribution in interstate or foreign commerce or through the mails, if—
    (A) the producing of such visual depiction involves the use of a minor engaging in sexually explicit conduct; and
    (B) such visual depiction is of such conduct.

Defendants had been convicted of violating that statute by shipping films involving adult-film performer Traci Lords, who it turned out was not an adult.

The defendants argued that the statute was facially unconstitutional in that it did not require scienter with regard to the age of the performers. The Ninth Circuit agreed and set aside the conviction, reading the Supreme Court case law as requiring scienter as to the nature and character of the material and holding that nature and character included the age of the performers. Based on its view of the natural reading of the act as requiring knowledge about transportation, shipment, receipt, or distribution but not requiring knowledge as to age, the statute was held unconstitutional. That would, indeed, seem the plain-language reading of the text.

When the case reached the Supreme Court, the Court stretched the scope of the adverb "knowingly" to include the age of the performer. The Court's reading of the language may not have been natural, but its conclusion was justified by a variety of factors. First, the Court concluded that the Ninth Circuit's reading would result in a number of "positively absurd" results, including liability for persons with no idea that they were even dealing with any form of sexual material, while knowingly transporting, shipping, and so on, such material, a result Congress presumably did not intend.[90] That argument, however, would not necessarily have gotten the Court to its eventual position. An outcome that would avoid such absurdities would be to require scienter with regard to the sexual nature of the material but not with regard to the age of the performers.

The Court's other two bases for its decision were stronger. The Court pointed to its "cases interpreting criminal statutes to include broadly applicable scienter requirements, even where the statute by its terms does not contain them."[91] Since the act at issue in *X-Citement Video* was a criminal statute involving significant penalties, it could not be seen as the sort of regulatory or public-welfare statute that might employ strict scrutiny. Lastly, the Court noted a canon of statutory construction that statutes should, when they can, be read so as to avoid constitutional difficulties: "[A] statute completely bereft of a scienter requirement as to the age of the performers would raise serious constitutional doubts. It is therefore incumbent upon us to read the statute to eliminate those doubts so long as such a reading is not plainly contrary to the intent of Congress."[92]

Thus, it appears that the Court, in the areas of obscenity and child pornography, requires that the defendant be shown to have been aware of the necessary facts, the nature of the material and age of the performers, but not be prescient with regard to any legal conclusions. If obscenity law is to be a guide in the development of hate speech law, the analog in that area should also hold. But application to hate speech may be a bit more difficult.

The difference, or at least one difference, is in the likelihood of mistake as to the nature of the material. One who has seen the content of a potentially obscene film is at least aware that the subject matter is sexual. If it turns out to be obscene, there is liability. There is a greater probability, although perhaps still small, that an individual may utter a comment reasonably taken as racist without realizing that it is racist. This lack of realization is different in kind from the failure to realize that sexual material is obscene. The speaker may not be aware that the term used has any racial meaning, in a way that a distributor of a sexual film who has seen the film cannot be mistaken. The speaker may, as an example in the next chapter will demonstrate, be unaware of, in a sense, the nature of the material. If so, despite knowing what sounds were uttered, the speaker is unaware of the nature of the speech as racist, sexist, or homophobic, in a sense similar to the distributor of a film who has not seen the content.

The lack of awareness of this accidental speaker of what would normally be hate speech puts him or her in a different position from the speaker who utters speech that he or she knows is targeted at a group on the basis of race, gender. or sexual orientation but believes not to be an appeal to degradation, not to be offensive under community standards, or to be protected by its serious value. That later speaker is in the same situation as Hamling and his codefendants. The lack of awareness of the likely legal outcome does not shield the speaker who recognizes the fact that the speech is directed at a target group.

At least in the criminal case, it should not be adequate for a conviction to show that the speaker made comments that appeal to a racist or degrading sentiment. The speaker should have to be shown to have intended to have spoken in a way that targets a group on the basis of race, gender, or sexual orientation. The speaker need not be shown to recognize that the speech was degrading in the sense suggested here, that the material was patently offensive under community standards, or that the speech lacked serious value. The jury may be inclined to find the speech to be hate speech, but if the jury does not conclude that the defendant knew the nature of his or her expression, there should be no liability.

The material in this chapter has addressed any application of criminal hate speech laws. These laws do not currently exist in the United States, but if they should eventually be approved and in places where similar regulation currently does exist, the analysis should prove useful. In the areas in the United States in which hate speech may lead to sanctions, such as in the employment context, there is not necessarily a requirement of scienter. It would, nonetheless, seem consistent with principles of fairness to bring the same considerations to bear. Although it may not be illegal to fire an at-will employee for speech that the employee did not know had any racial content, it seems inequitable.

8

Applications

This chapter applies the test developed in the preceding chapter to a number of examples. The examples flesh out the abstract analytical structure already presented. In most of the examples, the suggested conclusion is that the speech presented was not hate speech. That should not be taken as an indication that I do not have concerns over hate speech. Examples in which the speech should be considered hateful are numerous, ranging from the Nazi march in Skokie, Illinois, through cross burning, to an individual's referring to a coworker using racial epithets or a driver's shouting such words at a group standing on a corner, but these are rather easy to analyze. Except under very strange circumstances, they would all have to be considered hate speech.

The more interesting examples are those in which words that would commonly be used in a racist context are used in a way that should probably not be considered racist. These examples require a focus on, and a greater understanding of, the factors that have been set out in the preceding chapter. In that process, there will also be the occasion to question the reasoning behind those factors, and the examples may help explain their justification.

The first example was selected because it has also been addressed by Randall Kennedy, a prominent African American law professor, who also feels that in this case there may have been an overreaction to speech that in other contexts should be considered racist. His concurrence does not mean that others cannot feel differently. His view may be as idiosyncratic as the views to be presented here. What his agreement does demonstrate is that the view presented here is not a hopelessly Eurocentric one.

The Central Michigan University Basketball Case

Keith Dambrot was the head basketball coach at Central Michigan University during the 1992–93 season.[1] That year's team consisted of eleven African American and three white players; the coaching staff consisted of Dambrot, who is white, one black assistant coach, and one white assistant coach. There was also a white graduate assistant on the staff.

The incident that led to the dispute occurred in the locker room, either during halftime or at the end of a game that Central Michigan lost to Miami University. Dambrot said he had told his players that they had not been playing very hard. He also said to them, "Do you mind if I use the N word?" The players indicated that it would be all right, and the coach said, "you know we need to have more niggers on our team. . . . Coach McDowell is a nigger, . . . Sand[er] Scott who's an academic All-American, a Caucasian, I said Sand[er] Scott is a nigger. He's hard nose [sic], he's tough, et cetera."[2] Dambrot said that his intent had been to use the word in the "positive and reinforcing" manner that the players used the word toward each other in games, in the locker room, and on campus. The coach said he had used the word to mean a player who is "fearless, mentally strong and tough."[3]

It seems that Coach Dambrot had used the same word on at least one other occasion. After a practice, he had told the team that "he wanted the players to 'play like niggers on the court' and wished he had more niggers on the basketball court."[4] More problematically, he also said that "he did not want the team to act like niggers in the classroom."[5]

Dambrot's locker-room talk led to his dismissal as coach. A former member of the team heard about the comments and reported them to the university's affirmative-action officer, who asked Dambrot about the complaint. The coach admitted using the N-word but said he had done so in a positive manner. The AA officer saw the language as a violation of the university's discriminatory harassment policy, and the coach settled the complaint, accepting a five-day suspension without pay. The suspension served only to spread the news of the coach's language. There were two demonstrations on campus to protest the "racism" of the coach. Eventually the athletic director told Dambrot that the environment had become such that he would be unable to provide the leadership the program needed and that he would not be the coach for the 1993–94 season.

Dambrot sued the university over the loss of his job, a suit he effectively lost—"effectively" because, although he was victorious in his challenge to the university's speech code, his firing was found not to violate any of his constitutional rights. The court held that the speech code was vague and that it reached a significant amount of speech protected by the First Amendment and declared its enforcement unconstitutional. The First Amendment, however, does not apply in the same way to a state, including a state university, as an employer as it does to the state as a regulator of its citizens. Thus, although the university could not prohibit all the speech it wanted to, it might be able to fire the coach for that same speech.

The distinction may seem odd, but it is well established as a matter of First Amendment law.[6] The government has a stronger interest in the functioning of its workplaces than in the utterances of citizens generally. That does not mean that employee speech is never protected. When it regards a matter of public concern, it receives protection in a sort of balancing against the efficiency interests of the public employer. Here, however, the court found that the speech did not touch on a matter of public concern, and Dambrot received no protection.

> Focusing on the "content, form and context" of Dambrot's use of the word "nigger," this Court can find nothing "relating to any matter of political, social or other concern to the community." Dambrot's locker room speech imparted no socially or politically relevant message to his players. The *point* of his speech was not related to his use of the N-word but to his desire to have his players play harder. . . . Dambrot's use of the N-word was intended to be motivational and was incidental to the message conveyed. . . . A coach's distress about the degree of aggressiveness shown by his players on the basketball court is a reasonable matter of concern, certainly, to the coach, but not the kind of question that is fairly cast as a "public" issue.[7]

The coach also tried to bring his speech within the protection of the First Amendment by arguing that academic freedom protected his method of "instructing" his players. The court concluded that the university was not required to accept this teaching method.

Despite the legal conclusion that it was not unconstitutional for the university to fire the coach, there is still the issue of whether the university acted reasonably in doing so. That is, was it an overreaction, even if it was a permissible overreaction? Randall Kennedy concludes that it was, characterizing the decision of the athletic director as a misjudgment. Kennedy says that the initial response of telling Coach Dambrot to stop using the language was sufficient and was justified by concern that the use of the language would be misunderstood by the university community. When the reaction went further, it was excessive. In Kennedy's view, "The fact is that Dambrot, though imprudent, was obviously employing *nigger* in a sense embraced by his players—a sense in which the term was a compliment, not an insult. . . . [T]he CMU authorities capitulated too quickly to the formulaic rage of affronted blacks, the ill-considered sentimentality of well-meaning whites, and their own crass, bureaucratic opportunism."[8] Setting aside Kennedy's labels regarding the reactions, the criticism may be valid. An analysis of what was said by Coach Dambrot may show that it should not be considered racist, should not be seen to constitute hate speech, at least in part.

To address first the exhortation to "play like niggers on the court," there may have been an overreaction, and an analysis using the modified obscenity test shows why. Before that task, however, one other possibility should be addressed. It may be that certain words simply cannot be used in anything other than a racist way, and if that is so, the word used in this case is seemingly the best candidate for that status. Although Coach Dambrot said he intended to use the word in a positive manner, the view of the university's affirmative-action officer was that there was no positive way to use the word.[9]

The position that there is no nonracist way to use the N-word seems belied by its use by the players and by those in the music industry. It seems that the Central Michigan players referred to each other in the same manner. Although some people might find use of the word distasteful or unacceptable for other reasons, it seems unlikely that the players were addressing each other in a way that should be considered racist. Just as the coach was attempting to do, they were commenting positively on each other's play. This use as a positive comment is far from the sort of speech that indicates a belief in the inferiority of the target. It is not speech that is intended to degrade the target to a less than fully human level.

There has also been somewhat widespread use of the word by rappers. Again, it seems unlikely that those musicians, particularly African American rappers, are expressing racist sentiments to their fellow musicians or their audiences. Interestingly, it may be that the same cannot be said for lyrics by some of those same singers directed toward or regarding females. Although there is developing criticism of the language employed by rappers, it is not because the critics suspect the mostly African American musicians of being self-hating racists. The better basis for such criticism is that the white population will take away from black use of the word the belief that there is nothing wrong with its use. Coach Dambrot seems to have been caught in that sort of logical leap. The fact that his players may have used the same language did not make it automatically acceptable for their white coach to speak in the same way.

There is a difference between self-labeling and the labeling of others, but the difference ought to be in presumed intent, rather than an automatic license to some people and a complete bar to others. When the Central

Michigan players addressed each other with the N-word or complimented each other for "play[ing] like niggers," the reasonable assumption is that they were uttering some positive sentiments toward each other. With regard to rap stars, the reasonable assumption may be not so much that the utterances are positive but perhaps that at least they are not negative. For the white user of similar language the presumption is not there, and the use of the language is suspect. That is also why the rappers' language that may be seen as degrading toward women draws a stronger reaction. Since most rappers are male, the language is other-labeling and does not enjoy any presumption that it is a positive, or at least neutral, comment.

But a presumption should not be a definite conclusion, and applying the obscenity-based analysis to Coach Dambrot's language should prove useful. The first issue is whether, taken as a whole, the coach's comments were uttered with an intent to degrade on the basis of, in this case, race. Were the comments intended as an assertion that the target group was somehow less fully human than the group to which the speaker belongs? Under this prong of our test, the language would not seem to be hate speech. Although the affirmative-action officer may have been unable to accept any use of the word as positive, the coach seems to have intended a positive use. His players used the same language and intended it as positive. It was not a case of a neutral use by his players that might be reasonably be seen, even by his players, as negative when used by the coach. He used the phrase in the same way his players had. He also asked their permission to use the word, indicating his concern that he not be taken as uttering a negative. His recognition that that was a possible reaction may have counseled against using the language in question, but it should not be taken as making the use racist.

To turn to the second prong of the test, was the language offensive under community standards? This is an interesting issue that might seem to depend on how the community is defined. If the community is the audience to which the speech was addressed, there appears to have been no offense; that is, the members of the team seemed unoffended. If the community is the university, there did seem to be offense. It may be less clear what level of offense there may have been in the even wider community.

The specific audience seems to be the incorrect basis for the standard. An extreme example may be used to demonstrate that conclusion. Suppose the Ku Klux Klan held a rally and cross burning in an isolated location. Only members of the Klan were in attendance. There was speech that was hate filled on the basis of race and other factors, but none of the Klan members was offended. Indeed, they approved of the sentiments presented. The content or nature of the speech later becomes known to the outside community. Setting aside whether the speech should be punished, to claim that it was not racist because of its original audience seems nonsensical. This conclusion might be avoided by suggesting that the audience and the basis for a community standard changes when the speech becomes known outside the original audience.

The community, for the purpose of standards, should depend on the level at which the action is to be taken. For the original audience, the team, there seems to have been no offense. But when the speech became known outside the team, it is as if the speech had been delivered to the entire university. The university community was offended, even if the team and the still larger community may not have been. The community should then depend on the action taken. If the university takes only internal action, then its offense is what matters. If consideration outside the university is required, then the offense should be judged on the basis of a different community. For example, if university policy allows firing only for cause, that cause will be tested in court. In that case, again the level of offense in the wider community will determine whether the court sees the firing as reasonably based on cause.

In the case of a firing, there may be an issue with regard to specificity in the enforcement of hate speech regulations. A fired plaintiff is likely to claim that there was no way to know what speech would lead to that sanction. The Supreme Court, however, has addressed this sort of argument in a number of contexts. As discussed in the preceding chapter, in 1986 in *Bethel School District v. Fraser*,[10] the Court addressed the contention that a student facing discipline could not have known that the speech would lead to that reaction. The Court said that school disciplinary rules need not have the detail of a criminal code. The Court had said much the same in 1974 in *Arnett v. Kennedy*,[11] where the issue was discharge for cause of a government employee. That does not mean that no notice of what constitutes proscribed speech is required, but it does mean that some vagueness will be tolerated.

The third prong of the suggested test is whether the speech has serious literary, artistic, political, or scientific value and thus, even in the face of a determination of intent to degrade and of community offense in the first two prongs, should be protected. This may be the sort of defense Dambrot was invoking in suggesting that he was trying to instruct his players. Although the description of this aspect of the test did not specifically include instruction, if the instruction is aimed, as it usually is, at one of the factors in the test, such as science, literature, the arts, or politics, it should be protected. Thus, speech such as that presented by the coach may merit protection as an instructional technique, at least in some circumstances. Here, however, the university seems to have disavowed the use of such language for instructional purposes. Since the university's response was an employment action, its view on the proper performance of Dambrot's coaching duties seems to deny any protection under this factor. Of course, since the language does not meet the first two prongs of the test, it should not have been considered hate speech in the first place.

Although the results of applying the test come out the same way as Kennedy's assessment with regard to the locker-room comments on playing the game of basketball, an analysis of the comments about performance in the classroom may lead to a different result.[12] Whereas Dambrot's praising those who "play like niggers" on the court was intended as, and may well have conveyed, a message of encouragement that tied an often racist word to a positive description, his additional suggestion that the players not "act like niggers in the classroom" was uttered in a way that lacks the same positive tie.

The court explained the context for the classroom comment. When the coach was asked why he did not want his players to "act like niggers in the classroom," he said,

> Well, that's really a very easy question for me to answer, because we had had an incident early in the year where we had five or six basketball players, some of our bigger kids on our team, in a math class. And our kids were aggressive, tough, you know, a little bit loud, abrasive. And the lady was intimidated, because it was the first year that she ever had taught. And they almost got kicked out of the math class. . . . [I]t was my feeling that you can't be aggressive, tough, hard-nosed, abrasive in class, or you're going to get thrown out of classes, especially at a school like Central Michigan where the faculty members don't understand a lot about black people or have many black people in class. And I think our players understood what I meant by, "Don't be niggers in the classroom."[13]

The classroom comment might well be seen as invoking a negative stereotype. In fact, the direction not to behave in a certain way seems necessarily negative. Attaching it to any word indicating a racial group, let alone a word that is often or normally a racial epithet, would seem to make that negative statement stereotypical. Using what is commonly a racist term can only make it more so. Although perhaps not suggesting that his players were subhuman, the classroom comment does seem to be an expression of inferiority, a degradation to a level below that of the average student with regard to classroom behavior.

The coach could, despite this general position, argue that it does not apply in this case. The coach, through the context in which he used the word, could be seen as having assigned a nonracist meaning to the term. His use of the word in the context of playing basketball provided a meaning of being tough and aggressive, although in the classroom context loud and abrasive were seemingly added to the definition. Clearly, if he had used those adjectives to describe the behavior he did not want in the classroom, the direction would not have been racist. His argument, then, might be that his use of what would normally be a racist epithet should be seen only as a substitute for this combination of adjectives. Nonetheless, his use of a race-based and ordinarily racist substitute for the combination of adjectives seems problematic.

Further Consideration on Barring All Use of Racial Terms

Randall Kennedy rejects a blanket ban of the use of the word *nigger*, even when used by whites: "To condemn whites who use the N-word without regard to context, is simply to make a fetish of *nigger*."[14] As an example, Kennedy discusses correspondence between Carl Van Vechten and Langston Hughes in which Van Vechten, a white man, wrote of "niggers." Kennedy notes that Hughes did not object and asks if he should have. Kennedy's conclusion is that, because of Van Vechten's support of the Harlem Renaissance, his clear abhorrence of racial prejudice, and his support for improving the fortunes of African Americans, Hughes should not have objected.[15] That conclusion does not necessarily follow. Hughes could well, despite his relationship with Van Vechten and Van Vechten's record, have been uncomfortable with his use of the word. Kennedy seems right, nonetheless, in what is an unstated conclusion, that Van Vechten's speech was not racist. Although there may be a presumption of racist intent when the word is used by a white person, Kennedy seems to be arguing that the presumption is overcome by the speaker's record of racial enlightenment. For Kennedy, context matters.

For Kennedy, Coach Dambrot's use of the word seems to provide another example of a case in which the presumption of racist intent might reasonably be rejected. If the Van Vechten and Dambrot cases are not convincing, consider another case involving use of what is normally a racial epithet but that should probably be considered innocent, even though it should be, in a sense, banned.

We may have to go to a bygone era or to a remote part of the country with no access to mass media and an entirely white population, but consider a child who has no idea of the meaning of the word *nigger*. The child has heard a rhyme beginning "eeny, meeny, miny, moe" that is used to choose among individuals. That rhyme contains the word *nigger*. In reciting the rhyme, the child is using the word, but the use would not seem racist. The child has no idea of the meaning of, or the emotional impact of, the word. He should not be thought of as racist. He has no intent to express a belief that a particular group is less than fully human.

What is the proper response to this use of the word? It should be educational, and it may include a ban. The child's parent, hearing the recitation, should explain to the child that the word should not be used. A substitute line, in which one catches a "feller" or a "tiger" by the toe, might be suggested. Depending on how complete the explanation has been, the child may now know that the word is racist in most contexts. Any further use of the word would be more likely to be seen as racist than was the initial use. At any rate, the child now knows that the word is not proper in polite conversation.

There could also be instances when an adult has a similar lack of knowledge that a word has a racist meaning. Consider a professor who says that a character in a case or a novel was "gypped." A student of Romany descent in the class is seriously offended and reports the incident to the department head or the dean. The phrase *to gyp* has a racist connotation based on the presumed behavior of the Romany or Gypsies. It is also such a commonly used word that many to most people do not realize its racial overtones. While the professor's use of the word is in a context that degrades Gypsies as a class and could thus be seen as appealing to the degrading or subhumanizing interest suggested here to be the hallmark of hate speech, the lack of intent on the part of the speaker, indeed the lack of realization on the part of the speaker, suggests advising rather than sanctioning the professor.

There is also an interesting issue here with regard to the offensiveness of the comment under community standards. When a word has such widespread use, it may not rise to a sufficient level of offensiveness to allow for sanctions, at least in any criminal context. In the university setting, perhaps the greater expectation of understanding the basis for the word would include a greater likelihood of offensiveness under the standards of the university community. Thus, some sort of job-related action could be seen as appropriate, with counseling or advising seeming to be the best fit here.

Making sort of an opposite point, Kennedy presents an example of the use of a word that is not offensive but that was seen as offensive by some, or many, of those who heard it. The white director of a District of Columbia government department talked about budget problems and told his staff that they would have to be "niggardly" with their money. The use of that word, which certainly has no tie to race, led to a public outcry and his resignation.

Even having the meaning and etymology explained did not keep one reactant from wondering if the official had not noticed that he had to pass through "nigger," before getting to "-dly." Kennedy calls the incident an "infamous round of wrongheaded protest."[16]

Although neither the official nor the language may have been racist in this case, it is not clear that some action might not have been appropriate. The official should have recognized that some people would not understand the difference in the words or would assume that there was a linguistic tie. Whether or not he should have had to resign, some counseling probably would have been appropriate. Kennedy notes that a columnist asked whether the official, who is openly gay, would be bothered by a superior saying that he was "going to throw another faggot on the fire" or "go outside to smoke a fag."[17] It seems likely that the official would have experienced discomfort over these phrases, but of course here the words are the same words that are used in homophobic speech, not just somewhat similar sounding ones. It is true that, as with *niggardly*, the words were not used in an insulting manner, but discomfort could well be both strong and understandable. Counseling seems called for here as well, assuming a lack of degrading intent in the use of the words.

One more issue to note regarding *niggardly* is that a person might use the word in a racist way. Knowing that he or she cannot use the word *nigger*, a person might regularly use *niggardly* or other words that sound like racial epithets. In that case the speaker would never actually have used a racist word but would seem to be expressing racist sentiments. He or she would certainly have an impact on a member of the group toward which the sound-alike words might be addressed. Just as the use of a word that is ordinarily seen as racist should not be taken as conclusive with regard to the racist intent of the speaker, the fact that the words used are not the racial epithets they sound like should not lead to a necessary conclusion that the speech is not racist. In fact, speech can clearly be racist without the use of any epithets.

The Use-Mention Distinction

Consider the following hypothetical: A professor in a university Department of Native American Studies introduces to his class the issue of Native American concern over the use of tribal names and words such as "Braves" or "Redskins" for sports teams. One of the students expresses an inability to understand the concern, suggesting that "it's no big deal." The professor, hoping to make the point more accessible by broadening it, responds that for Native Americans a team name such as "Washington Redskins" is as offensive as Hispanic Americans would find "Sacramento Spics" or African Americans would find "Nashville Niggers." Two students in the class, one Hispanic American and one African American, find the professor's utterance of these terms offensive and complain to the professor's department chair. What should be the department chair's reaction?

An analysis of the situation requires an understanding of the use-mention distinction. Words may be either used or mentioned. In most ordinary conversation or writing, words are used. That is true of all words thus far in this paragraph and of most of the words in the preceding paragraph. However, sometimes one talks about words. In those situations, words may be mentioned instead of being used. When one is talking about a word, that is, mentioning the word, quotation marks or italics are generally used to indicate that the word is being mentioned rather than used.

If in referring to an individual a speaker employs what would generally be considered a racial epithet, the speaker is using a word while talking about a person. The basketball coach discussed earlier used the word that formed the basis for the complaint. Our professor of Native American studies did not use the words that formed the basis for the complaint against him. He mentioned the words. He was not talking about individuals. He was talking about words.

The *use* of a word is far more likely to be racist than the *mention* of the same word. That is not to say that all uses of a word that is ordinarily a racial epithet are in fact racist, as shown by Kennedy's reaction to the basketball coach's halftime talk. It is also not to say that all mentions of a word are not racist. If a person tells another, "the best labels to attach to you are," and follows that with a string of racial epithets, the fact that those epithets would be in quotation marks if they were written would not keep them from being racist. Despite the form of the sentence, the speaker is really speaking about the person, not about words.

Our professor's speech should not be seen as racist. He was not talking about people; he was speaking about words. And his discussion of words was not a subterfuge for the assignment of racial epithets to individuals. It was a serious discussion of the emotive impact of words and an attempt to educate a student who did not understand that impact. Our test for hate speech finds it not to be hate speech on at least two grounds. There is a lack of appeal to any racist sentiment. Words are not being used to disparage any individual. Indeed, the words in question on not being used at all. Second, there is serious value to the speech involved. It was intended as, and in fact was, educational. The remaining aspect of our test may not be quite as clear, but it seems unlikely that anyone who understood the context would conclude that the comments were offensive under community standards.

A Look at Serious Value

Kennedy provides examples of serious literary use of the word *nigger*. He notes that Harriet Beecher Stowe, Mark Twain, William Dean Howells, Edward Sheldon, Eugene O'Neill, Lillian Smith, Sinclair Lewis, Joyce Carol Oates, E. L. Doctorow, John Grisham, "and numerous other white writers have unveiled *nigger*-as-insult in order to dramatize and condemn racism's baleful presence."[18]

On this subject, Kennedy notes a controversy over the film director Quentin Tarantino.[19] Tarantino has characters in several of his films use the word "nigger"; in one case it is used by a black character, but in other cases it is used by white characters. Among Tarantino's critics was Spike Lee, whose own films use the same language. Lee claimed that as an African American he had more of a right to use the word. Kennedy discusses several bases for such a claim, dismissing them all. He concludes,

> The great failing of these theories is that, taken seriously, they would cast a protectionist pall over popular culture that would likely benefit certain minority entrepreneurs only at the net expense of society overall. Excellence in culture thrives, like excellence elsewhere, in a setting open to competition—and that includes competition concerning how best to dramatize the N-word. Thus, instead of cordoning off racially defined areas of the culture and allowing them to be tilled only by persons of the "right" race, we should work toward enlarging the common ground of American culture, a field that is open to all comers regardless of their origin.[20]

It is not only the differential application of rules regarding the use of potentially racist words that Kennedy seems to find objectionable. That difference can be explained on the basis of the presumptions of intent discussed earlier, and perhaps that is the best justification for the Spike Lee position. An African American using the objectionable word may be presumed not to be using the word in a racist way, whereas there may be a presumption that a European American, for example, is making a racist use of it. Kennedy, however, seems to reject that argument.

An even better argument for considering at least two of Tarantino's films objectionable, while accepting Lee's, may be in the characters themselves. In two of the Tarantino films, *True Romance* and *Pulp Fiction*, the objectionable line is uttered by a white character, and there may be a presumption of racism in its use. Spike Lee's films tend to involve black characters, whose use of the word may be seen as reflective of the vernacular and as nonracist. Thus, it is not the race of the director that matters but the potentially racist content of the lines themselves. That may still not be sufficient for Kennedy, since the depiction of any such racism by Tarantino could be seen as having the same value as the use of the same word by Mark Twain.

What is important here is the role Kennedy seems to see for serious value in the analysis of whether speech is racist. Continuing the discussion of criticism of Tarantino, Kennedy says that Lee's criticism is "off the mark." "It focuses on the character of Tarantino's race rather than the character of his work—brilliant work that allows the word *nigger* to be heard in a rich panoply of contexts and intonations."[21] Clearly, this is an appeal to the sort of serious literary, artistic, political, or scientific value in a work taken as a whole that would save that work from being considered obscene and, as has been argued here, should be extended to keep a work from being considered racist.

The issue of serious value has also arisen in the context of university codes limiting speech that, because of its racist or sexist nature, has an impact on students' ability to participate in and benefit from the educational process. In *Doe v. University of Michigan*,[22] a 1989 case, a federal district court considered the University of Michigan's policy on discrimination and discriminatory harassment. The policy varied, depending on where the speech occurred. With regard to classroom buildings, libraries, laboratories, and study centers, a person could be subject to discipline for

1. Any behavior, verbal or physical, that stigmatizes or victimizes an individual on the basis of race, ethnicity, religion, sex, sexual orientation, creed, national origin, ancestry, age, marital status, handicap or Vietnam-era veteran status, and that
   a. Involves an express or implied threat to an individual's academic efforts, employment, participation in University sponsored extra-curricular activities or personal safety; or
   b. Has the purpose or reasonably foreseeable effect of interfering with an individual's academic efforts, employment, participation in University sponsored extra-curricular activities or personal safety; or
   c. Creates an intimidating, hostile, or demeaning environment for educational pursuits, employment or participation in University sponsored extra-curricular activities.[23]

The university sought to reduce the vagueness in that language by also publishing a guide for students regarding the policy. The guide listed a number of examples of sanctionable conduct.[24]

The court found the university's policy unconstitutional, declaring that "the University could not ... establish an anti-discrimination policy which had the effect of prohibiting certain speech because it disagreed with ideas or messages sought to be conveyed."[25] Neither could the university bar the speech because it found it to be offensive. While these principles serve as general limitations on government power to restrict speech, the court felt that they applied with "special significance" within the university setting. The impact was simply too great on the "free and unfettered interplay of competing views ... essential to the institution's educational mission."[26]

Particularly troubling to the court was the fact that the policy had been applied to reach clearly protected speech. There had been a complaint filed against a graduate student in social work who was alleged to have harassed his fellow students on the bases of sexual orientation and sex. The student had, in a research class, stated that he believed homosexuality to be a disease and that he intended to develop a counseling plan to change homosexual clients into heterosexuals. He also said he had been counseling several gay clients to that end. His comments were not well received by classmates, who questioned both the validity and morality of his approach.

After the complaint was filed, the student was informed by the policy administrator that there had been an investigation and that there was sufficient evidence to justify a formal hearing. Perhaps oddly, the hearing panel found him guilty of sexual harassment but did not so find with regard to harassment on the basis of sexual orientation. The court took the university to task, because the university "saw no First Amendment problem in forcing the student to a hearing to answer for allegedly harassing statements made in the course of academic discussion and research."[27]

The court also noted that it had found only a single instance of a complaint involving an allegation of harassing remarks made within the classroom setting being dismissed because of a recognition that the comments were protected speech. A student in a class on the Holocaust suggested that Jewish people cynically use the Holocaust to justify the policies of Israel toward the Palestinian people. A complaint was filed by a Jewish student in the class, and the speaker refused to apologize for the comment. The policy administrator concluded that the comment was protected speech and was not covered by the policy.

Also of interest was the basis under which the plaintiff, Doe, had standing to sue the university. Doe was a graduate student in psychology, specializing in "the interdisciplinary study of the biological bases of individual differences in personality traits and mental abilities."[28] Doe said that he wanted to discuss questions regarding sex and race differences in his role as a teaching assistant in a Comparative Animal Behavior class. He said, in that regard,

An appropriate topic for discussion in the discussion groups is sexual differences between male and female mammals, including humans. [One] . . . hypothesis regarding sex differences in mental abilities is that men as a group do better than women in some spatially related mental tasks partly because of a biological difference. This may partly explain, for example, why many more men than women chose to enter the engineering profession.[29]

He argued that he might be subject to sanction for such comments, particularly since one of the examples in the university's guide to the policy was of a male student's remarking in a class, "Women just aren't as good in this field as men." Since some students would view his theories as sexist, he feared prosecution. Given the university's reactions to other instances of speech, such as those just presented, the court could not dismiss Doe's fears as speculative or conjectural.

The University of Wisconsin, in the same general time frame, developed its own antiharassment policies, policies that were challenged and found wanting in 1991 in *UWM Post v. Board of Regents*.[30] The policy provided that the university could discipline a student in "non-academic matters" in certain situations. Its rule provided sanctions

(2)(a) For racist or discriminatory comments, epithets or other expressive behavior directed at an individual or on separate occasions at different individuals, or for physical conduct, if such comments, epithets or other expressive behavior or physical conduct intentionally:
  1. Demean the race, sex, religion, color, creed, disability, sexual orientation, national origin, ancestry or age of the individual or individuals; and
  2. Create an intimidating, hostile or demeaning environment for education, university-related work, or other university-authorized activity.[31]

The university, within the rule itself, set out examples to illustrate situations and conduct intended to be covered by the rule. Among the examples of violations were intentionally making demeaning remarks to an individual on the basis of the person's ethnicity, remarks such as racial slurs, epithets, and jokes, when the purpose is to create a hostile educational environment. Persons would also be in violation for similar visual or written material with the same intent. Significantly, the policy said that it was not a violation in the context of a classroom discussion to express a derogatory opinion with regard to a racial or ethnic group. The difference was that such a remark was addressed not to an individual but to a group and, according to the explanation of the policy, lacked evidence of intent to create a hostile environment. Thus, under this policy, to be a violation the expression not only must be racist or discriminatory and demeaning but also must be directed at an individual, create a hostile environment, and do so intentionally.

Like the University of Michigan, the University of Wisconsin produced a guide setting out illustrations of violations and nonviolations. The guide included as a violation a student's calling a black dormitory floormate "nigger" whenever they passed in the hall. The guide said that the comment was directed at an individual and that the use and repetition demonstrated intent. Less clear, according to the guide, was a situation in which a group of students disrupted a class by shouting racial epithets. Although they were clearly subject to disciplinary action for disrupting a class, their liability under the new rules was less certain. That liability depended on whether the comments were directed to an individual in the class and were intended to demean and create an intimidating environment.

As examples of nonviolations, the guide included the sort of statement that raised a problem for the University of Michigan policy. The example given was a class discussion regarding women in the workplace in which a male student comments that he believes that women are, by nature, better equipped to be mothers than executives and should not be in upper-management positions. In concluding that that comment was not a violation, the guide said, "The statement is an expression of opinion, contains no epithets, is not directed to a particular individual, and does not, standing alone, evince the requisite intent to demean or create a hostile environment."[32] A second example, again similar to one that had raised a problem for the University of Michigan, involved a faculty member's suggesting in a genetics class discussion that certain racial groups may be genetically predisposed to alcoholism. The guide said that there would be no discipline under the policy not only because the policy applied to students rather than to faculty but also because the comment was the protected expression of an idea.

Like the University of Michigan policy, the University of Wisconsin policy was declared unconstitutional. Even with the examples given of protected speech not reached by the policy, the policy still went too far. Because the rule could be used to sanction speech that did not fall into a recognized exception to First Amendment protection, such as fighting words, it was overbroad and a violation of the First Amendment. Since both policies were declared unconstitutional, it might seem that there is little to learn by comparing the two. However, if the law should change at some point so as to allow limitations on hate speech, the distinctions would become important. Furthermore, in situations in which someone may be subject to sanctions for hate speech, such as in the employment context, the differences between speech with serious value and the simple utterance of epithets should be kept in mind.

Hate Speech Based on Gender and Sexual Orientation

Most of the discussion thus far has had to do with hate speech based on race, but the same considerations should apply when analogous speech focuses on gender or sexual orientation. Although some people may question how much sexist speech is based on hatred, there is certainly offense to be found in some utterances, and the considerations of the factors that are part of the obscenity test are also appropriate in this context.

As an example, the use of a name for a body part to refer to a woman seems to be the same sort of degradation discussed with regard to race. To reduce a woman to a body part is to deny, or at least belittle, the humanity of the woman. There is a disregard for the higher-order functioning of the target. The target is not seen as a thinking entity, as a person, and is instead referred to in terms that could apply to females of lower species as well. That would appear to be an expression of degradation, an assertion of subhuman status. If it is assumed, as seems reasonable, that such references are also seen as offensive, then they qualify as hate speech, unless there is also serious value.

A particularly interesting issue is the use of the word *bitch*. Given the proper referent of the word as a female dog, calling women "bitches" would also fit into the hate speech analysis presented here. Women are assigned a label that properly belongs to members of a subhuman species. Far worse than pornography's potential removal of humanity from the status of the divine, this may be seen as an assertion that women have less than even fully human status. The assumption that this word is also offensive under contemporary community standards may not be as clear as it is for the use of a body part, but there seems to be a developing recognition or acceptance of the offensiveness of the word when it is used to apply to women generally.

There is also the issue of the use of the word to apply to an individual woman based on her behavior or attitude. To call an individual a "bitch" might not seem to be the assignment of subhuman status to women in general, even if it is so viewed with regard to the individual. Thus, it might be seen as falling short of hate speech. That may not be the correct conclusion. With regard to a racist term, it would probably not be seen as a valid defense that the word was assigned to an individual because of his or her individual behavior, rather than because of his or her membership in a racial or ethnic group. While the motivation may have been directed toward the individual's behavior rather than an attitude toward a class, the use of the word to criticize the behavior seems to be the invocation of harmful stereotypes that is of the character of hate speech. The same conclusion should probably apply to the use of *bitch* to refer to an individual woman based on her behavior. There would, of course, remain the issue of offensiveness, and society may see the individual use as less offensive than the group designation.

There is also an issue that needs to be addressed with regard to some homophobic speech that may differ from racist or sexist speech. Most instances of homophobic speech may be analyzed in the same way as hate directed at race or gender. There are words that may be seen as the same sort of assertion of subhumanity as in the other cases. Even short of the use of epithets, there are clearly cases of speech that states, without those inflammatory words, a belief that homosexuals are of a lower order than heterosexuals. That seems to be as fully hate speech as the racial cases.

The issue that may be different from racist or sexist speech has to do with moral claims. No one reasonably asserts that it is immoral to be a member of a particular racial group or a gender. There is no personal choice there that can be the basis for criticism. With regard to sexual orientation, the same seems true. But some people are critical of homosexual activity on the basis of morality. Whereas an attack on those of homosexual orientation is clear hate speech, criticism of homosexual practices would, in the view of those offering such criticism, be the assertion of a moral claim. To limit such speech would raise issues regarding political, social, or religious suppression that may well counsel against concluding that it is hate speech. Such speech may also have serious value, which should save the speech from such a classification.

It must be admitted that the majority population may have trouble recognizing the offensive impact that speech may have on the minority, and in the area of homophobic speech this may be a particular problem. This does seem to have been the case with the offensiveness aspect of obscenity law as applied to homoerotic material. Although there may no longer be sufficient criminal prosecutions to demonstrate this point, the current practice of customs agents is relevant. Gay and lesbian pornography seems to be far more likely to be seized than straight materials.

The difficulties with this genre were well set out in 2000 in the Canadian Supreme Court case *Little Sisters Book & Art Emporium v. Canada*.[33] Little Sisters, a gay/lesbian bookstore, sued to end the treatment it had been receiving at the hands of Canadian Customs. Materials it imported, primarily from the United States, were held for extended periods by Customs. It appears that other erotica was not as likely to be seized or delayed. In fact, it appears that precisely the same material, when imported by a mainstream bookstore, did not face the same treatment. Although this fact may indicate negative treatment more of the store than of the material, Ronald Krotoszynski's analysis of the situation found that "[p]erhaps not surprisingly, erotica aimed at the gay and lesbian community struck many Customs inspectors as facially 'degrading' and 'dehumanizing.'"[34] He does not find this reaction to be unexpected: "Standards like 'dehumanizing' and 'degrading' are culturally situated; those applying the standard cannot replace their own aesthetic standards with those of a sexual minority."[35]

Little Sisters presents a case in which there was an inability to recognize gay and lesbian standards for degradation in limiting erotic material. The gay and lesbian community faced broader limitations on sexual material, and their freedom of expression was lessened. With regard to hate speech, there is a concern that the majority's inability to properly assess the level of offensiveness that their speech will have for gays and lesbians may provide less protection for gays and lesbians. If a person who utters such speech is unable to recognize offense, the result may be more protection for that speech, when perhaps it should have been limited.

Concluding Remarks

The relatively brief discussion in this chapter of applications of the obscenity-based test obviously is not exhaustive of all the varieties of hate expression people may utter. But the examples presented show the sort of analysis involved in examining an expression to determine its status as hate speech. The examples have focused on the sort of speech that degrades a population to less than fully human status. It is the same sort of degradation that some people have seen in pornography's degradation of humanity as a whole to an animal level, placing a gulf between humans and the divine. Although this view of pornography as obscenity may have less currency now, it serves to explain what some people have seen as unacceptable in that variety of expression. It also explains the parallel role of hate speech, which asserts a chasm not only between a particular population and the divine but between that population and the rest of humanity.

In addition to the examination of the degrading nature of hate speech, the examples have provided an opportunity to look to the other factors that must be considered, at least before any legal sanctions are invoked but also before a conclusion can be made that particular speech is racist, sexist, or homophobic. The examples also serve to justify those considerations.

There certainly may be differences in the conclusions different people may draw with regard to the same instance of expression. Even so, the analytic framework presented here is of value. Instead of two people disagreeing, without much basis to resolve their differences, the framework serves to provide a focus for understanding the disagreement. By looking at the factors drawn from the obscenity test, individuals can determine whether they disagree regarding the degrading nature of the speech or, for example, whether the value inherent in a particular instance of expression should serve to protect speech that they agree is degrading. If the disagreement is of the latter variety, the examples in which speech was seen as requiring protection can serve as the basis for debating the issue of serious value generally, through a comparison of the value found in the examples to the purported value in the expression under consideration. This new focused disagreement is more likely to be amenable to some resolution.

───────────────────────────────────── 9 ─────

Variable Obscenity,
Children, and Hate

The Special Problem of Children and Hate

Richard Delgado and Jean Stefancic argue in their book *Understanding Words That Wound* that children require special protection from hate speech.[1] They present that argument from the point of view of the minority child, who is "particularly susceptible to the wounds words can inflict."[2] Through hate speech, they note, young minorities are taught to hate themselves, as evidenced by stories of children trying to "scrub the color out of their skin."[3] Young children have fewer coping mechanisms, and they may simply become angry. Even more damaging, they may internalize the sentiments expressed.

Nonminority children can also be hurt by views they hear from others, especially if they internalize those sentiments. Racism may not be recognized as a mental disorder, but it is not the sign of a healthy mind. And just as it is minority youth who are most susceptible to injury from racist comments, it is nonminority youth who are most likely to adopt the racist comments they hear. Although Oscar Hammerstein was hardly an authority in psychology, he was correct in writing in his lyrics for the musical *South Pacific* that one must "be carefully taught" to hate.[4] His conclusion that this must be accomplished by the age of "six or seven or eight" may have been more a function of rhyme scheme than anything else. The portions of the brain that control judgment, inhibition, and executive function continue development beyond that age and might be affected by being taught hatred beyond the age of eight.[5] Some hate groups try to recruit more racists through music that appeals to older children,[6] so those groups clearly do not see their cause as lost by the time a child is eight and do believe that they may be persuasive with older children or perhaps even young adults.

These hate groups are not the first to recognize that children are the best target for any sort of indoctrination. And the recognition has belonged to those at both ends of the spectrum of good and evil. On the one end, Lenin is said to have said, "Give me four years to teach the children, and the seed I have sown will never be uprooted."[7] Hitler repeated the sentiment: "Give me the children, and I will give you a nation."[8] At the other end of the spectrum, St. Francis Xavier said, "Give me the children until they are seven, and anyone may have them afterwards."[9] All these expressions are variations of Virgil's saying, "As the twig is bent the tree inclines."[10]

There is and has long been, then, a recognition that the young present a particular target for those who would teach them any values. When the value that is being taught is a level of hatred that degrades others by treating their humanity as lesser than that of the majority, society should be especially concerned that the young be shielded from the expression. This is true for those young targets of hate speech who would be psychologically damaged by the speech. It is also true for those nonminority children who would come to believe the content of the hate speech at a time when they have not had the interactions with minorities to form their own understanding and while they are still in a state of emotional, psychological, and neural development.

Obscenity law provides some guidance here. Obscenity law recognizes that youths are particularly susceptible to pornographic images, and pornography may be obscene when distributed to youth, even when it would be perfectly legal to distribute the material to adults. The theory seems to be that the prurient interest of, for example, a sixteen-year-old male is more easily appealed to than that of an adult. This assumption seems to be true, but consideration of a younger child raises an interesting issue. A five-year-old will not experience an appeal to the prurient interest, at least in the sense that that interest speaks to arousal. Nonetheless, the exposure of young children to such images is clearly considered unacceptable and is often addressed by the same obscenity statute. Although prurience in the arousal sense may not be present for younger children, pornographic images in such a context may still appeal to a shameful interest by providing a degrading view of humanity. The young child is exposed to a purely animal side of humanity. Not only is the child not experiencing any nonanimal, romantic aspects; the child is incapable of understanding the higher-order aspects and is left only with the degrading aspects.

The degrading aspects of hate speech are also likely to have more impact on children. Assertions that imply that a population is less than fully human are likely to have the strongest impact on hearers who are unfamiliar with members of that target population. Knowing, particularly having positive interactions with, members of a minority population makes one far less susceptible to claims that that population is somehow flawed. A child, particularly one without experience with members of the target population, is more likely to be swayed by speech that degrades that population. Hate speech, like pornographic images, may have a sufficiently stronger impact on children as to make their exposure of particular concern.

This chapter explores the application of obscenity law to the case of hate speech and children. First, the concept of variable obscenity is presented. Then follows a discussion of the marketing of hate speech to children and a presentation of arguments for the protection of children, even if adults are left free to offer and receive such speech. Lastly, the issue of hate speech in the schools is discussed, and some recent language in cases on that issue is presented as indicating perhaps a coming recognition that such speech is sufficiently degrading as to be regulable.

The Concept of Variable Obscenity

The U.S. Supreme Court recognized the concept of variable obscenity in a 1966 case titled *Mishkin v. New York*.[11] Mishkin had been convicted for hiring others to prepare obscene books, publishing those books, and possessing the books with intent to distribute, all in violation of New York law. The books Mishkin published were cheap paperbacks prepared for him under rather specific instructions. Writers and artists were told that the sex depicted had to be "very strong, it had to be rough," that "sex scenes had to be unusual sex scenes," that there were to be "spankings and . . . sex in an abnormal and irregular fashion," and that they were to deal graphically with "the darkening of the flesh under flagellation."[12]

Among the defenses raised by Mishkin and disposed of by the Court was one of particular interest here. Mishkin claimed that the material at issue was not obscene under the then-applicable test. That test, adopted in 1957 in *Roth v. United States*,[13] like the current *Miller* test, required that the material appeal to the prurient interest of the average person. Here, however, the Court noted that

appellant's sole contention regarding the nature of the material is that some of the books involved in this prosecution, those depicting various deviant sexual practices, such as flagellation, fetishism, and lesbianism, do not satisfy the prurient-appeal requirement because they do not appeal to a prurient interest of the "average person" in sex, that "instead of stimulating the erotic, they disgust and sicken."[14]

The court rejected that contention. It did not hold that the material did appeal to the prurient interest of the average person. Instead, it explained that the "average person" approach had been adopted to reject the test received from the British, in the 1868 case *Regina v. Hinklin*,[15] which had focused on the effect the material would have on the most susceptible person in the community. The issue here was not whether the average person should be barred from reading material that would have an impact on the most susceptible, as it would have been under the *Hicklin* test. It was whether the lack of sexual impact on the average person should protect material that has an appeal to those who are, in a sense, differently susceptible, to those with special deviant interests.

On that issue, the Court said, "Where the material is designed for and primarily disseminated to a clearly defined deviant sexual group, rather than the public at large, the prurient-appeal requirement of the *Roth* test is satisfied if the dominant theme of the material taken as a whole appeals to the prurient interest in sex of the members of that group."[16] The Court noted that there was no claim made that the material at issue did not appeal to the prurient interest of its target audience. The instructions to those who prepared the books indicated an intent to have such appeal, as did the fact that Mishkin provided the preparers with manuals on sexual deviations.[17]

The impact of this case may not seem clear, but it was a step toward recognizing that material might be treated differently not only when distributed to a deviant group but also when distributed to children. That more relevant position was adopted by the Court in the 1968 case *Ginsberg v. New York*.[18] Sam Ginsberg and his wife operated Sam's Stationery and Luncheonette in a community on Long Island, New York. At the store, they sold magazines, including what the Court called "girlie" magazines. On two occasions, Sam sold such magazines to a sixteen-year-old. He was charged under a New York law barring, among other things, the sale to a person under seventeen of a magazine that contained nudity and was harmful to minors.[19] "Harmful to minors" was defined in a way that mirrored the then-existing test for obscenity for materials distributed to adults:

> "Harmful to minors" means that quality of any description or representation, in whatever form, of nudity, sexual conduct, sexual excitement, or sadomasochistic abuse, when it:
> (i) predominantly appeals to the prurient, shameful or morbid interest of minors, and

(ii)   is patently offensive to prevailing standards in the adult community as a whole with respect to what is suitable material for minors, and

(iii)   is utterly without redeeming social importance for minors.[20]

The magazines at issue depicted provocatively posed nude females but were not, the Court recognized, obscene for an adult audience. The issue before the Court was, then, whether materials that were legal for adult distribution could be the subject of criminal sanction when sold to children under seventeen.

Here the Court turned to the concept of variable obscenity. It cited and quoted an article by William Lockhart and Robert McClure that had been cited in *Mishkin* as well but was of particular relevance here:

> Variable obscenity . . . furnishes a useful analytical tool for dealing with the problem of denying adolescents access to material aimed at a primary audience of sexually mature adults. For variable obscenity focuses attention upon the make-up of primary and peripheral audiences in varying circumstances, and provides a reasonably satisfactory means for delineating the obscene in each circumstance.
>
> Material which is protected for distribution to adults is not necessarily constitutionally protected from restriction upon its dissemination to children. In other words, the concept of obscenity or of unprotected matter may vary according to the group to whom the questionable material is directed or from whom it is quarantined. Because of the State's exigent interest in preventing distribution to children of objectionable material, it can exercise its power to protect the health, safety, welfare and morals of its community by barring the distribution to children of books recognized to be suitable for adults.[21]

The Court also drew on other commentators to support the position that children may, or should, be treated differently. Of particular interest were those who took strong stances on allowing adult access to pornographic material and arguing against any obscenity exception to First Amendment protection when adults were involved. The Court quoted Thomas Emerson:

> Different factors come into play, also, where the interest at stake is the effect of erotic expression upon children. The world of children is not strictly part of the adult realm of free expression. The factor of immaturity, and perhaps other considerations, impose different rules. Without attempt-

ing here to formulate the principles relevant to freedom of expression for children, it suffices to say that regulations of communication addressed to them need not conform to the requirements of the first amendment in the same way as those applicable to adults.[22]

A quotation from Louis Henkin, characterized by the Court as a commentator who rejected the imposition of a single moral standard on adults, added weight to the argument:

> One must consider also how much difference it makes if laws are designed to protect only the morals of a child. While many of the constitutional arguments against morals legislation apply equally to legislation protecting the morals of children, one can well distinguish laws which do not impose a morality on children, but which support the right of parents to deal with the morals of their children as they see fit.[23]

Recognizing the right of parents to restrict their children from seeing this sort of material, the Court also recognized that parents may need the help of the state in preventing the provision of the material by third parties.[24] Furthermore, the Court said that the state had its own interests in the well-being of its youth. The question of whether pornographic material harms that well-being may not have been fully resolved, but the Court said that the fact that obscene material is unprotected allowed the legislature to act, so long as it had a rational basis for such a belief. Although the existing studies did not demonstrate any causal link between obscenity and impaired moral or ethical development, the Court noted that the studies also did not disprove such a link. Under those circumstances, the Court said, "We do not demand of legislatures 'scientifically certain criteria of legislation,'" and found a rational relationship between the statute and the well-being of minors.[25]

Whatever might have been the state of science at the time, the Court was willing to recognize the right of the legislature to act on the premise that children are different. They may be more susceptible to the impact of material that would have less effect on adults. The conclusion of this case applies directly, of course, only to sexual material, but the potential for greater impact of expression on youth is likely to be similar in other areas. The legal question is whether the restrictions on youths' access to materials can be extended to other areas. In the case of sexual material, adult access may be restricted when the material is sufficiently extreme. The holding of *Ginsberg* was that less explicit material may be withheld from youths. If hate speech may not be limited for adults, there is not then a lesser standard to apply to children. If on the other hand, limits are allowed for the dissemination of hate speech to adults, stronger limits might well be allowed when the speech is directed at minors.

Marketing Hate to Children

Limitations on the dissemination of hate to children are likely to have to be backed by criminal sanctions. If hate speech in the adult community were ever to become the subject of criminal bans, then the differences that obscenity law provides for material directed toward children rather than adults would have application here as well. Even if hate speech is not regulated in the adult community, there are reasons why there is a need to impose limits on providing the same sort of expression to children.[26]

If, as Oscar Hammerstein said, children have to be taught to hate, there are those who are more than willing to provide the instruction. Not only are there individuals so inclined; there are organized groups with "educational" programs to that end. Perhaps among the most successful efforts at passing on racial hatred and the doctrine of white supremacy have been those of groups that have used music.[27] The first major distributor of racist music in the United States was Resistance Records. The label was established by William Pierce, the leader of the National Alliance. That is the same William Pierce who was an author of *The Turner Diaries,* a book that figured prominently in the bombing of the Federal Building in Oklahoma City.

Resistance Records has marketed such groups as Nordic Thunder, Angry Aryans, Blue-Eyed Devils, and RaHoWa (an acronym for "Racial Holy War"). Available CDs include titles such as *Racially Motivated Violence, Holocaust 2000, Retribution, Born to Hate,* and *On the Attack,* with song titles such as "Race Riot," "Third Reich," and "White Revolution."

Examples of the lyrics show the messages the songs convey. Angry Aryans' song "Browntown Burning Down" speaks of driving through a blackened ghetto, which has been destroyed as a result of allowing "the niggers to run free" and "Zulu tribal clashes," of "Negro in flames," and the expectation of "White racial violence."[28] The same group's song "Racially Debased," speaking of the birth of a "mud brown child," talks of the child's being a "mongrel, with African hair," and of the mother's getting the beating of her life, with hands around her neck as "air slowly dwindles away."[29] Nordic Thunder's song "United, White and Proud" speaks of being "[o]n the attack" and ready to "take our Nation back," of "bashing the fags," and of their causing all "the muds to be on the run."[30] RaHoWa's "White Revolution" tells "slimy jew[s]" that they will wish they had never been born; and since the "jews" "sent in the niggers," the same will be true for the "ugly coon[s]."[31] Blue Eyed Devils' song "Final Solution" addresses its concerns with the "Jewish hordes" and calls for sending "every foe to his grave" and indicates that the Nazi regime knew what to do to "set our race free"; it calls for a "White revolution" and ends with "Sieg Heil."[32] The same group's "Murder Squad" calls for "kill[ing] the Jew" and sending "the filth to an early demise."[33]

The music distribution business is not just a profit center for the National Alliance, although it is that as well. It has been an instrument for recruiting alienated whites to be the next generation of supremacists. In an interview, William Pierce "expressed his hope that 'resistance music' would influence young people who are not yet politically motivated. He said: 'Through music I want to give them more awareness and a better understanding of what needs to be done. Music is truly a mass medium which reaches and influences everyone, not just those who are already politically committed.'"[34]

William Pierce died in 2002, and the National Alliance may have lost some of its momentum, but Resistance Records has carried on.[35] The change in leadership at Resistance Records also opened the way for competition in the hate-music market. Panzerfaust Records entered the arena and took up the approach of using music to recruit youths, but with an interesting new bent.

In September 2004, . . . Panzerfaust announced "Project Schoolyard USA," an explicit attempt to target children for recruitment by using hate music. Panzerfaust created a special compilation CD of hate music that it offered for sale for just pennies, intending that white supremacist groups would buy large numbers of the CD and distribute them to children at schools, concerts, and other venues.[36]

It appears that Panzerfaust Records has now gone out of business, perhaps triggered by the disclosure that Anthony Pierpont, one of its cofounders, is partially of Mexican descent.[37]

Resistance Records has also marketed a video game titled *Ethnic Cleansing* that combines all the hatred of the rest of its materials with the type of simulated violence in video games that concerns many people regarding the real-world effects of that violence. A player of *Ethnic Cleansing* may choose the guise of one of a number of racist characters and then proceeds through the streets of a city, shooting black and Hispanic characters in an attempt to get to their Jewish masters in the subways and, by killing them, save the white race. The company's website describes the game: "The most politically incorrect video game ever made. Run through the ghetto blasting away various blacks and spics in an attempt to gain entrance to the subway system, where the jews have hidden to avoid the carnage. Then, if YOU'RE lucky . . . you can blow away jews as they scream 'Oy Vey!', on your way to their command center."[38]

This sort of material is beyond distasteful. It is assaultive in the sense that various minority scholars have described. It is also clearly degrading. It cannot be seen as anything other than a statement that the various minority targets are less than human or at least less human than the white population. It harms the minority child who hears and perhaps internalizes the message of inferiority, and it harms the psychological state of the nonminority child.[39] If the supremacist message is not to be passed on to the next generation, then at a minimum, children need to be shielded from these efforts at recruitment.

So what can be done to shield children? Certainly, if hate speech were ever to become treated as violative of the law, there would be a strong opportunity to limit the access of these hatemongers to children. Even if the content of these songs were somehow seen as not sufficiently reprehensible as to allow the prohibition of distribution to adults, there could still be a prohibition against distribution to children. The theory of variable obscenity allows society to protect children from sexual images that may legally be distributed to adults. Were hate speech to become limitable, there ought to be an equivalent doctrine for variability with regard to children. If this material may be distributed to adults, there could still be the possibility that, when the intent, the offensiveness, and the lack of serious value are judged from the standpoint of a minor, the material would be considered unacceptable for that audience.

The First Amendment and Children

An interesting question arises in the event that hate speech does not become regulable for adults. Might it, nonetheless be regulable for children? I have argued elsewhere[40] that the freedom of expression that is so important for the adult community need not carry over to children. The importance of the freedom of expression for the adult community simply looses force when the issue is expression directed to the young.

The greatest importance for free speech is tied to self-governance. A country cannot really be free and self-governing if its people lack the freedom to discuss political issues and debate the direction the state or culture should take. As Alexander Meiklejohn puts it,

It is that mutilation of the thinking process of the community against which the First Amendment to the Constitution is directed. The principle of the freedom of speech springs from the necessities of the program of self-government. It is not a Law of Nature or of Reason in the abstract. It is a deduction from the basic American agreement that public issues shall be decided by universal suffrage.[41]

Those who participate in self-governance must have the freedom to obtain the information necessary for that participation. Without the opportunity to hear from those who have views that differ from the dominant opinion, there is no opportunity to act to change that opinion and the policies it may have motivated.

Children, however, do not participate in self-governance; they are denied the vote. Although informed decision-making may sometimes require input from children, it does not require that children be the recipients of speech. Those who want to use the political process to change the world should address their views toward voters. This may seem an odd argument, since there seems to be little harm to children from political speech. The difficulty, however, is in determining what constitutes political speech. The Supreme Court, some time ago, determined that entertainment was protected by the First Amendment, because the line between entertainment and political speech is too difficult to draw.[42] That understanding of the First Amendment leaves children open to expression of far greater concern than speeches before a political convention. Courts have concluded that it includes, for example, protecting a right to play violent video games.[43]

Judge Richard Posner, in one of the cases striking down limitations on children's access to violent video games, said that children do have First Amendment rights. He noted that the right to vote attaches at the age of eighteen and that children must have the freedom to form political views before that age so that they can cast informed votes. He went on to say that the state cannot help parents limit children's access, because the child's right is independent of the parent. He suggested that this sort of limitation, in the form of indoctrination by the Hitler Jugend, led to the fanaticism of German soldiers in World War II. And he concluded, "People are unlikely to become well-functioning, independent-minded adults and responsible citizens if they are raised in an intellectual bubble."[44]

It is true that children cannot be kept in the dark until the moment they gain their majority. It would then take some time for them to gain the information necessary to be informed voters. There may need to be a period of time prior to their eighteenth birthdays when children have more freedom to receive expression. That would speak in favor of any limits being removed at an earlier age, perhaps at seventeen. That leaves the child with a year to play as many violent video games or listen to as much hate speech as it takes to become a competent voter.

Self-governance is not the only value that people have found behind the constitutional guarantee of free expression. Also recognized by some as equally fundamental is the role of free expression to the autonomy of the individual,[45] which is built on a belief that every individual has a right to self-realization and self-determination, including a right to express one's thoughts and to receive any expression one desires. This is an attractive position, so far as adult recipients of expression are concerned. A societal determination that adults should not receive certain expression may be seen as a determination by society that it knows better than the individual what the individual's best interests are. It is what would be considered a paternalistic attitude toward the individual. But think about what is wrong with paternalism. It is a belief that another individual or society must act as one's father, must determine what is best for you and guide you along the right path. When the target of such paternalism is an adult, it is an expression of some form of inequality that may rightly be taken as insulting. When the target of paternalism is a child, the insult is lacking. The child is not the equal of the adult even in the ability to determine his or her own best interests. This is certainly true of choice of diet and may well also be true in the selection of reading or viewing material.

These autonomy-based approaches largely grow out of the work of John Stuart Mill. Mill discusses the utility of free expression as a means toward reaching the truth,[46] but his autonomy theory seems to make an exception for children. Phrased generally, his view is that society should not try to control the individual's lifestyle decisions, which would certainly include the choice of expression to receive, unless harm is done to others. Without that harm, "neither one person, nor any number of persons, is warranted in saying to another human creature of ripe years, that he shall not do with his life for his own benefit what he chooses to do with it."[47] Note the use of "of ripe years" in this quotation. This is not simply a slip of the pen. When Mill argues against punishing purely self-regarding behavior, behavior that is not harmful, he provides as one reason that society has other ways of bringing its "weaker members" up to its behavioral standards:

Society has had absolute power over them during the early portion of their existence: it has had the whole period of childhood and nonage in which to try whether it could make them capable of rational conduct in life. The existing generation is master both of the training and the entire circumstances of the generation to come. . . . If society lets any considerable number of its members grow up mere children, . . . society has itself to blame for the consequences.[48]

Thus, one of the reasons for adult autonomy is the lack of autonomy for children.

Another rationale for free expression has been the search for truth and the concept of the marketplace of ideas. This is what Justice Holmes had in mind in his dissent in the 1919 case *Abrams v. United States,* in which he wrote that the First Amendment provides society with the benefit of a free trade in ideas and that "the best test of truth is the power of thought to get itself accepted in the competition of the market."[49] The marketplace metaphor also finds a home in Justice Brandeis's 1927 concurrence in *Whitney v. California,* in which he says the remedy for bad speech is more speech, rather than suppression: "If there be time to expose through discussion the falsehood and fallacies, to avert the evil by the process of education, the remedy to be applied is more speech, not enforced silence."[50] Again, however, the rationale loses force when applied to children. More speech may be an inadequate remedy to an idea that is very attractive to a mind without the experience to anticipate consequences or to understand subtle distinctions. This may, of course, also be true for some adults, but we presume an equality for adults that does not carry over to children. When expression shows the potential of being sufficiently harmful to children, maybe the best remedy is suppression of that expression to children. In fact, if an idea can win the day only by its appeal to the less rational child, perhaps allowing its expression to children is a subversion of the marketplace of ideas rather than a proper functioning of that marketplace.

There are alternative rationales offered for the guarantee of free expression. Thomas Emerson, in his analysis of a variety of reasons behind the freedom, adds a suggestion that free expression serves as a sort of social control. The allowing of expression serves as a safety valve for those who would otherwise be inclined to action. This argument speaks most strongly for expression by, rather than expression to, individuals. For children, limits on expression to them seem no more likely to lead to revolution than limits on ice cream or, to use another media example, limits on hours of television viewing.[51]

It should be noted that there would be a danger in allowing the state to determine, on its own, what is suitable speech for children. That danger could, in the extreme, be a regimentation reminiscent of the Hitler Youth movement that concerned Judge Posner. In the less extreme, it would be the sort of concern that explains the Supreme Court's 1969 decision in *Tinker v. Des Moines Independent Community School District*,[52] a case growing out of the decision by a school system not to allow black armbands in protest of the conflict in Vietnam, while allowing other accessories with political meaning. If the state allows the expression of one view to children and suppresses others, the potential dangers that motivate free expression will have their impact on the younger generation.[53]

This problem can be ameliorated by recognizing that the authority to limit the expression presented to children should not apply to the child's parents. Perhaps the best approach to limiting the provision of hate speech to children would be to address only the direct provision to children of material such as the hate music previously discussed. Parents who are so inclined might be allowed to buy the material and give it to their children. This exception for parents is not because of any belief that parents should present such material to children but because of a concern over the slippery slope of what other type of materials might be prohibited by the state. If parents remain free to provide the material, then despite Judge Posner's concern over regimentation, the ideas will not be denied completely to the next generation, and the children who are so "enlightened" can then bring those views to their contemporaries as they become adults.[54]

In addition to the lessened importance of free expression to children, when the standard rationales for free speech are analyzed, there is also more potential harm to children in that expression. It has long been recognized that children are a work in progress, insofar as moral development is concerned. Moral reasoning, the ability to think about moral problems, takes time to develop, so influences on children at a time before this development is complete or even when it is well along may have greater consequences than they would on adults.

The stages of moral development were recognized by the Swiss psychologist Jean Piaget, who presented children of various ages with questions regarding a number of stories and studied their responses.[55] Each story was about a person causing a harm, but the seriousness of the harm and the intentions of the actor varied. The results showed that children under ten focused on the consequences, rather than on the intention. Only as children became older did they begin to take into account the motives of the actor in discussing that person's culpability.

Piaget's work was extended by Lawrence Kohlberg, who found that moral development continues through the teen years and even into young adulthood.[56] Children progress from what Kohlberg calls the preconventional or premoral stage to the conventional and then the postconventional stages of moral reasoning, each stage having two substages.[57] At the preconventional stage, children focus on punishment and reward. At the conventional level, children recognize the existence of social order and societal rules, and intentions and motives, as well as the perspectives of others, come to play a role in moral reasoning.[58] Some children, but more likely young adults, may reach the "postconventionalist or principled" stage.[59] In that stage, the individual understands the nature of rules and laws. In the second substage of the postconventional stage, a stage that may actually be reached by only very few people, the individual comes to the recognition that there are ethical principles that govern conduct and that when the principles and the law conflict, the principles should control. In Kohlberg's later work, he says that the postconventional stage appears in the postcollege years, rather than in adolescence, and that the second substage of that highest stage is more of a theoretical ideal and that in applying a refinement of the standards, none of the individuals he studied, with one possible exception, had attained that level.[60]

Carol Gilligan has criticized Kohlberg's work as a male-centered theory, and she argues that the moral development of females may progress differently.[61] She presents her own theory of stages of development, focusing not on rights and rules but on responsibility to others. Although the results of her study of female subjects' consideration of hypothetical situations differ from Kohlberg's, there are still stages in moral reasoning as the female subjects grew older and progressed. Although the end point of that development may differ from that of males, there is still moral growth throughout childhood and into adolescence and even young adulthood.

The psychological theories that show an extended period of moral development have recently gained support from advances in neuroscience. It had long been thought that the physical development of the brain was complete in rather early childhood and that the teenage brain was a finished product. The advances in neuroscience show that the teenage brain is, in fact, far from complete and that the incompletion is in an area that is central to inhibition and judgment.[62]

What had long been known is that there is a period of intense change in the human brain in infancy and early childhood. A newborn has the same density of synapses, the connections between nerve cells, as a mature adult, at least in portions of the brain. During infancy, between birth and a point between one and two years of age, synaptic density increases to become 50 percent higher than that of an adult. During childhood, this overblooming of synapses is pruned until the adult level is again reached. Although the initial overblooming is simply a product of contact between neurons and seems random, the environment plays a role in the stabilization of the synapses and in determining which will survive the pruning process. As stated in an article by Peter Huttenlocher and Arun Dabholkar, who study synaptic paring, "Stabilization of randomly made synapses appears to be activity dependent. Synaptic contacts that are not included in neuronal circuits are gradually eliminated. . . . Synapse elimination, in contrast to synaptogenesis, seems to be at least to some extent environmentally regulated."[63]

The availability of functional magnetic resonance imaging (fMRI) has allowed for a more detailed understanding of the development of the brain and in particular an examination of what occurs in the preteen and teen years.[64] Whereas the overblooming in most regions of the brain was limited to infancy, with paring lasting into early in the second decade of life, an examination of another region yielded a different story. What was discovered was a second period of overblooming, a period of rapid development, around the onset of puberty, followed by a gradual pruning through adolescence and even into young adulthood.

An early longitudinal study of the brains of youths, a study that compared the same brains at different ages, examined 145 individuals between 4.2 and 21.6 years of age.[65] Biennial fMRIs showed an increase in the gray matter of the cortex in the preadolescent years and a decrease in the postadolescent period, also showing that the peaks of development vary from region to region of the cortex. Another study compared the brains of those between twelve and sixteen with those between twenty-three and thirty and found significant differences relevant to the issue here. As stated by Elizabeth Sowell and her colleagues, "In regions of the frontal cortex, we observed reduction in gray matter between adolescence and adulthood. . . . [T]he frontal lobes are essential for such functions as response inhibition, emotional regulation, planning and organization. Many of these aptitudes continue to develop between adolescence and young adulthood."[66]

The new brain science allows us to see the behavior of adolescents as more than the product of hormonal changes. It has become clear that the brains of adolescents, in the areas most relevant to self-control and judgment, are different from those of adults. Linda Spear notes similarity among species in this development:

This remodeling of the brain is seen in adolescents of a variety of species and entails not only brain growth, including the formation of additional connections between nerve cells, but also a prominent loss (or pruning) of such connections in particular neural regions. Among the brain areas prominently remodeled . . . is the prefrontal cortex, a brain region thought to be involved in various goal-directed behaviors . . . and in emotional processing. . . . Along with a decline in the relative size of the prefrontal cortex during adolescence, there is a substantial remodeling of connections between neurons—with some connections lost and others added.[67]

As the author concludes, given brain differences, it would be "astonishing indeed if adolescents did *not* differ from adults in various aspects of their motivated behavior."[68] The science is summed up by another author, the science reporter Barbara Strauch:

Over a span of roughly ten to twelve years, the adolescent brain, through a series of sometimes subtle and sometimes breathtakingly dramatic shifts, is transformed from child to adult. The grey matter of an adolescent's frontal lobes grows denser and then abruptly scales back, molding a leaner learning machine. The brain fine-tunes its most human part, the prefrontal cortex, the place that helps us cast a wary eye, link cause to effect, decide "maybe not"—the part, in fact, that acts grown-up.[69]

It has been recognized among educators, as well as psychologists, that environment plays a role in the development of the brain. Although genetics also plays a role, environment is seen as making a 40 to 70 percent contribution to the total development of the cognitive regions of the brain.[70] In the overblooming and pruning of synapses in the brain's cognitive regions, experience determines which synapses are pruned and which remain as part of the brain's wiring.[71] It would be odd, indeed, if the same environmental impact were not present in the selection of synapses to be pruned or to remain in the prefrontal cortex.

The impact of hate speech can be found in both periods of brain development. In the earlier cognitive development, we learn about and wire our understanding of the world. If the child's environment is one of hate speech, it seems that there would have to be an impact on the child's understanding of the role and status of the targets of that hate. In the later period of development, in which the older child learns to exercise judgment and inhibition, again an atmosphere of hatred seems certain to have an impact on how that judgment and inhibition will be exercised or not exercised in the future. As explained in an interview with David Fassler, then chair of the American Psychiatric Association's Council on Children, Adolescents and Their Families, "As science continues to show how behavior and brain structure dance in tandem—anatomy influences emotions and experiences, and emotions and experiences, in turn, alter the fundamental architecture of the brain—we do have to be more concerned . . . about certain kinds of experiences teenagers may have."[72]

There is one brain study that may be of particular concern here.[73] The study used functional magnetic resonance imaging in examining brain activity in a group of children and adolescents as they tried to identify the affective content of facial expressions. Although the expressions shown were all expressions of fear, they were sometimes misidentified as portraying anger, confusion, surprise, or happiness. The magnetic resonance imaging showed that the part of the brain that was involved in the task was the amygdala, which is a part of the limbic system that, as Abigail Baird and her colleagues explain, has "evolved to detect danger and produce rapid protective responses without conscious participation . . . [and is] essential for the expression of automatic and somatic fear responses."[74] The authors conclude that their findings suggest that "one role of the amygdala during development may be to recognize facial expression and, through experience, learn to assign a label to facial expression."[75]

Given the rapid-response, automatic, and somatic nature of this recognition of facial affect, the hard wiring of the brain in childhood and adolescence should be of great concern. If in a hate-filled environment the brain learns to attach negative emotions to the appearance of the faces of those of a different race or ethnicity, there will be a negative response to members of those groups operating below the level of consciousness. To avoid this result, there may need to be limits on the exposure of children and adolescents to hate material, including limits on exposure to the sort of racism mongered by the hate-music industry.

Hate Speech and the Schools

There are recent comments from federal judges in cases regarding in-school hate speech that may indicate a coming acceptance of limits. Most interesting is what the views seem to say about the sort of degradation that has been the central topic of this chapter. But, before turning to those cases, a look at the Supreme Court case law in the area is necessary to establish the background for those decisions.

An analysis of the regulation of hate speech in the public schools must begin with the Supreme Court's 1969 decision in *Tinker v. Des Moines Independent Community School District*.[76] *Tinker* grew out of a protest against the United States' involvement in Vietnam. As a part of the protest a number of students had decided to wear black armbands. The district's principals decided that students who wore an armband would be asked to remove it and would be suspended if they refused. A number of students did refuse and challenged their penalties under the First Amendment.

The Supreme Court began its analysis by noting that the special characteristics of the schools must be taken into account in any free expression analysis but said that these rights do exist in school: "It can hardly be argued that either students or teachers shed their constitutional rights to freedom of speech or expression at the schoolhouse gate."[77] It was important to the Court, in holding that the students' rights had been violated, that the protest had been silent and passive. There was no disruption of any class, and though there was some hostility expressed by other students outside the classroom, there were no threats of violence or actual violence. The district may have feared disturbance, but the Court said that was not enough. Any disagreement with the views of the majority may cause trouble or raise fear of disturbance, at least in the form of an argument. That is something we must abide. "In order for the State in the person of school officials to justify prohibition of a particular expression of opinion, it must be able to show that its action was caused by something more than a mere desire to avoid the discomfort and unpleasantness that always accompany an unpopular viewpoint."[78] In that regard, the Court said, "the record fails to yield evidence that the school authorities had reason to anticipate that the wearing of the armbands would substantially interfere with the work of the school or impinge upon the rights of other students."[79] The Court added that there was no evidence of "interference, actual or nascent, with the schools' work or of collision with the rights of other students to be secure and to be let alone."[80]

Tinker seemed to establish rather strong rights on the part of students, but later cases cut back on those rights. In 1986, the Court decided *Bethel School District v. Fraser*,[81] a case growing out of what was characterized as a lewd speech given at a high school assembly in nomination of a fellow student for a student government office. The Court described the speech as "an elaborate, graphic, and explicit sexual metaphor."[82] Students' reactions ran from hooting, yelling, and sexually suggestive gestures on the part of some to embarrassment on the part of younger students, and the speaker was punished.

The Supreme Court, in holding in favor of the school, pointed to the role of the schools in inculcating the fundamental values and civility needed for democracy to flourish. Those fundamental values clearly include tolerance of divergent political and religious views, but they must also take into account, in the case of a school, the sensibilities of fellow students. The Court recognized that society has an interest in teaching students the boundaries of socially appropriate behavior.[83] This analysis seems to distinguish between political speech and racist invective at least as well as it does between political speech and the vulgarity that was the focus of that case.

The most recent of this line of cases, in 2007, has become known as the "Bong Hits 4 Jesus" case. The case, *Morse v. Frederick*,[84] gets its name from a banner unfurled at a high-school-sponsored event. The torch relay for the 2002 Winter Olympics in Salt Lake City was to pass through Juneau, Alaska. The principal of Juneau-Douglas High School, a school on the route of the torch, decided to make an event of the relay by allowing students and staff to leave class to line the street down which the relay would proceed.

As the torch and its accompanying camera crews passed, a senior at the high school unfurled a fourteen-foot-long banner reading, "BONG HiTS 4 JESUS." The legend was easily seen by students and others. The principal ordered that the banner be taken down. When the student refused, he was suspended from school. The action was based on a belief that, in violation of school rules, the banner promoted drug use.

The Court found that the student's free expression rights had not been violated, accepting as reasonable the principal's belief that the sign advocated the use of drugs. The Court also distinguished this advocacy of drug use from taking a political position on the legalization of marijuana.[85] Given the Court's understanding of the message, the question became whether the schools can restrict student speech reasonably believed to promote drug use. The Court determined that doing so was not a violation of the First Amendment, and in making this determination, gave its most recent view of the meaning of the school speech cases.

With regard to *Tinker*, the Court found that the facts there "quite stark, implicating concerns at the heart of the First Amendment."[86] The speech in *Tinker* was political expression, the protection of which is "at the core of what the First Amendment is designed to protect."[87] Proceeding on to *Fraser*, the Court said the mode of analysis employed there "is not entirely clear."[88] While the Court "was plainly attuned to the content of Fraser's speech, citing the 'marked distinction between the political "message" of the armbands in *Tinker* and the sexual content of [Fraser's] speech,' . . . the Court also reasoned that school boards have the authority to determine 'what manner of speech in the classroom or in school assembly is inappropriate.'"[89] Declining to resolve completely the lack of clarity, the Court was willing to "distill . . . two basic principles":

> First, *Fraser's* holding demonstrates that "the constitutional rights of students in public school are not automatically coextensive with the rights of adults in other settings." . . . *Fraser's* First Amendment rights were circumscribed "in light of the special characteristics of the school environment." Second, *Fraser* established that the mode of analysis set forth in *Tinker* is not absolute. Whatever approach *Fraser* employed, it certainly did not conduct the "substantial disruption" analysis prescribed by *Tinker*.[90]

The school district in *Morse* argued that *Fraser* should be interpreted to allow the suppression of the speech at issue because it was offensive in the sense used in *Fraser*, but the Court declined.[91] Agreeing that Frederick's speech was offensive would have been stretching the class of speech *Fraser* allowed to be suppressed, perhaps beyond the breaking point. Racist speech, however, can be included in the *Fraser* concept with far greater ease. Such speech is easily more offensive than the sexually suggestive but not explicit speech in *Fraser*.

An interesting additional slant on the school speech cases and the disruption that was central to *Tinker*, the most protective of speech among the cases, is provided by the 1954 school-desegregation case *Brown v. Board of Education*.[92] The Court in *Brown* concluded that educational segregation, in itself, deprives minority children of equal educational opportunity, that separate but equal was an impossibility.[93] As the Court said, "To separate [school children] . . . solely because of their race generates a feeling of inferiority as to their status in the community that may affect their hearts and minds in such a way unlikely ever to be undone."[94] Segregation was recognized as implying racial inferiority, and that would affect motivation to learn and retard educational and mental development.

At issue in *Brown* was, of course, legally established segregation, rather than the sting of racist speech, but the effect may well be the same. In fact, it may well be that racist speech directed at a child in the classroom or in the cafeteria could have a stronger impact than a child's finding him- or herself in a single-race school, particularly if the legal details of that result are not explained to the child. Even if a child recognizes the legal basis for segregated schools, the legal sanctioning of racist speech, if the schools do not attempt to stop it, may lead to the same belief that society has accepted a theory of racial inferiority. It is reasonable to conclude that hate speech has a negative impact on the educational process, that it is inherently disruptive of the schools' mission. Unless *Tinker* is limited to violence and the effects of noise, this seems to be a sufficient interference with the education process to allow limitations.

This suggestion can find support in *Fraser*. The Court there, speaking of the use of sexual metaphor, said that the speech "[b]y glorifying male sexuality . . . was acutely insulting to teenage girls."[95] As with *Brown*, marginalization, this time of females, could be seen as having a negative impact on their education. The impact of such speech, and of racist speech, does disrupt the education process and should serve as a basis, even sticking to the *Tinker* disruption rationale, for limits on such expression in the schools.

When the lower federal courts began to examine the constitutionality of school limitations on hate speech, primarily symbols that might be seen as racist, they focused on the test in *Tinker*. In fact, they focused on only one part of that test, disturbance or substantial interference with the work of the school. The outcome was generally determined by whether there had been a history of race-based disturbances.

After the Court's more recent cases, the lower courts have begun to recognize that *Tinker* also referred to conduct that "impinge[s] upon the rights of other students" or "colli[des] with the rights of other students to be secure and to be let alone." That aspect of the test may allow limits on speech, even without the likelihood of a physical disturbance and without a history of racial conflict.

One of the better statements of this new approach is found in a vacated 2006 opinion by the U.S. Court of Appeals for the Ninth Circuit. Although the opinion was vacated, it sets out in a stronger manner than any of the opinions by other courts the arguments that the Supreme Court's precedents allow limiting hate speech in the schools. It should be pointed out that the order to vacate was not out of any stated disagreement by the Supreme Court with the analysis of the Ninth Circuit. Instead it was a procedural decision.[96]

The case, *Harper v. Poway Unified School District*,[97] involved T-shirts, in a high school, that condemned other students on the basis of their sexual orientation. There had been a history of conflict over issues of sexual orientation at Poway High School. As a way to further tolerance, the school allowed a group called the Gay-Straight Alliance to hold a "Day of Silence."[98] The day was not uniformly well received. There was a series of incidents, including antihomosexual comments and altercations, with the altercations leading to suspensions. A week after the "Day of Silence" another group of students organized a "Straight-Pride Day." The message of tolerance was replaced by T-shirts with comments derogatory toward homosexuals, leading to more altercations.

The next year a second "Day of Silence" was planned. On that day, a student who believed the real purpose of the day was to promote homosexual activity, wore a T-shirt with the handwritten words "I WILL NOT ACCEPT WHAT GOD HAS CONDEMNED" on the front and "HOMOSEXUALITY IS SHAMEFUL 'Romans 1:27'" on the back. The next day he came to school in a T-shirt with the handwritten words "BE ASHAMED, OUR SCHOOL EMBRACED WHAT GOD HAS CONDEMNED" on the front and the same legend as on the prior day on the back.

The second day the student was sent to the principal's office. The principal decided that, given the conflicts of the previous year, he would not let the student wear what he saw as an inflammatory T-shirt on campus. The student filed suit, alleging a number of constitutional violations, including his right to free speech. The federal district court refused to grant a preliminary injunction against the school. The basis for the district court's denial of the injunction, and one that the appellate court could have quite easily and simply affirmed, was that the school had a sufficient basis to predict a substantial disruption of and interference with the education mission. Given the history surrounding the "Day of Silence" in the previous year and the ongoing conflict in the schools, surely *Tinker* would permit this limit on student speech. Rather than affirming on that basis, however, the Ninth Circuit based its decision on the other aspect of *Tinker*.

The court used language from *Tinker* looking to whether the speech activity that the school sought to suppress "'intrudes upon . . . the rights of other students' or 'colli[des] with the rights of other students to be secure and to be let alone.'"[99] The court said that the wearing of the T-shirt so collided with the rights of other students in a fundamental way:

Public school students who may be injured by verbal assaults on the basis of a core identifying characteristic such as race, religion, or sexual orientation, have a right to be free from such attacks while on school campuses. As *Tinker* clearly states, students have the right to "be secure and to be let alone." Being secure involves not only freedom from physical assaults but from psychological attacks that cause young people to question their self-worth and their rightful place in society.[100]

The court went on to note that the impact is not only on psychological health and well-being but on educational development as well. School administrators do not have to tolerate this negative impact, and the court concluded that the school had a right to bar the T-shirt in question on the ground that it was "injurious to gay and lesbian students and interfered with their right to learn."[101]

Although the analysis I have provided in this chapter is based on *Fraser*, rather than on *Tinker*, that analysis would certainly come to the same result as the majority view in *Harper*. The *Harper* majority's expression of the concerns could hardly be improved on. Under either approach, there is the recognition that students may be sufficiently affected as to allow limits on hate speech. It may be sufficient that the target students' right to receive an education is affected, and it seems also that allowing such limits would come within the *Fraser* concerns over schools' teaching civility. Either way, minorities would be protected from hate speech in the schools.

The suggested use of *Fraser* in this context, rather than the *Harper* court's use of *Tinker*, gains support from the Eleventh Circuit's 2003 opinion in *Scott v. School Board of Alachua County*.[102] The issue was a student suspension for displaying the Confederate flag. The Eleventh Circuit held that the ban was not a violation of the student's free expression rights, and it did so without laying out a basis for real concern over material and substantial disruption. The court noted that the freedom of expression "stands against the unique backdrop of a public school." Although students do not lose their First Amendment freedoms at the schoolhouse door, "those rights should not interfere with a school administrator's professional observation that certain expressions have led to, and therefore could lead to, an *unhealthy* and potentially unsafe learning environment for the children they serve."[103] An unhealthy environment, as distinguished from an unsafe environment, does not seem to require the fear of a substantial disturbance that *Tinker* seems to envision. Psychological impact may well be sufficient.

Just one more case shows that more courts seem to be coming to recognize this right of school authorities to protect their minority students from derogatory comments. In *Zamecnik v. Indian Prairie School District #204 Board of Education*,[104] a 2007 case, a federal district court considered another case growing out of a "Day of Silence." The day had been celebrated at the high school for several years, sponsored by the Gay/Straight Alliance. Some of the students wore labels indicating their participation and remained silent during the day, except when required to speak in class or to a member of the staff. Some of the students and staff wore shirts bearing the message "Be Who You Are."

The legal issue arose when a student group wanted to hold a "Day of Truth" the day after the "Day of Silence." The school agreed that they could do so on the same basis as the previous day. They could remain silent and could display pins, shirts, and the like with a message of "Be Happy, Be Straight" or "Straight Alliance." A student who professed religious beliefs against homosexuality went beyond these messages and wore a T-shirt that had "MY DAY OF SILENCE, STRAIGHT ALLIANCE" on the front and "BE HAPPY, NOT GAY" on the back. School officials made the student black out the "NOT GAY" portion of the message.

When the case went to court, the court found no violation of the student's constitutional rights. The court said, "school officials may prohibit a public high school student from displaying negative statements about a category of persons, including homosexuals, that are inconsistent with the school's educational goal of promoting tolerance."[105] The court distinguished the message displayed from the message "Be Happy, Be Straight." The latter was said to be a positive statement about being straight, not a directly negative comment about being gay.[106] If school officials had prevented that positive statement, as alleged, there would have been a violation. "Since, on the previous day students were permitted to display messages supporting being homosexual, the next day's suppression of a message supporting being heterosexual should be understood as viewpoint discrimination."[107]

The district court's denial of an injunction was appealed to the U.S. Court of Appeals for the Seventh Circuit, and the appellate court, with Judge Richard Posner writing, ruled that the injunction should have been granted.[108] Interestingly, however, the disagreement between the courts was over application, rather than theory. As to application, the Seventh Circuit noted that the expression "Be Happy, Not Gay" could be seen as a play on words, since *gay* is not only a word indicating homosexual orientation but also a synonym of *happy*.[109] The court also concluded that the comment might not even be seen as derogatory, since it really said no more than the "Be Happy, Be Straight" shirt that the school would have allowed. Although there may be a strong nonpropositional difference between two sentences seemingly making the same point, the "Be Happy, Not Gay" shirt was not seen as an offensive way to say the same thing as a "Be Happy, Be Straight" shirt. In this court's view, "Be Happy, Not Gay" "is only tepidly negative; 'derogatory' or 'demeaning' seems too strong a characterization."[110] It was, at any rate, seen as "highly speculative" that the shirt in question would "poison the educational atmosphere."[111]

The plaintiff's success on appeal was only partial. The Seventh Circuit refused to enjoin more generally the enforcement of the school's rule, and much of the court's analysis in that regard agreed with the position taken by the district court and espoused here. The Seventh Circuit sided with the right of the schools to place some limits on student speech beyond the lewd speech of *Fraser* or the drug-oriented speech of *Morse*.

> Neuqua Valley High School . . . has prohibited only (1) *derogatory* comments on (2) unalterable or otherwise deeply rooted personal characteristics about which most people, including—perhaps especially including—adolescent schoolchildren, are highly sensitive. People are easily upset by comments about their race, sex, etc., including their sexual orientation, because for most people these are major components of their personal identity—none more so than a sexual orientation that deviates from the norm. Such comments can strike a person at the core of his being.[112]

The court recognized that there was evidence that at least suggested that "adolescent students subjected to derogatory comments about such characteristics may find it even harder than usual to concentrate on their studies and perform up to the school's expectations."[113] And the court said, "Mutual respect and forbearance enforced by the school may well be essential to the maintenance of a minimally decorous atmosphere for learning."[114]

These more recent decisions are speaking in terms of degradation. Courts are seemingly coming to realize that schools should be allowed to limit student speech that degrades others on the basis of core characteristics. To express derision on the basis of one's race, gender, or sexual orientation is to belittle another on the basis not of what he or she has done but on the basis of who he or she is. It is the sort of degradation of the target population to a level lower than fully human that is the modern equivalent of obscenity's degradation of humanity to a level lower than the divine. Just as the schools have been allowed to limit sexual speech, they should be allowed to limit the far more degrading varieties of hate speech sometimes found there.

As the Twig Is Bent . . .

Although this chapter has focused on children, concerns over children and hate speech are not divorced from concerns over adult hate speech. There are, however, both similarities and differences in these concerns. The offensiveness that motivates the suppression of obscene material seems even stronger when children are the target audience. As with sexual depictions, the offensiveness of hate speech should also be seen as even stronger when directed at children. Furthermore, although hate speech is harmful to both adult and child recipients, children are likely to be more susceptible. Just as the prurient interest of the child may be more easily appealed to, the degrading impact of hate speech is likely to be stronger for the child than for the adult. Whereas the adult target of hate speech may be most likely to experience some combination of disgust and anger, there seems to be more danger that the child will internalize any negative ascriptions. Shielding children can contribute to their having a positive sense of self-worth that will make for not only a better childhood but a better adult life.

Hate speech involving children may be more destructive than hate speech involving adults, but that is not the only reason for a special emphasis on such speech. Limiting the expression of hatred by children is likely to lead to less hate speech when those children become adults. That is, Virgil may well be correct in saying, "As the twig is bent the tree inclines."

With adults, especially if those adults grew up in an environment in which hate speech was tolerated or even taught, the only thing likely to limit hate speech is the fear of punishment. There may never be an internalization of the values behind the suppression of hate speech. And there is likely to be continued hatred that even the fear of punishment will not lessen. Although punishment might reduce the level of actual hate speech, the person inclined toward hate speech is likely to see the possibility of such punishment simply as evidence of the subjugation of people of his or her race, gender, or sexual orientation. With children, however, internalization of the values behind the suppression of hate speech seems far more likely. If children grow up in an environment in which hate speech is not accepted and in which toleration and diversity are encouraged, they are far more likely to become adults who do not need the fear of sanctions to behave civilly toward their fellow citizens and coworkers. That would, unquestionably, be a better world.

Conclusion

In February 2009, Eric Holder, the Attorney General of the United States, delivered a speech to employees at the Justice Department marking Black History Month. In the speech he called for a conversation on race and said that the United States is "a nation of cowards" in the discussion of racial matters.¹ The speech may be seen as repeating a similar call by now-president Barack Obama, who during the Democratic presidential primary season "urged the nation to break 'a racial stalemate we've been stuck in for years' and bemoaned the 'chasm of misunderstanding that exists between the races.'"² This book is narrower than what was called for in either speech. It is a discussion of racist speech, but it does not address racial relations more generally. It is also, in a sense, broader. It is not a discussion solely of racist speech; it includes sexist and homophobic speech as well.

Although the effort undertaken in this book is not as broad as the conversation requested by Holder and Obama, it is a necessary first step toward that conversation. The conversation will not take place unless there can be some agreement on tone and vocabulary. For many of us, one of the labels we would least like to have ascribed to us is "racist." To avoid that label, we may simply choose to say nothing. As *New York Times* writer Charles M. Blow put it, "white people don't want to be labeled as prejudiced, so they work hard around blacks not to appear so. . . . [M]any whites . . . are so worried about appearing prejudiced that they act colorblind around blacks, avoiding 'talking about race, or even acknowledging racial difference,' even when race is germane."³

A reluctance to talk about race seems natural when racist speech is so hard to define. Most of us recognize such speech as wrong, but we may lack a real understanding of the nature of that wrong, and we certainly lack clarity in delimiting the speech that should reasonably be seen as offensive. We operate primarily on intuition. *Chicago Tribune* writer Dawn Turner Trice, writing on race generally, said, "for too many of us, race remains a Rorschach test in that we still can look at the same thing and see something totally different."⁴ If that is true of race generally, it seems even more true with regard to speech that might be seen as racist by some and as innocent by others.

This book has attempted to provide a conceptual framework for recognizing and analyzing racist, sexist, and homophobic speech. In doing so, it has journeyed over two thousand years into the past. Answers have been sought beginning in an era in which hate speech would have presumably been considered perfectly natural and acceptable. After all, the Greeks considered nonspeakers of Greek to be barbarians, and the Greeks and Romans primarily considered those of other lands and ethnicities to be suitable for little more than slavery. These Greek and Roman cultures differed greatly from our modern culture, which places more value in diversity and, for the most part, sees all human beings as equals. So it might seem odd to believe that the classical cultures could provide much guidance in analyzing hate speech.

What Greek and Roman culture can teach us is the nature of obscenity. Beginning our examination of obscenity in an era in which there was significant pornography but, in fact, no obscenity was the first step in understanding what it is that, in some cultures and eras, leads to the acceptance of pornography, whereas other cultures and eras consider pornography to be obscene. The hallmark of pornography is sexual depiction, and the hallmark of obscenity is shame and degradation. But what gives depictions of sex, and sex itself, the celebratory acceptance enjoyed in Greece, in contrast to the secretive and degrading reaction in later Europe?

The thesis of this book has been that pornography becomes obscene when it can be the source of a degraded view of humanity. The Greeks and Romans could celebrate sex and pornography because they had gods who were themselves sexual creatures. Human sexual activity and the depiction of humans in such acts did not serve to differentiate humanity from the gods and place humans on the animal side of any divine/animal rift. In fact, as religious myths regarding mixtures of gods, humans, and animals show, there was no such rift.

With the onset of Christianity and its monotheistic God, sex and sexual depiction suddenly did distinguish humans from God. With a nonsexual God, human sexuality and its depiction showed our animal side. Initially, the concern was with the clergy, a group that had to be seen as closer to God than the average person is. While sex faced general renunciation in the early Church, official limitations on sexual activity were imposed, or at least were sought to be imposed, only on the clergy. History also shows a focus for obscenity prosecutions on depictions involving clergy.

As humanity began to find its place in nature during the Enlightenment, it might have been expected that there would be less concern over depictions that show our animal nature. Indeed, there does seem to have been a growth in pornography in the era. In the late 1800s, however, there was an increase an obscenity prosecution. The suggestion here has been that this increase was a response to evolutionary thinking. While humanity may have been becoming comfortable with its animal side, the idea that we are nothing more than animals, that we evolved from and along with other animals, may simply have been too much to take. The reaction was an increase in attempts to suppress pornography.

This distinction I have drawn between monotheistic and polytheistic religions and the acceptance of sexuality and sexual depiction has been reinforced with an examination of other cultures. The polytheistic aspects of several Asian religions have been matched with an acceptance of sexual conduct and depiction that would be expected of such religious belief systems. Even within Europe, the later coming of Christianity to the northern regions, with the result of a later presence of a polytheistic religion, has been suggested as explaining differences in attitudes toward sexuality in the Scandinavian countries. Judaism and Islam, the other major monotheistic religions, shared to some degree the attitudes of monotheistic Christianity. The difference between those two religions and Christianity has been explained by the existence in Christianity of God made human and made chaste human. Again, differences are explained by the degrading nature of sex and sexual depiction. For Christians, they may distinguish human from Christ and, hence, from God. For Jews and Muslims, there may be distinction from God but not from the major human figures of the religion. If men such as Abraham, Moses, and Mohammed were holy and were sexual, sex would not be seen to be as degrading as it would for Christians.

In the latter half of the twentieth century, humans seemed to become much more accepting of our animal status. There has certainly become a greater acceptance of pornography, with obscenity prosecutions becoming uncommon. But there has been a new contender to fill the spot once occupied by pornography as expression that degrades. That contender is, of course, hate speech. But hate speech degrades in a way that differs from the degradation of obscenity.

Pornography, when it was viewed as obscene or degrading, degraded all of humanity. It is true that the early focus of obscenity law was on protecting the clergy, but sexual imagery in the eras in which it was obscene said something about all humankind. All of humanity moved toward the animal side of the divine/animal split. Even if the concern was only that the clergy not be so depicted, the images said something about all of humanity.

Hate speech is not the assertion of a degraded view of all of humanity. It is based on a belief that the target population, whether on the basis of race, gender, or sexual orientation, is of a lower order than the group to which the speaker belongs. It is a degradation to a less than fully human level of the subpopulation. It affords the dignity seen as properly due human beings to most of the population, while denying that dignity to its target group. This is a degradation that seems far worse than that represented by sexual obscenity. Rather than moving all of us away from the divine, it moves some of us away from humanity.

Since hate speech is the modern form of degrading speech, the law that has developed for what has historically been considered degrading speech can provide guidance for any regulation of hate speech. Obscenity law is the law of offense, and hate speech is offensive for the same reasons as sexual obscenity. One has been seen as offensive because of the degraded view it presents of humanity. The other should similarly be viewed as offensive because of the degraded view of its target population.

The prurient interest so central to determination of sexual obscenity is rather easily converted to an appeal to a degrading view of the target of hate speech. The other factors, the requirement of statutory or regulatory definition, the role of community standards, and the need to protect expression with serious value also carry over easily from obscenity to hate speech. Lastly, the concept of variable obscenity, with stronger limitations when material is made available to children, can be adapted to hate speech delivered to children. Those who are most susceptible deserve more protection.

Most people recognize that there is something wrong with hate speech, but for most of us it may simply be an intuition, even if a rather obvious one. With regard to specific instance, we are left with Dawn Turner Trice's "Rorschach test," less a matter of analysis and more one of gut-level reaction. This book has attempted to provide an analytic framework for analyzing hate speech generally and with regard to specific instances. With this help, rather than simply recognizing that something is wrong with a particular utterance, there can be an examination of just what it is that is wrong. If there is disagreement regarding a particular instance, the framework can serve to focus and perhaps resolve that disagreement. Only then can people stop talking past each other and have a real conversation about such speech. And once that point is reached, a national discussion regarding race becomes more probable and potentially fruitful.

Notes

NOTES TO THE INTRODUCTION

1. Charles R. Lawrence, "If He Hollers Let Him Go: Regulating Racist Speech on Campus," 1990 *Duke L.J.* 431.

2. *Id.* at 462. Lawrence cites several cases, including Fisher v. Carousel Motor Hotel, Inc., 424 S.W.2d 627 (Tex. 1967), which he characterizes as upholding a damages award for assault and battery on the theory that battery protects not only physical security but dignity as well.

3. *Id.* at 452–53.

4. Richard Delgado & Jean Stefancic, *Understanding Words That Wound* 13 (Boulder, CO: Westview, 2004).

5. *See* Mari J. Matsuda, "Public Response to Racist Speech: Considering the Victim's Story," 87 *Mich. L. Rev.* 2320, 2336–37 (1989).

6. Brian Mullen & Joshua M. Smyth, "Immigrant Suicide Rates as a Function of Ethnophaulisms: Hate Speech Predicts Death," 66 *Psychosomatic Medicine* 343, 346 (2004).

7. *See* Frederick A. Schauer, *The Law of Obscenity* 2 (Washington, DC: Bureau of National Affairs, 1976).

8. *See id.* at 3; H. Montgomery Hyde, *A History of Pornography* 71, 153 (New York: Farrar, Straus & Giroux, 1964); *see also* David Loth, *The Erotic in Literature: A Historical Survey of Pornography as Delightful as It Is Indiscreet* 65–66 (New York: Julian Messner, 1961).

9. Frederick A. Schauer, *supra* note 7 at 5 (citing Dominus Rex v. Curl, 2 Str. 789, 93 Eng. Rep. 849 (1727)).

10. *Id.* at 6.

11. *See* David Tribe, *Questions of Censorship* 56–57 (London: George Allen & Unwin, 1973).

12. *See id.* at 57–58.

13. Frederick A. Schauer, *supra* note 9, at 6.

14. *Id.* at 13.

15. Harry M. Clor, *Obscenity and Public Morality: Censorship in a Liberal Society* 225 (Chicago: University of Chicago Press, 1969).

16. *Id.* at 226.

NOTES TO CHAPTER 2

1. David Loth, *The Erotic in Literature: A Historical Survey of Pornography as Delightful as It Is Indiscreet* 47 (New York: Julian Messner, 1961).

2. Peter Webb, *The Erotic Arts* 71 (New York: Farrar, Straus & Giroux, 1983).

3. Robert F. Sutton, Jr., "Pornography and Persuasion on Attic Pottery," in Amy Richlin, ed., *Pornography and Representation in Greece and Rome* 3, 4 (New York: Oxford University Press, 1992).

4. *See id.* at 8.

5. Peter Webb, *supra* note 2, at 54.

6. *See* Kenneth J. Dover, *Greek Popular Morality in the Time of Plato and Aristotle* 206 (Oxford, UK: Basil Blackwell, 1974).

7. See Harvey A. Shapiro, "Eros in Love: Pederasty and Pornography in Greece," in Amy Richlin, ed., *supra* note 3, at 53, 53.

8. Peter Webb, *supra* note 2 at 54.

9. H. Montgomery Hyde, *A History of Pornography* 41 (New York: Farrar, Straus & Giroux, 1964).

10. *See* Poul Gerhard, *Pornography in Fine Art from Ancient Times up to the Present* 3–5 (Los Angeles: Elysium, 1969). Gerhard notes as a humorous detail that the placement of the decorations in the bottom of the cups makes them visible only when the contents are finished. *See id.* at 3. Perhaps that fact is the reason such images were placed there, since the image might provide an incentive for a child to finish his or her drink.

11. Peter Webb, *supra* note 2, at 54.

12. David Tribe, *Questions of Censorship* 32 (London: George Allen & Unwin, 1973) (quoting D. H. Lawrence, *Pornography and Obscenity* 5–6 (1929)).

13. *See* David Loth, *supra* note 1, at 48.

14. Aristophanes, *Lysistrata,* in *Four Plays by Aristophanes* 335 (William Arrowsmith, Richard Lattimore & Douglass Parker, trans.) (New York: New American Library, 1984).

15. *Id.* at 406–07.

16. *Id.* at 419.

17. *Id.* at 434–35.

18. *Id.* at 444–45.

19. Aristophanes, *Lysistrata* (Robert Henning Webb, trans.) (Charlottesville: University of Virginia Press, 1963).

20. *Id.* at 85. The German accent seems to have been used to show that Sparta's dialect differed from that of Athens. *See id.* at 7 n.10. Parker's translation uses a backwoods accent for the same purpose.

21. *Id.* at 91.

22. *Id.* at 94.

23. Aristophanes, *The Clouds,* in *Four Plays by Aristophanes, supra* note 14 at 7, 71.

24. *Id.* at 127.

25. *Id.* at 157–58 n.63.

26. The lines Arrowsmith shows as delivered by Aristophanes may instead be spoken by the Chorus, but those lines are still said to represent the author's view. *See id.* at 156–57 n.61.

27. *Id.* at 63.

28. *Id.* at 160 n.90.

29. *Id.* at 90–91.

30. *Id.* at 91.

31. Bella Zweig, "The Mute Nude Female Characters in Aristophanes' Plays," in Amy Richlin, ed., *supra* note 3, at 73, 74.

32. *See id.* at 75.

33. For the role of hetaerae in Greek society, *see infra* notes 53–56 and accompanying text.

34. Bella Zweig, *supra* note 31, at 79.

35. *See id.* at 91.

36. *See* H. Montgomery Hyde, *supra* note 9, at 40 (citing James C. N. Paul & Murray L. Schwartz, *Federal Censorship*104 (1961)).

37. *Id.* at 41.

38. Richard A. Posner, *Sex and Reason* 41 (Cambridge, MA: Harvard University Press, 1992).

39. *See* Peter Webb, *supra* note 2, at 56.

40. *Id.* at 57.

41. Vern L. Bullough, *The History of Prostitution* 37 (New Hyde Park, NY: University Books, 1964).

42. There is some suggestion that the fact that most of the historical and literary record comes from Athens may have resulted in an inaccurate view of the sex practices in the other city-states. Athenian writers are said to have "told denigrating stories about wife-swapping among the Spartans, implying that both the moral and legal standards of Sparta were vastly inferior to those of Athens." *See* James A. Brundage, *Law, Sex, and Christian Society in Medieval Europe* 14 (Chicago: University of Chicago Press, 1987).

43. *See* Richard A. Posner, *supra* note 38, at 39.

44. H. Montgomery Hyde, *supra* note 9, at 41.

45. *See* Richard A. Posner, *supra* note 38, at 39.

46. *See* Kenneth J. Dover, *supra* note 6, at 209.

47. David Cohen, *Law, Sexuality, and Society: The Enforcement of Morals in Classical Athens* 140 (Cambridge: Cambridge University Press, 1991).

48. *Id.* at 133.

49. *See* H. Montgomery Hyde, *supra* note 9, at 34. Translated somewhat differently: "We have mistresses for our enjoyment, concubines to serve our person, and wives for the bearing of legitimate offspring." *See* James A. Brundage, *supra* note 42, at 13.

50. It appears that there was a legal requirement, under a law of Solon, that men have sexual relations with their wives at least three times a month. See James A. Brundage, *supra* note 42, at 13.

51. *See* Richard A. Posner, *supra* note 38, at 40.

52. *See* David Cohen, *supra* note 47, at 221 ("Athenian laws [regarding sex] are relatively few, and apart from adultery, primarily concern sexual transactions involving force, and the abuse of children. . . . Athenian law . . . in principle did not punish immoral behavior *as such*, rather only immoral behavior which either harmed those unable to protect themselves or directly transgressed against the clearly demarcated public sphere.") (emphasis in original). Athenian law did have provisions excluding individuals from political life if they had accepted sexual roles unworthy of a citizen, for example, engaging in prostitution or adulterous acts by a citizen's wife. *See id.* at 222, 225.

53. *See id.* at 40.

54. *See* H. Montgomery Hyde, *supra* note 9, at 35.

55. *Id.* at 34. It appears that Phryne did not participate in the nudity which was common in the public baths or at the festival of Poseidon, so the sudden exposure seemed to have had an even greater effect. *See id.* at 34–35.

56. *See id.* at 35.

57. Indeed, these relationships may have been the only significant romantic attachments for at least many men. *See* David Cohen, *supra* note 47, at 134.

58. Kenneth J. Dover, *supra* note 6, at 213. Lesbianism seems to have been treated differently. Posner says the Greeks found it "unnatural and revolting"; *see* Richard A. Posner, *supra* note 38, at 43. Hyde says that lesbianism "was not idealized as was the male relationship nor is it known to have inspired any literature; it was merely tolerated as an eccentricity." H. Montgomery Hyde, *supra* note 9, at 43. Whether tolerated or held to be disgusting, lesbianism does not seem to have had the acceptability of male homosexuality. It is worth noting, however, as Dover does, that "every surviving word of Classical Greek was written by a man" and that the female point of view has not survived. Kenneth J. Dover, *supra* note 6, at 95.

59. This might seem to conflict with the focus of sex laws on protecting, among few others, children. There seems, however, to have been a distinction between pederasty, the desire of adult males for adolescent boys, and pedophilia, sexual activity between an adult male and a preadolescent boy. *See* Richard A. Posner, *supra* note 38, at 42.

60. *See id.* at 43; Kenneth J. Dover, *supra* note 6, at 215.

61. Kenneth J. Dover, *supra* note 6, at 215.

62. David Loth, *supra* note 1, at 48.

63. There are a great many references available on the Greek gods and on Greek legends generally. A particularly good reference is Edith Hamilton, *Mythology* (New York: Little, Brown, 1942), which covers both Greek (and as a result Roman) and Norse mythology.

64. *See id.* at 79.

65. *See id.* at 36.

66. *Id.* at 33.

67. *See id.* at 227.

68. Pollux may have been the only one actually to be a lesser god. *See infra* note 69.

69. Although Castor and Pollux are sometimes thought of as twins, they would actually seem to be half brothers. Pollux was clearly immortal, and Castor had a form of semi-immortality, to the degree that immortality can be "semi." The love of Pollux for Castor was sufficiently strong that he split time in Hades with him. *See* Edith Hamilton, *supra* note 63, at 45.

70. *See id.* at 64.

71. *See id.* at 348.

72. *See id.* at 429.

73. *See id.* at 430.

74. *See id.* at 431.

75. *See id.* at 417.

76. *See id.* at 47–48.

77. *See id.* at 48.

78. *See id* at 44.

79. *See id.* at 48.

80. *See id.* at 430.

81. *Id.* at 376.

82. *Id.* at 393.

83. *Id.*

84. *See id.* at 432.

85. *See id.* at 469.

86. *See id.* at 277–78.

87. Hamilton says that Aeneas is the son of Venus, the Roman equivalent of Aphrodite. *See id.* at 320. Given the centrality of Aeneas to the mythical history of Rome, the change to Roman divinities seems appropriate.

88. *See id.* at 264.

89. *See id.* at 267.

90. Hamilton lays out genealogies for the royal houses. *See id.* at 470–72.

91. *See id.* at 393–94.

92. There is an online collection of over six hundred of Aesop's fables to be found at www.aesopfables.com. They primarily rely on the English translations of the fables by Ambrose Bierce and by the Reverend George Townsend. The only fables to be discussed in the text are rather familiar examples that have become part of our culture as well.

93. Joyce E. Salisbury, *The Beast Within: Animals in the Middle Ages* 106 (London: Routledge, 1994).

94. *See generally* Richard C. Beacham, *The Roman Theatre and Its Audience* (London: Routledge, 1991).

95. *See id.* at 4–5.

96. *See id.* at 129.

97. *See id.* at 136.

98. *See id.* at 137.

99. *See* Richard A. Posner, *supra* note 38, at 45.

100. *See* Peter Webb, *supra* note 2, at 64.

101. *Id.* at 67.

102. *Id.* at 68.

103. *See* Molly Myerowitz, "The Domestication of Desire: Ovid's *Parva Tabella* and the Theater of Love," in Amy Richlin, ed., *supra* note 3, at 131, 133.

104. *See id.* at 141. Myerowitz's article also contains photographs of some of the erotic decor she discusses.

105. *See id.* at 139.

106. *See also supra* notes 3–4 and accompanying text, on the export of pornographic pottery from Greece to the Etruscans.

107. *See* Poul Gerhard, *supra* note 10, at 9.

108. H. Montgomery Hyde, *supra* note 9, at 45.

109. *See* Vern L. Bullough, *supra* note 41, at 50.

110. *See id.*

111. *See* Molly Myerowitz, *supra* note 103, at 145.

112. H. Montgomery Hyde, *supra* note 9, at 56.

113. *See* Richard A. Posner, *supra* note 38, at 44.

114. *See id.* at 44–45.

115. *See id.* at 44.

116. *But see* William E. H. Lecky, *History of European Morals* 168 (New York: George Braziller, 1955) ("The Roman gods were not, like those of the Greeks, the creations of an unbridled and irreverent fancy . . . ; they were for the most part simple allegories, frigid personifications of different virtues, or presiding spirits imagined for the protection of different departments of industry.").

117. Edith Hamilton, *supra* note 63, at 49.

118. *Id.* at 50.

119. James A. Brundage, *supra* note 42, at 19.

120. *See id.* at 28.

121. William E. H. Lecky, *supra* note 116, at 291.

122. *See id.* at 166.

123. Roger Scruton, *Sexual Desire: A Moral Philosophy or the Erotic* 1 (New York: Free Press, 1986). Scruton takes the position that animals do not experience sexual arousal, only sexual urges, nor do they experience anger or engage in social behavior, even if it may look that way. Interestingly, he cites Charles Darwin's observation that blushing is a peculiarly human reaction that separates us from the animals. Darwin's work in which that observation is presented, *The Expression of Emotions in Man and Animals* (London, 1872), is, in most other regards, in conflict with Scruton's view. Darwin's work is discussed in chapter 4 of this volume.

124. 354 U.S. 476, 488 n.20 (1957) (quoting ALI, Model Penal Code, s 207.10(2) (Tent. Draft No. 6, 1957)).

NOTES TO CHAPTER 3

1. As Richard Posner puts it, in contrasting the Christian view of sexuality from the pagan, "Almost all that is distinctive in that attitude can be derived from the essential although not original ethical move made by Christianity (for Christianity got it from Judaism), which was to conceive of man—and woman too—as having been created in the image of God and thus of having a quasi-divine dignity." Richard A. Posner, *Sex and Reason* 46 (Cambridge, MA: Harvard University Press, 1992).

2. *Id.* Interestingly, Posner notes that despite the similarity of the Christian and Jewish religions in their monotheism, the Jewish religion did not reject sexual pleasure. Although there may have been more regulation among the Jews than among the Greeks and Romans, sexual pleasure was not disapproved and celibacy was thought to be an inferior state to marriage. *See id.* at 49.

3. Joyce E. Salisbury, *The Beast Within: Animals in the Middle Ages* 138 (New York: Routledge, 1994).

4. Peter Brown, *The Body and Society: Men, Women and Sexual Renunciation in Early Christianity* 432 (New York: Columbia University Press, 1988).

5. Joyce E. Salisbury, *supra* note 3, at 78–79 (quoting St. Augustine, *City of God* 577 (H. Bettenson, trans., 1972); Thomas Aquinas, *Summa Theologica* II, Q. 98, 493–94 (Fathers of the English Dominican, trans., 1957)).

6. *See* Vern L. Bullough, "Introduction: The Christian Inheritance," in Vern L Bullough & James Brundage, eds., *Sexual Practices and the Medieval Church* 1, 6 (Buffalo, NY: Prometheus Books, 1982).

7. *See id.* at 7.

8. *See* Joyce E. Salisbury, *supra* note 3, at 159–60.

9. *See id.* at 160–61.

10. Robin Lane Fox, *Pagans and Christians* 355 (New York: Knopf, 1987).

11. *Id.*

12. *Id.* at 362.

13. Fox says that Mary's virginity was asserted in the Gospel of St. James, which existed in the early second century. *See id.* at 363.

14. James A. Brundage, *Law, Sex, and Christian Society in Medieval Europe* 57 (Chicago: University of Chicago Press, 1987).

15. *See id.*

16. Peter Brown, *supra* note 4, at 34.

17. *See* Robin Lane Fox, *supra* note 10, at 363–64.

18. *Id.* at 364.

19. Peter Brown, *supra* note 4, at 54.

20. 1 Corinthians 7:9.

21. Peter Brown, *supra* note 4, at 55.

22. Although St. Paul is characterized as holding that "wedded sex might . . . be an aid to salvation" (James A. Brundage, *supra* note 14, at 61), again it is a defensive aid. Although the ideal might be abstinence, most people could not meet that ideal. By restricting sex to marriage, those Christians could still be saved.

23. Brundage says, speaking of St. Paul, that "[h]is strong disapproval of sexual misconduct did not necessarily represent a revulsion at its moral enormity; rather Paul seemed to feel that those who spent their time and energy in pursuit of sexual pleasure had their priorities wrong and should be attending instead to preparations for the final judgment." James A. Brundage, *supra* note 14, at 60. This seems an odd conclusion, a sort of a hurry-up Stoicism in the face of the coming of the end of the world. There does seem to be a moral revulsion in addition, perhaps, to a belief that time is wasting. Indeed, on the same page, Brundage says that Paul considered illicit sex to be almost as serious as murder, certainly a sin for more than its time-wasting aspect. *Id.*

24. Peter Brown, *supra* note 4, at 55.

25. *See* Robin Lane Fox, *supra* note 10, at 356–57.

26. *Id.* at 357.

27. *See id.* Fox says that the common theme of these stories has the Apostle convincing the wife of a pagan governor or other notable to abstain and that the result is the, perhaps not surprising, martyrdom of the Apostle. *See id.*

28. *See* James A. Brundage, *supra* note 14, at 63. Brundage also notes the existence of other Christian groups that argued that "Christianity implied free love and lack of sexual restraint and preached a doctrine that involved total sharing of resources, including sexual favors, among the faithful." *Id.*

29. Peter Brown, *supra* note 4, at 92–93.

30. Peter Brown notes that radical disciples of Tatian the Encratite said that the loss of paradise was directly the result of sex. "They asserted that Eve had met the serpent, who represented the animal world, and that the serpent had taught Eve to do what animals do—to have intercourse." *Id.* at 93–94. "Encratite exegesis presented sexuality itself, as such, with the abiding sign of an unnatural kinship with the animal world that the serpent had forced on Adam and Eve." *Id.* at 95. Thus, the Fall was not simply breaking a rule laid down by God; it was the result of adopting an animal-like nature. It was choosing to separate from God, from the divine, and move to the animal side of the divine-animal split.

31. James A. Brundage, *supra* note 14, at 64 (citing Tertullian, *De exhortatione castitatis* 11.1).

32. *Id.* (citing Tertullian, *De cultu feminarum* 1).

33. *Id.* at 66.

34. As an interesting side note, it appears that second marriages were not well thought of. St. Paul had held that bishops could not remarry, and Tertullian extended the prohibition to all. *See id.* at 68. This applied not only to marriage after divorce but to widows as well.

35. James A. Brundage, *supra* note 14, at 66–67 (citing Justin Martyr, *Apologia* 1.29, for the first sentence and a variety of authors for the second).

36. Peter Brown, *supra* note 4, at 351.

37. James A. Brundage, *supra* note 14, at 82.

38. *Id.* at 90.

39. Margaret R. Miles, *Carnal Knowing: Female Nakedness and Religious Meaning in the Christian West* 94 (Boston: Beacon, 1989). Miles notes that Martin Luther seems not to have been far from St. Augustine on this issue, saying that there would be sex in the Garden but that it would be without lust. *See id.* at 106 (citing Luther, *Lectures on Genesis* LW I, 56).

40. In a later era, the thirteenth century, St. Albert the Great (Albertus Magnus) rejected this position. He did not see sex as unnatural and did not believe that the nature of sex had changed as a result of original sin. He did not see a difference between sexual desire and arousal in Eden and in the then-current world. *See* James A. Brundage, *supra* note 14, at 421. Albertus Magnus was more than just a religious leader. He can be seen as a scientist and as an early Renaissance man, and his views may be more those of the coming Enlightenment than of the early Christian era. He was also the teacher of St. Thomas Aquinas, and his influence continued in the works of St. Thomas.

41. Richard A. Posner, *supra* note 1, at 46–47.

42. *Id.* at 47.

43. *See* Robin Lane Fox, *supra* note 10, at 347.

44. *See id.* at 348–49.

45. *Id.* at 348.

46. *Id.*

47. "[T]he philosophers were writing for a tiny minority whose ethical ideal was not their contemporaries'. . . . What we know through laws, histories and inscriptions refutes the idea that a widespread change in pagan sexual practice or attitudes was gathering its own momentum." *Id.* at 350.

48. *See id.* at 362.

49. James A. Brundage, *supra* note 14, at 75.

50. Robin Lane Fox, *supra* note 10, at 362.

51. *See* Edward Schillebeeckx, O.P., *Celibacy* 52 (C. A. L. Jarrot, trans.) (New York: Sheed and Ward, 1968).

52. *Id.* at 21.

53. *See* A. W. Richard Sipe, *A Secret World: Sexuality and the Search for Celibacy* 35 (New York: Brunner/Mazel, 1990).

54. *See id.* at 35–36.

55. *See id.* at 36.

56. *See id.* at 25.

57. *See id.* at 36–37.

58. *See id.*

59. *Id.* at 38.

60. *Id.*

61. *See id.* at 41–47.

62. *Id.* at 41.

63. *Id.*

64. *See id.* at 44.

65. *Id.* at 44. *See also* Edward Schillebeeckx, *supra* note 51, at 36 (noting that there was a prohibition in the sixth century not against clerics' being married but against bishops' having children, a prohibition that prevented the division of Church property).

66. *See* Edward Schillebeeckx, *supra* note 51, at 60.

67. A. W. Richard Sipe, *supra* note 53, at 44. Schillebeeckx says that, until the twelfth century, there was not really a rule of celibacy but only a rule of continence (Edward Schillebeeckx, *supra* note 51, at 40), a rule that had, it seems, been regularly violated, as evidenced by the birth of children to priests who purportedly had been living as brother and sister with their wives. *See id.* at 39.

68. *See* A. W. Richard Sipe, *supra* note 53, at 45. Schillebeeckx, seemingly speaking of a somewhat earlier era, notes a bishop of Liege complaining that, if he were to enforce the rules on clerical continence, he would have to dismiss all his clergy and that some bishops resorted to just asking their priests who could not give up their wives to at least be discrete. *See* Edward Schillebeeckx, *supra* note 51, at 43.

69. Interestingly, Sipe sees two outcomes of all these efforts, at least one of which would have been unintended and may be seen to have continued to the present. "Ironically, the legislation against marriage and sexual activity for clerics produced two notable side effects in the Church: (1) an increase in the transgressions against chastity and the rearticulated rule of celibacy; and (2) a continuing degradation of women." A. W. Richard Sipe, *supra* note 53, at 39. Further, in discussing the 1545 Council of Trent, Sipe says, "Predictably, the more sexuality was outlawed, the more it flourished. Pope Julius III (1550–1555) had a homosexual involvement with a 15-year-old boy whom he named a cardinal." *Id.* at 47.

70. *See* James A. Brundage, *supra* note 14, at 552.

71. Vern L. Bullough, *The History of Prostitution* 128 (New Hyde Park, NY: University Books, 1964).

72. Richard A. Posner, *supra* note 1, at 49.

73. David Loth, *The Erotic in Literature* 66 (New York: Julian Messner, 1961).

74. *See* Richard A. Posner, *supra* note 1, at 50.

75. *See id.*

76. Pierre J. Payer, "Sex and Confession in the Thirteenth Century," in Joyce E. Salisbury, *Sex in the Middle Ages: A Book of Essays* 126, 128 (New York: Garland, 1991).

77. *See id.* at 127.

78. *See* Richard A. Posner, *supra* note 1, at 50; see also Pierre J. Payer, *supra* note 76, at 127 ("The usual reason for exercising care in questioning is to avoid having penitents leave confession worse off than when they entered because of having learned novel ways of sinning.").

79. Richard A. Posner, *supra* note 1, at 49.

80. David Loth, *supra* note 73, at 66.

81. *See* Pierre J. Payer, "Confession and the Study of Sex in the Middle Ages," in Vern L. Bullough & James A. Brundage, *Handbook of Medieval Sexuality* 3, 13 (New York: Garland, 1996).

82. *See* Pierre J. Payer, *supra* note 76, at 131–32. Here, too, a distinction from the animals may have been important in determining what positions were acceptable for vaginal intercourse. Salisbury notes that early Christians sought to determine how and why animals copulate and to teach adherents to have whatever sexual intercourse they might have in ways that differed from the animals and thus to preserve a gulf between human and animal. *See* Joyce E. Salisbury, *supra* note 3, at 77.

83. Robin Lane Fox, *supra* note 10, at 352.

84. *Id.* at 355.

85. *See* James A. Brundage, *supra* note 14, at 555.

86. *Id.*

87. David Loth, *supra* note 73, at 58.

88. *Id.* at 59–60.

89. *Id.* at 60.

90. *Id.* at 68.

91. Giovanni Boccaccio, *The Decameron* 89 (G. H. McWilliam, trans.) (Harmondsville, UK: Penguin, 1972).

92. *Id.* at 90.

93. *Id.* at 91.

94. *Id.*

95. *See id.* at 25.

96. *Id.* at 316–17.

97. *Id.* at 317.

98. *Id.*

99. *Id.*

100. *Id.* at 240–41.

101. H. Montgomery Hyde, *A History of Pornography* 153 (New York: Farrar, Straus & Giroux, 1964).

102. *See id.* at 71.

103. *See id.* at 65.

104. *See* Richard A. Posner, *supra* note 1, at 51 ("The Reformation attacked Catholic sex theory as too severe and Catholic sex practice as too lax.").

105. Joyce E. Salisbury, *supra* note 3, at 153–54 (quoting Andreas Capellanus, *The Art of Courtly Love* 149 (New York: Columbia University Press, 1964)).

106. *See* Ian Frederick Moulton, *Before Pornography: Erotic Writing in Early Modern England* 28 (Oxford: Oxford University Press, 2000).

107. *Id.* at 104.

108. *See id.* at 119.

109. Prior to this era there seems to have been a general lack of nudity in artistic depiction, although there certainly were some depictions of nude figures engaged in debauchery. Brundage notes a marked contrast between the nudity of ancient art and of the Renaissance, on one hand, and in this era, on the other. *See* James A. Brundage, *supra* note 14, at 424–25.

110. *See* Lynn Hunt, introduction to Lynn Hunt, ed., *The Invention of Pornography: Obscenity and the Origins of Modernity 1500–1800* 1, 25 (New York: Zone Books, 1993).

111. *Id.* at 24.

112. *See id.* at 122.

113. For a brief discussion of this group of *poligrafi, see id.* at 138–39.

114. See Ian Frederick Moulton, *supra* note 106, at 119.

115. *See* Lynn Hunt, *supra* note 110, at 25.

116. It has been noted in this regard that "[w]hile the Index of Forbidden Books . . . was primarily designed to exercise from the Catholic world heretical works and the writings of Protestants, it tangentially addressed the moral content of art and literature." Paula Findlen, "Humanism, Politics and Pornography in Renaissance Italy," in Lynn Hunt, ed., *supra* note 110, at 49, 55. Findlen quotes the Canons and Decrees of the Council of Trent (1563) to the effect that "[b]ooks which professedly deal with, narrate or teach things lascivious or obscene are absolutely prohibited, since not only the matter of faith but also that of morals, which are usually easily corrupted by the reading of such books, must be taken into consideration." *Id*. Perhaps Raimondo but not Romano got caught up in that tangential sweep.

117. *See* Poul Gerhard, *Pornography in Fine Art from Ancient Times up to the Present* 41 (Los Angeles: Elysium, 1969).

118. *See* H. Montgomery Hyde, *supra* note 101, at 75.

119. *Id*.

120. Peter Webb, *The Erotic Arts* 104 (New York: Farrar, Straus & Giroux, 1983).

121. *See id*. at 105–07.

122. *See* Roger Thompson, *Unfit for Modest Ears: A Study of Pornographic, Obscene and Bawdy Works Written or Published in England in the Second Half of the Seventeenth Century* 5 (Totowa, NJ: Rowman and Littlefield, 1979).

123. Posner makes a similar point that anything related to the body is questionable. *See supra* note 1.

NOTES TO CHAPTER 4

1. Ian Frederick Moulton, *Before Pornography: Erotic Writing in Early Modern England* (Oxford: Oxford University Press, 2000).

2. *Id*.

3. *Id*. at 36.

4. Lynn Hunt, introduction to Lynn Hunt, ed., *The Invention of Pornography: Obscenity and the Origins of Modernity, 1500–1800* 1, 10–11 (New York: Zone Books, 1993).

5. Peter Wagner, *Eros Revised: Erotica of the Enlightenment in England and America* 5 (London: Secker & Warburg, 1988).

6. *See* H. Montgomery Hyde, *A History of Pornography* 83 (New York: Farrar, Straus & Giroux, 1964).

7. *Id*. at 94–95.

8. This growth in pornography in England is chronicled in Roger Thompson, *Unfit for Modest Ears: A Study of Pornographic, Obscene and Bawdy Works Written in England in the Second Half of the Seventeenth Century* (Totowa, NJ: Rowman and Littlefield, 1979).

9. Sarah Toulalan, *Imagining Sex: Pornography and Bodies in Seventeenth-Century England* 1 (Oxford: Oxford University Press, 2007).

10. *See id*. at 42. It has been argued that concerns over moral orthodoxy became a part of the struggle between the Catholic Church and Protestantism as to religious orthodoxy. "Protestantism and Catholicism vied with each other to demonstrate not only that one or other represented genuine doctrine but that from this 'true' Christianity 'moral' benefits flowed." David Tribe, *Questions of Censorship* 55 (London: George Allen & Unwin, 1973).

11. Sarah Toulalan, *supra* note 9, at 43.

12. *See id.* at 260.

13. *See id., e.g.,* at 180, 238, 239.

14. *See id.* at 260. The story seems to be the same as that for a French work, *L'academie des dames,* also translated from the Latin.

15. The Italian material of the sixteenth century seems not to have had much impact in England. The works were available in Italian and are said to have been widely available in that language, but they were not translated into English. *See* Ian Frederick Moulton, *supra* note 1, at 120. The *Sonetti* are said to be the most infamous erotic works in England in their era, with the adjective *Aretine* coming into use to describe erotic images; however, they were not widely circulated in England, to the point that "[w]hile the existence of the sonnets and engravings was well known in Elizabethan London, there is little proof that any English person owned or had even seen a copy." *Id.* at 123.

16. *See* H. Montgomery Hyde, *supra* note 6, at 155.

17. *Id.* at 157.

18. *Id.* at 97.

19. *Id.* at 163.

20. 383 U.S. 413 (1966).

21. Lynn Hunt, *supra* note 4, at 33.

22. *Id.* at 34.

23. *See* Sarah Toulalan, *supra* note 9, at 45.

24. Lynn Hunt, "Pornography and the French Revolution," in Lynn Hunt, ed., *supra* note 4, at 301, 306.

25. *Id.* at 307.

26. *Id.*

27. *Id.* at 305.

28. *Id.* at 302.

29. Peter Webb, *The Erotic Arts* 148–51 (New York: Farrar, Straus & Giroux, 1983).

30. *See id.* at 151–58.

31. Peter Wagner, *supra* note 5, at 294–302, discusses the topic of early American pornography.

32. Felice Flanery Lewis, *Literature, Obscenity, and Law* 1 (Carbondale: Southern Illinois University Press, 1976).

33. *See* Frederick F. Schauer, *The Law of Obscenity* 2–3 (Washington, DC: Bureau of National Affairs, 1976).

34. *See id.* at 4; *see also* Leo M. Alpert, "Judicial Censorship of Obscene Literature," 52 *Harv. L. Rev.* 40, 40–41 (1938).

35. The case is reported in two places, 83 Eng. Rep. 1146 (K.B. 1663) and 82 Eng. Rep. 1036 (K.B. 1663).

36. *See* Leonard W. Levy, *Blasphemy: Verbal Offense against the Sacred, from Moses to Salman Rushdie* 214 (New York: Knopf, 1993).

37. A description of Sedley's antics may be found in *id.*; Frederick F. Schauer, *supra* note 33, at 4; Leo M. Alpert, *supra* note 34, at 41–42.

38. This language is from a discussion of the case found at 1 Keble 620 (1662).

39. 88 Eng. Rep. 953 (Q.B. 1708).

40. Leo M. Alpert, *supra* note 34, at 43.

41. 11 Mod. Rep. at 142, 88 Eng. Rep. at 953. This rule, of course, was to change. The position was overruled in Dominus Rex v. Curl, 93 Eng. Rep. 849 (K.B. 1727).

42. Fortescue's Reports 98, 92 Eng. Rep. 777 (1708) (alternative report of Queen v. Read).

43. 93 Eng. Rep. 849 (K.B. 1727).

44. *See* Frederick F. Schauer, *supra* note 33, at 5.

45. *See* Leo M. Alpert, *supra* note 34, at 44.

46. *See* Leonard W. Levy, *supra* note 36, at 307.

47. *See* Peter Wagner, *supra* note 5, at 72.

48. *See* Alec Craig, *Suppressed Books: A History of the Conception of Literary Obscenity* 30 (Cleveland: World, 1963).

49. Frederick F. Schauer, *supra* note 33, at 6.

50. The King v. John Wilkes, 95 Eng. Rep. 737 (K.B. 1764).

51. *See* Frederick F. Schauer, *supra* note 33, at 6.

52. See Leo M. Alpert, *supra* note 34, at 44.

53. *Id.* at 45.

54. *See* Frederick F. Schauer, *supra* note 33, at 6.

55. (1868) L.R. 3 Q.B. 360.

56. 3 Q.B. at 371.

57. *See* Felice Flanery Lewis, *supra* note 32, at 2.

58. 2 Serg. & R. (Pa.) 91 (1815).

59. 2 Serg. & R. at 91–92.

60. 2 Serg. & R. at 91.

61. 2 Serg. & R. at 101–02.

62. 2 Serg. & R. at 103.

63. 17 Mass. 335 (1821).

64. Frederick F. Schauer, *supra* note 33, at 10.

65. *See* 304 U.S. 476, 481 n.9 (1957).

66. *See* 304 U.S. at 485.

67. *See* Frederick F. Schauer, *supra* note 33, at 12.

68. Schauer discusses Comstock's influence. *See id.* at 12–14.

69. An Act for the Suppression of Trade in and the Circulation of Obscene Literature and Articles of Immoral Use, ch. 258, 17 Stat. 598 (1873).

70. Frederick F. Schauer, *supra* note 33, at 13.

71. Quoted in James Jackson Kilpatrick, *The Smut Peddlers* 35 (New York: Doubleday, 1960).

72. Richard A. Posner, *Sex and Reason* 52 (Cambridge, MA: Harvard University Press, 1992).

73. *See* H. Montgomery Hyde, *supra* note 6, at 166–67.

74. *Id.* at 164.

75. *See id.* at 164–65; Lynn Hunt, *supra* note 4, at 304.

76. *See* H. Montgomery Hyde, *supra* note 6, at 165.

77. *See id.* at 166–67.

78. Lynn Hunt, *supra* note 4, at 302.

79. Quoted in *id.* at 304.

80. *See supra* notes 68–71 and accompanying text. Morris Ernst suggests that the trends in England and in the United States were unrelated, saying, "through a historical coincidence the psychotic rampages of Anthony Comstock coincided with new legislation in England which was trying to define the contours of the obscene." Morris L. Ernst,

foreword to Alec Craig, *supra* note 48, at 7, 8. Coincidence seems an unsatisfactory explanation, if there is any theory that allows an explanation of the contemporaneous movements.

81. *See* Frederick F. Schauer, *supra* note 33, at 10.

82. See Michel Foucault, *The History of Sexuality, Volume I: An Introduction* 7 (Robert Hurley, trans.) (New York: Pantheon Books, 1978).

83. *See id.* at 49 ("We must therefore abandon the hypothesis that modern industrial societies ushered in an age of increased sexual repression.").

84. *See* H. Montgomery Hyde, *supra* note 6, at 165.

85. *See* Richard A. Posner, *supra* note 72, at 52.

86. *See* Frederick F. Schauer, *supra* note 33, at 2.

87. Ian Frederick Moulton, *supra* note 1, at 28.

88. *See id.* at 104. Moulton offers in support of this position the 1596 High Commission order in which the Archbishop of Canterbury, John Whitgift, stated an intention to regulate

> divers copies books or pamphlets . . . latlie printed and putt to sale, some conteyn-
> ing matter of Ribaldrie, some of superstition and some of flat heresie. By means
> whereof the simpler and least advised sorts of her majesties subjects are either
> allured to wantonness, corrupted in doctrine or in danger to be seduced from that
> dutifull obedience which they owe to her highness. (*Id.* at 103.)

89. *See supra* notes 3–5 and accompanying text.

90. *See* Morris L. Ernst, introduction to H. Montgomery Hyde, *supra* note 6, at vii, viii.

91. Joyce E. Salisbury, *The Beast Within: Animals in the Middle Ages* 2 (New York: Routledge, 1994). Interestingly, Salisbury notes that there are no representations of apes, our closest animal relations, in early Christian art and no portrayals of apes mimicking human behavior but that after the twelfth century apes are depicted as degenerate images of humanity. *Id.* at 142. Thus, a relationship between humans and animals seems to have been recognized in that era.

92. *Id.* at 167.

93. *Id.* at 2 (quoting James Rachels, *Created from Animals: The Moral Implications of Darwinism* 4 (New York: Oxford University Press, 1991)).

94. *See* Carl Sagan & Ann Druyan, *Shadows of Forgotten Ancestors* 273 (New York: Random House, 1992).

95. *Id.* at 274 (quoting a February 14, 1747, letter from Linnaeus to J. G. Gmelin quoted in George Seldes, *The Great Thoughts* 247 (Bromley, UK: Columbus Books, 1985)).

96. *See* Peter J. Bowler, *Evolution: The History of an Idea* (Berkeley: University of California Press, 3rd ed. 2003).

97. Quoted in Gerhard Wichler, *Charles Darwin: The Founder of the Theory of Evolution and Natural Selection* 23 (New York: Pergamon, 1961).

98. Some scholars also find the germ of the idea of natural selection in the work of Erasmus Darwin. *See* Peter J. Bowler, *supra* note 96, at 85.

99. *See* Carl Sagan & Ann Druyan, *supra* note 94, at 36.

100. *See* Edward J. Larson, *Evolution: The Remarkable History of a Scientific Theory* 14–15 (New York: Modern Library, 2004).

101. *See* Peter J. Bowler, *supra* note 96, at 77–79.

102. *See id.* at 38–39.

103. *See* Edward J. Larson, *supra* note 100, at 91.

104. *See id.* at 63.

105. *See* Carl Sagan & Ann Druyan, *supra* note 94, at 38.

106. Although an 1858 paper on natural selection by Wallace may have led to the hurried publication by Darwin of his theory, Darwin is said to have developed his theory of natural selection some twenty years earlier. *See* Peter J. Bowler, *supra* note 96, at 173–74.

107. *See* Carl Sagan & Ann Druyan, *supra* note 94, at 50.

108. Peter J. Bowler, *supra* note 96, at 207.

109. *See* Edward J. Larson, *The Creation-Evolution Debate: Historical Perspectives* 2 (Athens: University of Georgia Press, 2007)

110. Peter J. Bowler, *supra* note 96, at 207.

111. Quoted in Edward J. Larson, *supra* note 100, at 67.

112. Peter J. Bowler, *supra* note 96, at 52.

113. *See id.* at 211.

114. *See* Edward J. Lawson, *supra* note 100, at 67.

115. *See* Carl Sagan & Ann Druyan, *supra* note 94, at 50.

116. James Rachels, *supra* note 93, at 4.

117. Charles Darwin, *The Expression of Emotions in Man and Animals* (1872; repr., London: Julian Friedmann, 1979).

118. Peter J. Bowler, *supra* note 96, at 214–15.

119. Charles Darwin, *supra* note 117, at 132.

120. *Id.*

121. *Id.* at 361–62.

122. *Id.*

123. *Id.* at 363.

124. *Id.*

125. *Id.* at 364.

126. *Id.* at 311.

127. *Id.* at 338.

128. The impact seems, in scope, to go beyond the religious and to have touched on the self-perceptions of humanity in a variety of ways. George Levine, who has written on the impact of evolutionary theory on novelists, says, "[Darwin] can be taken as the figure through whom the full implications of the developing authority of scientific thought began to be felt by modern nonscientific culture. Darwin's theory thrust the human into nature and time, and subjected it to the same dispassionate and material investigations hitherto reserved for rocks and stars." George Levine, *Darwin and the Novelists: Patterns of Science in the Victorian Fiction* 1 (Cambridge, MA: Harvard University Press, 1998).

The relationship between humanity and the animals seemed to lead to a blurring of the lines between good and evil in characters in Victorian novels. Again, in the words of Levine,

> All living things in Darwin's world are quite literally related, and, as he will say in a variety of ways, graduate into each other. Isolated perfection is impossible. . . . Fiction's emphasis on the ordinary and the everyday, its aversion to traditional forms of heroism and to earlier traditions of character "types," all reflect the tendency obvious in Darwin's world to deny permanent identities or sharply defined categories—even of good and evil. Note how rarely in Trollope or . . . in Eliot genuinely evil characters appear. Typical stories are of decline or of development.

Id. at 17. Novels were less likely to have plots representing a simple struggle between good and evil characters. Novelists investigated, instead, the struggle between good and evil in the individual, which might be seen as a struggle between divine nature and animal nature in humans.

129. *See* Peter J. Bowler, *supra* note 96, at 208.

130. Carl Sagan & Ann Druyan, *supra* note 94, at 270 (quoting Thomas N. Savage & Jeffries Wyman, "Observations on the External Characters and Habits of the Troglodytes Niger and on Its Organization," *Boston Journal of Natural History* (1843–44), *quoted in* Thomas H. Huxley, *Man's Place in Nature and Other Anthropological Essays* (New York: D. Appleton, 1900)).

131. Carl Sagan & Ann Druyan, *supra* note 94, at 270.

132. *Id.* at 272.

133. Reay Tannahill, *Sex in History* 98 (New York: Penguin Putnam, 1980).

134. Vern L. Bullough, *Sexual Variance in Society and History* 99 (New York: Wiley Interscience, 1976).

135. *See* Vern L. Bullough & Bonnie Bullough, *Sin, Sickness, & Sanity: A History of Sexual Attitudes* 56 (New York: New American Library, 1977).

136. *See* Peter Wagner, *supra* note 5, at 16–17.

137. *Id.* at 19.

138. Vern L. Bullough, *supra* note 134, at 498.

139. *Id.*

140. *Id.* at 545.

141. Vern L. Bullough & Bonnie Bullough, *supra* note 135, at 59.

142. Edgar Gregerson, *Sexual Practices: The Story of Human Sexuality* 28 (London: Franklin Watts, 1983) (emphasis in original).

143. *See* Vern L. Bullough & Bonnie Bullough, *supra* note 135, at 63.

144. *See* Vern L. Bullough, *supra* note 134, at 547.

145. Carl Sagan & Ann Druyan, *supra* note 94, at 270 (quoting Thomas N. Savage & Jeffries Wyman, *supra* note 130).

146. *See* Nicola Beisel, *Imperiled Innocents: Anthony Comstock and Family Reproduction in Victorian America* 54 (Princeton, NJ: Princeton University Press, 1997).

147. *Id.* (quoting New York Society for the Suppression of Vice, *Thirteenth Annual Report* 9 (1887)).

148. *See id.* at 55.

149. Edward DeGrazia provides a detailed discussion of obscenity prosecutions aimed at serious literary works. *See* Edward DeGrazia, *Girls Lean Back Everywhere: The Law of Obscenity and the Assault on Genius* (New York: Random House, 1992).

150. *See, e.g.,* Epperson v. Arkansas, 393 U.S. 97 (1968); Scopes v. State, 289 S.W. 363 (Tenn. 1927).

151. Cass R. Sunstein, *Democracy and the Problem of Free Speech* 211 (New York: Free Press, 1993).

152. *See* "Evolution, Creationism, Intelligent Design," Gallup website, www.gallup.com/poll/21814/Evolution-Creationism-Intelligent-Design.aspx.

153. *See* Edwards v. Aguillard, 482 U.S. 578 (1987).

154. *See supra* note 103 and accompanying text.

155. The initial case in this area was Kitzmiller v. Dover Area School District, 400 F.Supp.2d 707 (M.D. Pa. 2005).

1. Vern L. Bullough, *The History of Prostitution* 79 (New Hyde Park, NY: University Books, 1964).

2. There are a number of sources on the Hindu gods that present the field with varying levels of complexity. For a more complete, and more complex, view, see Alain Daniélou, *The Gods of India: Hindu Polytheism* (New York: Inner Traditions International, 1985). At a more simple level, the British Broadcasting Company website includes an examination of the Hindu gods; *see* "Hinduism," www.bbc.co.uk/religion/religions/hinduism. Another, somewhat intermediate, source is found at the website of the Kashmiri Overseas Association; *see* "Hindu Deities," www.koausa.org/Gods.

3. *See* "Hindu Deities," *supra* note 2.

4. There is also a concept known as Brahman, which is the force of God that is in all things.

5. *See* "Brahma," BBC website, www.bbc.co.uk/religion/religions/hinduism/deities/brahma.shtml.

6. *See* Alain Daniélou, *supra* note 2, at 235–36.

7. *See id.* at 236.

8. "Hindu Deities," *supra* note 2.

9. *See* "Vishnu," BBC website, www.bbc.co.uk/religion/religions/hinduism/deities/vishnu.shtml.

10. *See* "Lord Vishnu," Kashmiri Overseas Association website, www.koausa.org/Gods/God3.html.

11. *See* Alain Daniélou, *supra* note 2, at 168–69.

12. *See id.*

13. *See id.*

14. *See infra* notes 23–26 and accompanying text.

15. *See* Alain Daniélou, *supra* note 2, at 173.

16. *See id* at 261.

17. *See id.* at 176.

18. *See id.* at 263.

19. *Id.* at 177.

20. *See id.* at 263.

21. *See id.* at 179.

22. *See* Vern L. Bullough, *Sexual Variance in Society and History* 250 (New York: Wiley, 1976).

23. When thought of as the goddess of beauty, Lakshmi is given the name Sri. *See id.* at 261.

24. *See* "Lakshmi," BBC website, www.bbc.co.uk/religion/religions/hinduism/deities/lakshmi.shtml.

25. *See* Alain Daniélou, *supra* note 2, at 261.

26. *See* "Lakshmi," *supra* note 24.

27. Outside the three major gods, Kama may be the champion in this category. He is the god of lust, the husband of Desire, the brother of Anger, and the father of Thirst. *See* Alain Daniélou, *supra* note 2, at 312.

28. "Shiva," BBC website, www.bbc.co.uk/religion/religions/hinduism/deities/shiva.
shtml.

29. *See id.*

30. *See id.*; Alain Daniélou, *supra* note 2, at 263.

31. *See* "Shiva," *supra* note 28.

32. *See id.*

33. Alain Daniélou, *supra* note 2, at 173.

34. *See id.* at plate 15.

35. Having four arms does not make Ganesh unique. His father, Vishnu, is also depicted as having four arms.

36. It might seem that Hinduism treats the cow as a god or goddess, or at least as sacred, which would serve as another merger of god and animal, but it is not clear that the cow is really seen as divine. The cow is, at least, revered as being the foundation of civilization. And in one of Vishnu's incarnations, Krishna is a cowherd or protector of cows. *See* "Holy Cow: Hinduism's Sacred Animal," PBS Nature website, www.pbs.org/wnet/nature/holycow/hinduism.html. But a recognition of the role of the cow and a respect for animals and even the cow's tie to Krishna may differ from a belief that the cow is divine.

37. Peter Webb, *The Erotic Arts* 73 (New York: Farrar, Straus & Giroux, 1983). Webb credits a lecture by Philip Rawson as a source for his comments.

38. *See id.* at 74–75.

39. *Id.* at 76. The marriage of these temple women to the god met the Hindu requirements of marriage. *See* Vern L. Bullough, *supra* note 1, at 87.

40. *See* Peter Webb, *supra* note 37, at 76.

41. *See* Vern L. Bullough, *supra* note 1, at 87.

42. Peter Webb, *supra* note 37, at 78.

43. *See* H. Montgomery Hyde, *A History of Pornography* 90–91 (New York: Farrar, Straus & Giroux, 1964).

44. Peter Webb, *supra* note 37, at 78.

45. *See id.* at 79.

46. Vern L. Bullough, *supra* note 22, at 253.

47. *Id.* at 251.

48. Vern L. Bullough, *supra* note 1, at 82.

49. *See id.* at 82–83.

50. *Id.* at 84.

51. *See id.* at 84–85.

52. *See id.* at 82–85. Bullough says of this hetaerae-like class of women,

> As women who had sacrificed what was regarded as specially honorable in a woman, they were held in low estimation by society; but as custodians of the fine arts, which had ceased to be cultivated by respectable women, they were admired and respected. . . . [They] were often employed as tutors for the daughters of the rich in order that they too might learn enjoyment of the arts. (*Id.* at 85–86.)

53. *See id.* at 86. In some sects, sex with a prostitute was seen as particularly beneficial:

> In such sects promiscuous intercourse is spoken of as an act of devotion to the deity and regarded as obligatory for all members. The best possible union occurs

when the woman is as different as possible from the man. Thus the union of a man with his own wife is more or less devoid of merit for the true devotee. . . . Beyond this union there are succeeding grades of sexual intercourse, each representing, so to speak, a higher stage: adultery, virgin taking, union with a high-caste woman, union with low-caste women and prostitutes, incest, union with a demoness, and ultimately, the seventh and highest grade, union with the goddess herself. (Vern L. Bullough, *supra* note 22, at 258–59.)

54. Peter Webb, *supra* note 37, at 79.

55. *See* Vern L. Bullough, *supra* note 1, at 92–93.

56. *Id.* at 93.

57. Bullough suggests that the Buddhist view of female superiority in sexual matters, as picked up from Hinduism, was left out of Buddhism's Chinese variety in order to avoid antagonizing Confucians. *See id.* at 94.

58. *Id.* at 96.

59. *Id.* at 103.

60. *Id.* at 95.

61. Peter Webb, *supra* note 37 at 88.

62. *Id.* at 86–87.

63. *Id.* at 87.

64. *See id.*

65. *See id.* at 89.

66. *Id.* at 90.

67. *See id.* at 90–91.

68. *See* George Ryley Scott, *Far Eastern Sex Life: An Anthropological, Ethnological and Sociological Study of the Love Relations, Marriage Rites and Home Life of the Oriental Peoples* 16 (London: Gerald G. Swan, 1943).

69. *See id.* It should be said that Scott writes with a view that is far more judgmental than would be expected of a modern anthropologist. *See, e.g., id.* at 17 (speaking of the Chinese and saying, "it is doubtful if a more superstitious race exists among the so-called civilized peoples.").

70. Peter Webb, *supra* note 37, at 93.

71. *See id.*

72. *See id.* at 92.

73. George Ryley Scott, *supra* note 68, at 25–26.

74. Peter Webb, *supra* note 37, at 92.

75. *Id.*

76. *See id.* at 93–96.

77. *Id.* at 92.

78. *See id.* at 97–101.

79. Poul Gerhard, *Pornography in Fine Art from Ancient Times up to the Present* 19 (Los Angeles: Elysium, 1969)

80. *Id.* at 21.

81. *See id.* at 27.

82. *See id.* at 19–27.

83. *Id.* at 19.

84. *See id.* at 21. There may be changes in the most modern times, in the post–World War II era. Interestingly, one of the legal cases that may show this change, Expression (The Lady Chatterley's Lover Decision), Hanreishu, XI, No. 3, 997 (Criminal), focuses on a sense of shame that comes from recognizing the animal side of human nature. The opinion also seems to indicate a willingness of the court to find a work obscene, even if the general public fails to see the objectionable nature of the material. This may again, as in the Christian era, reflect a difference between a more philosophical class and the mass of the population.

85. George Ryley Scott, *supra* note 68, at 104.

86. *Id.* at 123.

87. *See* Peter Webb, *supra* note 37, at 98.

88. *See, generally,* Grethe Jacobsen, "Sexual Irregularities in Medieval Scandinavia," in Vern L. Bullough & James Brundage, eds., *Sexual Practices and the Medieval Church* 72 (Buffalo, NY: Prometheus Books, 1982).

89. *See id.* at 72–73.

90. *See* Edith Hamilton, *Mythology* 445 (New York: Little, Brown, 1942).

91. *See* Raymond I. Page, *Norse Myths: The Legendary Past* 10 (London: British Museum Press, 1990).

92. *See id.*

93. Edith Hamilton, *supra* note 90, at 443.

94. For a listing and brief description of the Norse gods, *see id.* at 454–65.

95. *See* "Norse Gods—A Who's Who," BBC website, www.bbc.co.uk/dna/h2g2/classic/A13392911. This website provides a rather complete listing of Norse gods and some descriptions of their acts.

96. The Vanir and the Aesir had been at war, and at the end of the war, several gods were sent by each side to the other. *See id.*

97. *See id.*

98. When Baldar died and was sent off on his flaming burial ship, Thor is said to have thrown a dwarf onto the ship. *See id.*

99. The events that follow may be found at "Norse Gods—A Who's Who," *supra* note 95.

100. Another story holds that the first people were created from trees, an ash tree for the first man and an elm for the first woman. *See* Edith Hamilton, *supra* note 90, at 460.

101. Peter Webb, *supra* note 37, at 28. Webb credits John H. Field for his section on ancient and primitive cultures.

102. *Id.*

103. *Id.* at 27.

104. *See* Grethe Jacobsen, *supra* note 88, at 73.

105. *See id.* at 82.

106. *Id.* There was a system of diminishing fines. The first man to have intercourse with a single woman could be fined four and one-half marks; the second man with that woman, three marks; the third, a half mark; and no fine for later men. *See id.* at 82–83. It seems, then, that any wrong that was seen in the act was related to some sort of damage to the marriage marketability of the female.

107. Jenny Jochens, "Old Norse Sexuality: Man, Women, and Beasts," in Vern L. Bullough & James A. Brundage, eds., *Handbook of Medieval Sexuality* 369 (New York: Garland, 1996).

108. *Id.* at 370.

109. Grethe Jacobsen, *supra* note 88, at 85.

110. Cathy Jorgensen Itnyre, "A Smorgasbord of Sexual Practices," in Joyce E. Salisbury, *Sex in the Middle Ages: A Book of Essays* 135, 145 (New York: Garland, 1991).

111. David Loth, *The Erotic in Literature: A Historical Survey of Pornography as Delightful as It Is Indiscreet* 51 (New York: Julian Messner, 1961).

112. Louis M. Epstein, *Sex Laws and Customs in Judaism* (New York: Bloch, 1948).

113. *See id.* at 4.

114. *See id.*

115. *See id.* at 7–9.

116. *See id.* at 26.

117. *See, e.g.,* Poul Gerhard, *supra* note 79; Peter Webb, *supra* note 37. There are discussions of what is sometimes characterized as pornographic text in the Old Testament (*see, e.g.,* David Loth, *supra* note 111, at 51–53), but visual images are lacking.

118. *See* Louis M. Epstein, *supra* note 112, at 37.

119. *See id.* at 152–54.

120. *See id.* at 157–63.

121. *See* Peter Webb, *supra* note 37, at 18. Here, Webb credits John H. Field.

122. *Id.* at 19.

123. *See id.* at 20.

124. *Id.* at 22.

125. David Biale, *Eros and the Jews: From Biblical Israel to Contemporary America* 12 (Berkeley: University of California Press, 1997).

126. *See* Louis M. Epstein, *supra* note 112, at 163–64.

127. *See id.* at 165–66.

128. *See id.* at 168–69.

129. There was, of course, the birth of Abraham's son long after Sarah's normal period of fertility. Since infertility could therefore not be conclusively presumed from a woman's age, it could be argued that continuing to have sex past the usual age of fertility was still tied to procreation. But there seems to be more to it. The acceptance seems to have been simply a recognition of the importance of sexual pleasure within the marital relationship. And it was considered a positive good, rather than being the lesser evil compared to infidelity, as it was described by some Christian writers.

130. Bullough offers explanations for bans on certain sexual practices as based on the Jewish people's drive to separate from other neighboring cultures. He suggests that condemnation of cross-dressing was tied to pagan practices in which the goddess Atargatis was worshiped by cross-dressed devotees. *See* Vern L. Bullough, *supra* note 22, at 79–80. He also suggests that the treatment of homosexual acts was influenced by the prevalence of the practice among pagans. *See id.* at 82. "Among the Hebrews, the denunciation seems to be not so much against homosexuality as such as against the idolatry associated with it, or they sprang from fears of assimilation." *Id.* at 86.

131. *See* David Biale, *supra* note 125, at 61. Biale notes that this accepted role for sex within marriage was a modification of the asceticism of Talmudic culture that is particularly remarkable for the school of Ashkenazic pietists, who affirmed marital eroticism while denouncing other earthly pleasures. *See id.* at 78.

132. *See id.* at 86.

133. *See id.* at 88–89.

134. *Id.* at 101.

135. *Id.* at 102.

136. *Id.* at 33.

137. *Id.* at 34.

138. *Id.*

139. Poul Gerhard, *supra* note 79, at 19.

140. Vern L. Bullough, *supra* note 22, at 205 (quoting H. R. P Dickson, *The Arab of the Desert: A Glimpse into the Badawin Life in Sau̓di Arabia* 162 (London: George Allen & Unwin, 1949)).

141. Vern L. Bullough, *supra* note 22, at 212–13, quotes Koran XXIV at 30 as follows: "And say to the believing women that they cast down their looks and guard their privy parts and display not their ornaments, except those that are external; and let them pull their veils over the opening of their chemises at their bosoms and not display their ornaments to their husbands and fathers."

142. *Id.* at 213.

143. *See id.* at 216. Indeed, even touching the skin of a member of the opposite sex, other than that of a wife or relative, was seen as an act requiring ablution. *See id.* at 218.

144. *See id.* at 222.

145. *See id.* at 217.

146. *Id.* at 231.

147. Peter Webb, *supra* note 37, at 81.

148. *Id.*

149. *See id.* at 82.

150. *Id.*

151. *See* Vern L. Bullough, *supra* note 22, at 211 (citing Koran XXII at 5 and XXIII at 30).

152. *Id.*

153. *Id.* at 206–07.

154. *See id.* Bullough also notes that the stories are made unlikely by the fact that Muhammad did not marry until he was twenty-five and then to a woman who was fifteen years older than he was. He was faithful to his wife, until she died, whereupon he took several other wives—perhaps as a way of establishing political alliances—who may have been widows and at least some of whom may have been beyond childbearing age. *See id.* at 208. Muhammad's behavior seems not to have been that of a libertine.

155. *Id.* at 207.

156. *See id.*

NOTES TO CHAPTER 6

1. *See* Kevin W. Saunders, *Violence as Obscenity: Limiting the Media's First Amendment Protection* (Durham, NC: Duke University Press, 1996).

2. All the facts and quotes from this section are drawn from the rather short report of the case: Knowles v. Connecticut, 3 Day 103, 1808 WL 89 (Conn. 1808).

3. Dictionaries define *mountebank* as a person who mounts a bench and sells medicine or claims the ability to cure diseases. More generally, the word may apply to a hoaxster or charlatan. Law in the colonial era spoke of mountebank sermons, so the more general

definition may be the better one here. *See, e.g.,* The King v. Sir Charles Sedley, in which Sedley was accused of having preached blasphemy, abused the scriptures, and preached a "Montebank" sermon. The case is reported at 83 Eng. Rep. 1146 (K.B. 1663) and at 82 Eng. Rep. 1036 (K.B. 1663). Given that other law in the era spoke of mock sermons, the use of the word in this context seems clear.

4. The statute is presented in the case report. *See* 1808 WL 89 at 1.

5. *See* 1808 WL 89 at 4.

6. There was an additional ground for appeal raising the procedural issue of whether the information charged two offenses. Having reversed on other grounds, the court had no need to address the contention.

7. *See* 1808 WL 89 at 3.

8. 354 U.S. 476 (1957).

9. *See* 354 U.S. at 483.

10. That is not to say that sexual content would have been the only other basis the court might have considered. There were a number of other statutes and cases cited by the *Roth* Court. *See* 354 U.S. at 482–83. Interestingly, these cases also did not all have to do with sexual content. There was an 1815 case among the *Roth* Court's citations that did focus on sex. In Commonwealth v. Sharpless, 2 Serg. & R. (Pa.) 91 (1815), the defendant had been charged with exhibiting a "a certain lewd, wicked, scandalous, infamous, and obscene painting, representing a man in an obscene, impudent, and indecent posture with a woman, to the manifest corruption and subversion of youth, and other citizens of the commonwealth." 2 Serg. & R. at 91–92. The focus of most of the rest of the matter cited had to do with heresy or blasphemy, which could again be seen as questioning the relationship between humanity and God.

11. *See* American Amusement Machine Ass'n v. Kendrick. 115 F.Supp.2d 943 (S.D. Ind. 2000), *rev'd,* 244 F.3d 572 (7th Cir.), *cert. denied,* 534 U.S. 994 (2001).

12. *See, e.g.,* Virginia v. Black, 538 U.S 343 (2003).

13. International Covenant on Civil and Political Rights, *opened for signature* December 16, 1966, 999 U.N.T.S. 171, S. Exec. Doc. E, 95-2 (1978) (entered into force March 23, 1976).

14. *Id.* at art. 19, § 2.

15. *Id.* at art. 20, § 2.

16. International Convention on the Elimination of All Forms of Racial Discrimination, *opened for signature* March 7, 1966, 660 U.N.T.S. 195 (entered into force March 12, 1969).

17. *Id.* at art. 4. Article 5 contains rights to the freedoms of thought, conscience, religion, opinion and expression, and peaceful assembly and association.

18. Recommendation R(97) 20 of the Committee of Ministers of the Council of Europe on "Hate Speech," October 30, 1997.

19. Additional Protocol to the Convention on Cybercrime, Concerning the Criminalisation of Acts of a Racist and Xenophobic Nature Committed through Computer Systems, January 28, 2003, Europ. T.S. No. 189.

20. *Id.* at art. 3, § 1.

21. *Id.* at art. 3, §§ 2, 3.

22. For an examination of hate speech laws in a number of countries, *see* Michel Rosenfeld, "Hate Speech and Constitutional Jurisprudence: A Comparative Analysis," 24 *Cardozo L. Rev.* 1523 (2003).

23. 1 C.R. (4th) 129 (1990).

24. (1986) 1 S.C.R. 103, 50 C.R. (3d) 1.

25. 1 C.R. (4th) at para. 92.

26. 1 C.R. (4th) at para. 95.

27. 1 C.R. (4th) at para. 137.

28. 1 C.R. (4th) at para. 140.

29. Michel Rosenfeld, *supra* note 22, at 1546.

30. *See id.*

31. 1998 chapter 42.

32. ETS 5, *opened for signature* April 11, 1950.

33. For a discussion of free expression in German law, *see* Edward J. Eberle, "Human Dignity, Privacy, and Personality in German and American Constitutional Law," 1997 *Utah L. Rev.* 963; Ronald J. Krotoszynski, "A Comparative Perspective on the First Amendment: Free Speech, Militant Democracy, and the Primacy of Dignity as a Preferred Constitutional Value in Germany," 78 *Tulane L. Rev.* 1549 (2004).

34. The Basic Law may be found in translation at www.iuscomp.org/gla/statutes/GG.htm.

35. Ronald J. Krotoszynski, *supra* note 33, at 1553–54 (quoting Ernst Benda, "The Protection of Human Dignity (Article 1 of the Basic Law)," 53 SMU L. Rev. 443, 444 (2000)).

36. *Id.* at 1589.

37. *See* BVerfGE 2, 1 (1952), available in translation in Donald P. Kommers, *The Constitutional Jurisprudence of the Federal Republic of Germany* 218 (Durham, NC: Duke University Press, 2d ed. 1997).

38. BVerfGE 90, 241–55, Decision of the First Senate in accordance with § 24 Federal Constitutional Court Act, 1 BvR 23/94, April 13, 1994, available in translation at www.utexas.edu/law/academics/centers/transnational/work_new/german/case.php?id=621.

39. BVerfGE 82, 11 BvR 680, 681/86, April 3, 1990, available in translation at www.utexas.edu/law/academics/centers/transnational/work_new/german/case.php?id=630.

40. Ronald J Krotoszynski, *supra* note 33, at 1597.

41. Alexander Tsesis, "The Boundaries of Free Speech," 8 *Harv. Latino L. Rev.* 141, 159 (2005) (review of Richard Delgado & Jean Stefancic, *Understanding Words That Wound* (Boulder, CO: Westview, 2004)) (citing United Nations Committee on the Elimination of Racial Discrimination, Reports Submitted by States Parties under Article 9 of the Convention: Thirteenth Periodic Report of States Parties Due in 1997, Austria).

42. Alexander Tsesis, "Hate in Cyberspace: Regulating Hate Speech on the Internet," 38 *San Diego L. Rev.* 817, 858 (2001).

43. *See* Christopher D. Van Blarcum, "Internet Hate Speech: The European Framework and the Emerging American Haven," 62 *Washington & Lee L. Rev.* 781, 824 (2005).

44. The facts of this case are most easily found, at least for an English-speaking reader, at Yahoo! Inc. v. La Ligue Contre le Racisme et L'antisemitisme, 169 F.Supp.2d 1181 (N.D. Cal. 2001). On appeal, the Ninth Circuit reversed the district court's ruling, but the decision was not based on the difference in First Amendment analysis. Rather, the appellate court concluded that the district court's order should not have issued, because of lack of contacts with the United States of the complainants in the original French case and now defendants in the U.S. case. See 379 F.3rd 1120 (9th Cir. 2004). Even that was not the end of the case. The Ninth Circuit then granted en banc review, and the opinions it issued showed a very fractured court. A majority of eight judges concluded that the district court had, in fact, had personal jurisdic-

tion over the defendants, but of those eight, three held that the action was not yet ripe for review. The overall result was the dismissal of the suit without prejudice. There was a group of five judges who would have exercised jurisdiction and declared enforcement of the judgment to be a violation of the First Amendment. *See* Yahoo! Inc. v. La Ligue Contre le Racisme et L'antisemitisme, 433 F.3d 1199 (9th Cir.) (en banc), *cert. denied*, 547 U.S. 1163 (2006).

45. *See* Richard Delgado, "Are Hate-Speech Rules Constitutional Heresy? A Reply to Steven Gey," 146 *U. Pennsylvania L. Rev.* 865 (1998)

46. *See* Kathleen E. Mahoney, "Hate Speech: Affirmation or Contradiction of Freedom of Expression," 1996 *U. Illinois L. Rev.* 789.

47. *See* Mari J. Matsuda, "Public Response to Racist Speech: Considering the Victim's Story," 87 *Michigan L. Rev.* 2320 (1989).

48. *See* Michel Rosenfeld, "Extremist Speech and the Paradox of Tolerance," 100 *Harvard L. Rev.* 1457 (1987) (reviewing Lee C. Bollinger, *The Tolerant Society: Freedom of Speech and Extremist Speech in America* (New York: Oxford University Press, 1986)).

49. Ronald J. Krotoszynski, *supra* note 33, at 1598–99.

50. 343 U.S. 250 (1952).

51. 343 U.S. at 251 (quoting § 224a of Division 1 of the Illinois Criminal Code, Ill. Rev. Stat.1949, c. 38, § 471).

52. 343 U.S. at 252.

53. 343 U.S. at 254.

54. 343 U.S. at 258.

55. Justice Douglas, in a dissent that would be expected of such a champion of free expression, added an interesting comment recognizing the harms that can come from racist speech, concluding that some such speech could be indictable. He said,

> Hitler and his Nazis showed how evil a conspiracy could be which was aimed at destroying a race by exposing it to contempt, derision, and obloquy. I would be willing to concede that such conduct directed at a race or group in this country could be made an indictable offense. For such a project would be more than the exercise of free speech. Like picketing, it would be free speech plus. (348 U.S. at 284 (Douglas, J., dissenting).)

56. 578 F.2d 1197 (7th Cir.), *cert. denied*, 439 U.S. 916 (1978).

57. 505 U.S. 377 (1992).

58. 505 U.S. at 380.

59. 505 U.S. at 392.

60. 538 U.S. 343 (2003).

61. There is an additional basis under which a cross burning could lead to criminal liability. A cross burning at a Ku Klux Klan rally might, under the right circumstances, be held to be the advocacy of criminal behavior. Although Virginia v. Black and Brandenburg v. Ohio, 395 U.S. 444 (1969), both demonstrate that burning a cross at a Klan rally is insufficient in itself to justify criminal charges, *Brandenburg* does say that incitement of imminent lawless action may be prosecuted. Thus, a cross burning that was part of an attempt to incite a crowd to immediate violence and was likely to do so would not enjoy the protection of the First Amendment.

62. 315 U.S. 568 (1942).

63. 315 U.S. at 573.

64. 315 U.S. at 573 (quoting the state court opinion).

65. Russell Working, "Illegal Abroad, Hate Web Sites Thrive Here: 1st Amendment Lets Fringe Groups Use U.S. Sites to Spread Their Message around the World," *Chicago Tribune* A1 (Nov. 13, 2007), available at 2007 WLNR 22413864.

66. *Id.*

67. *Id.* (discussing the reaction of Peter Lazenby, a reporter for the *Yorkshire Evening Post*).

68. 315 U.S. at 573 (quoting the state court opinion).

69. 315 U.S. at 572.

70. 78 Stat. 253, as amended, 42 U.S.C. § 2000e et seq.

71. 477 U.S. 57 (1986).

72. 477 U.S. at 64.

73. 477 U.S. at 67 (internal citation omitted).

74. 510 U.S. 17 (1993).

75. 510 U.S. at 21.

76. 510 U.S. at 21–22.

77. 510 U.S. at 22.

78. *See, e.g.,* Shanoff v. Illinois Department of Human Services, 258 F.3d 696 (7th Cir. 2001), in which the suit went forward on that basis of a claim that Shanoff's supervisor had subjected him to abusive and insulting comments based on his Jewish race and religion.

79. *Harris,* 510 U.S. at 21.

80. *See* Burlington Industries, Inc. v. Ellerth, 524 U.S. 742 (1998).

81. 524 U.S. at 765.

82. Smith v. Auburn University, 201 F.Supp.2d 1216, 1226 (M.D. Ala. 2002) (citing Splunge v. Shoney's, Inc., 97 F.3d 488, 490 (11th Cir. 1996) (quoting Steele v. Offshore Shipbuilding, 867 F.2d 1311, 1316 (11th Cir.1989))).

83. *See* 42 U.S.C.A. § 2000e.

84. *See, e.g.,* Connick v. Myers, 461 U.S. 138 (1983).

85. International Convention on the Elimination of All Forms of Racial Discrimination, art. 4, *opened for signature* March 7, 1966, 660 U.N.T.S. 195 (entered into force March 12, 1969).

86. Recommendation R(97) 20 of the Committee of Ministers of the Council of Europe on "Hate Speech," October 30, 1997.

87. Additional Protocol to the Convention on Cybercrime, Concerning the Criminalisation of Acts of a Racist and Xenophobic Nature Committed through Computer Systems, art. 2, §1, January 28, 2003, Europ. T.S. No. 189.

88. There is a treaty on discrimination against women which might be cited in an argument that gender-based hate speech is to be prohibited. The Convention on the Elimination of All Forms of Discrimination against Women, opened for signature December 18, 1979, 1249 U.N.T.S. 13, includes a provision, as Article 5, that is on point. Article 5 states,

> State Parties shall take all appropriate measures: (a) To modify the social and cultural patterns of conduct of men and women, with a view to achieving the elimination of prejudices and customary and all other practices which are based on the idea of the inferiority or the superiority of either of the sexes or on stereotyped roles for men and women.

Certainly, gender-based hate speech seems to fit into the harmful practices being addressed.

89. 515 U.S. 557 (1995).

90. 530 U.S. 640 (2000).

91. Bjørnar Borvik, *The Norwegian Approach to Protection of Personality Rights: With a Special Emphasis on the Protection of Honour and Reputation* 133 (Bergen, Norway: Fagbokforlaget, 2004) (translating the Penal Code of May 22, 1909, No. 10, Art. 135a.). Borvik notes that Norway will soon provide a sentence of up to three years for expression "threatening or insulting anyone, or inciting hatred or persecution of or contempt for anyone because of his or her a) skin colour or national or ethnic origin, b) religion or life stance, c) homosexual orientation, or d) disability." Personal correspondence from Borvik, translating Section 185 of the General Civil Penal Code of May 20, 2005, not yet in force but, according to Borvik, probably taking effect in 2011 or 2012. Thus, hate speech on disability will also then be included.

NOTES TO CHAPTER 7

1. 413 U.S. 15 (1973).

2. The Court, in Paris Adult Theatre I v. Slaton, 413 U.S. 49 (1973), also allowed a prohibition of the exhibition of obscene material in a theater that admitted only adults and provided notice of the sort of film being exhibited. In Stanley v. Georgia, 394 U.S. 557 (1969), the Court set a limit on the state's interests and held that a prohibition on private possession in one's home is unconstitutional.

3. This was not the Court's first stab at defining obscenity. It had offered a definition in Roth v. United States, 345 U.S. 476 (1957), and had modified that definition in Memoirs v. Massachusetts, 383 U.S. 413 (1966).

4. *Miller,* 413 U.S. at 24 (citation omitted).

5. 413 U.S. at 32–33 (citations omitted).

6. 481 U.S. 497 (1987).

7. 481 at 500 (quoting *Miller,* 413 U.S. at 34).

8. 481 at 500–01.

9. Justice Scalia, in a concurring opinion, questioned the possibility of applying an objective test—and the reasonable person test is considered to be such an objective test—to matters of literary or artistic value, noting that "[s]ince ratiocination has little to do with esthetics, the fabled 'reasonable man' is of little help in the inquiry." 481 U.S. at 504–05 (Scalia, J., concurring).

10. 354 U.S. 476 (1957).

11. 354 U.S. at 481.

12. *See* 354 U.S. at 482 n.12.

13. *See* 354 U.S. at 483.

14. 354 U.S. at 484.

15. 354 U.S. 508 (Douglas, J., dissenting).

16. 354 U.S. at 509.

17. 354 U.S. at 509–10.

18. 354 U.S. at 512 (quoting William B. Lockhart & Robert C. McClure, "Literature, the Law of Obscenity and the Constitution," 38 *Minn. L. Rev.* 295, 371 (1954) (last quoted language only)).

19. 413 U.S. 49 (1973) (Brennan, J., dissenting).

20. 413 U.S. at 79.

21. 413 U.S. at 84 (quoting Jacobellis v. Ohio, 378 U.S. 184, 197 (1964) (Stewart, J., concurring) (last quoted language only; alteration of *Jacobellis* language in *Slaton*)).

22. 413 U.S. at 87–88 (quoting Ginsberg v. New York, 390 U.S. 629, 674 (1968) (Fortas, J., dissenting)).

23. 413 U.S. at 103 (footnote omitted).

24. 413 U.S. at 106.

25. 413 U.S. at 106–07 (quoting Thomas I. Emerson, *The System of Freedom of Expression* 496 (New York: Vintage Books, 1970) (insertion in opinion)).

26. This is not to suggest that there is no force behind feminist arguments that much of what constitutes pornography specifically degrades women, although even the Indianapolis ordinance struck down in American Booksellers Association v. Hudnut, 771 F.2d 323 (7th Cir. 1985), *aff'd,* 475 U.S. 1001 (1986), allowed men who had been treated as women ordinarily were in pornography to have the same cause of action available to women. To the degree that a pornographic depiction treats women purely as objects, it may be seen as especially degrading to women. It not only places women in a place removed from the divine but also reduces the women so depicted from the level of human to object.

27. *See* Ginsberg v. New York, 390 U.S. 629 (1968).

28. *See* Paris Adult Theatre I v. Slaton, 413 U.S. 49 (1973).

29. *Roth,* 354 U.S. at 487 n.20.

30. 354 U.S. at 487 n.20 (quoting *Webster's New International Dictionary* (unabridged, 2d ed., 1949)).

31. 354 U.S. at 487 n.20 (quoting ALI, Model Penal Code, § 207.10(2) (Tent. Draft No. 6, 1957) (comment at 10 and the discussion at p. 29 et seq.)).

32. *See* Harry M. Clor, *Obscenity and Public Morality: Censorship in a Liberal Society* 210 (Chicago: University of Chicago Press, 1969); Andrea Dworkin, "Against the Male Flood," 8 *Harv. Women's L.J.* 1, 7 (1985).

33. *See* Harry M. Clor, *supra* note 32, at 210 (citing Havelock Ellis, *On Life and Sex* 100 (New York: Garden City, 1939); Walter Allen, *To Deprave and Corrupt* 147 (London: Souvenir, 1962) ("Obscenity seems originally to have meant that which could not be represented upon the stage. It is related to ancient Greek theories of drama.") (quoted in Richard H. Kuh, *Foolish Figleaves? Pornography in—and out of—Court* 336–37 n.1 (New York: Macmillan, 1967)).

34. *Id.* at 225.

35. *Id.* at 231 (quoting Joseph Heller, *Catch-22* 449–50 (New York: Simon & Schuster, 1955).

36. *Id.* at 234.

37. *Id.* at 225.

38. *Id.*

39. *Id.*

40. *Id.* at 226.

41. *Id.* at 230.

42. This statement is not intended to dispute the position that much of what is available as pornography degrades woman, rather than or more than men. To the degree that that is true of particular, or all, pornography, it, too, would then single out a particular subpopulation for degradation. For a discussion of the feminist attack on pornography, in the context of the history of obscenity presented herein, *see* Kevin W. Saunders, "The United

States and Canadian Responses to the Feminist Attack on Pornography: A Perspective from the History of Obscenity," 9 *Ind. Int'l & Comp. L. Rev.* 1 (1998).

43. *See supra* chapter 1, notes 1–6 and accompanying text.

44. International Covenant on Civil and Political Rights, *opened for signature* December 16, 1966, 999 U.N.T.S. 171, S. Exec. Doc. E, 95-2 (1978) (entered into force March 23, 1976).

45. *Id.* at art. 19, § 2.

46. *Id.* at art. 20, § 2.

47. International Convention on the Elimination of All Forms of Racial Discrimination, *opened for signature* March 7, 1966, 660 U.N.T.S. 195 (entered into force March 12, 1969).

48. *Id.* at art. 4. Article 5 contains rights to the freedoms of thought, conscience, religion, opinion and expression, and peaceful assembly and association.

49. Recommendation R(97) 20 of the Committee of Ministers of the Council of Europe on "Hate Speech," October 30, 1997.

50. Additional Protocol to the Convention on Cybercrime, Concerning the Criminalisation of Acts of a Racist and Xenophobic Nature Committed through Computer Systems, January 28, 2003, Europ. T.S. No. 189.

51. *Id.* at art. 2, § 1.

52. Del. Code Ann. 11 § 1364 (2)(a) (1981). *See also, e.g.,* Ga. Code Ann. § 16-12-80(b)(3)(A) (1996) ("Acts of sexual intercourse, heterosexual or homosexual, normal or perverted, actual or simulated"); Idaho Code Ann. § 18-4101(A)(2)(a) (1976) ("ultimate sexual acts, normal or perverted, actual or simulated"); Mont. Code Ann. § 45-8-201(2)(a) (1989) ("a representation or description of perverted ultimate sexual acts, actual or simulated [or] a patently offensive representation or description of normal ultimate sexual acts, actual or simulated"); Nev. Rev. Stat. § 201.235(4)(c)(1) (1979) ("ultimate sexual acts, normal or perverted, actual or simulated"). The prominence of such a definition is no doubt due to the guidance supplied by the Supreme Court in *Miller* indicating that such language would provide an adequate definition. *See Miller,* 413 U.S. at 25.

53. Colo. Rev. Stat. Ann. § 18-7-101(2)(b)(I) (2004).

54. Tenn. Code Ann. § 39-17-901(10)(14)(A) (1989).

55. Mich. Comp. Laws Ann. § 752.364(4)(1)(b)(3) (West 1985).

56. Colo. Rev. Stat. Ann. § 18-7-101(2)(b)(II) (2004). *See also, e.g.,* Del. Code Ann. 11 § 1364(2)(b) (1953) ("masturbation, excretory functions, and/or lewd exhibitions of the genitals"); Idaho Code Ann. § 18-4101(A)(2)(b) (1976) ("masturbation, excretory functions, or lewd exhibition of the genitals or genital area"); Mont. Code Ann. § 45-8-201(2)(a)(iii) (1989) ("masturbation, excretory functions, or lewd exhibition of the genitals"); Nev. Rev. Stat. 201.235(4)(c) (1979) ("(2) Depicts or describes in a patently offensive way masturbation, excretory functions, sadism or masochism. (3) Lewdly exhibits the genitals.").

57. 478 U.S. 675 (1986).

58. The case is seen as departing from the protection of free expression afforded students in Tinker v. Des Moines, 393 U.S. 503 (1969). There is disagreement about the nature of the departure, either as simply a weakening of *Tinker* or a different treatment for school-sponsored speech, or as a sort of indecency exception to the rule in *Tinker. See, generally,* Kevin W. Saunders, *Saving Our Children from the First Amendment* 228–55 (New York: New York University Press, 2003).

59. 478 U.S. at 686 (quoting New Jersey v. T.L.O., 469 U.S. 325, 340 (1985) (internal citation omitted)).

60. 416 U.S. 134 (1974).

61. 416 U.S. at 159.

62. *Id.*

63. 416 U.S. at 161.

64. 458 U.S. 747 (1982).

65. 458 U.S. at 761 (quoting Memorandum of Assemblyman Lasher in Support of [the Statute] (insertion in *Ferber*)).

66. 458 U.S. at 773.

67. The ordinance defined *pornography* as

the graphic sexually explicit subordination of women, whether in pictures or in words, that also includes one or more of the following:

(1) Women are presented as sexual objects who enjoy pain or humiliation; or

(2) Women are presented as sexual objects who experience sexual pleasure in being raped; or

(3) Women are presented as sexual objects tied up or cut up or mutilated or bruised or physically hurt, or as dismembered or truncated or fragmented or severed into body parts; or

(4) Women are presented as being penetrated by objects or animals; or

(5) Women are presented in scenarios of degradation, injury, abasement, torture, shown as filthy or inferior, bleeding, bruised, or hurt in a context that makes these conditions sexual; or

(6) Women are presented as sexual objects for domination, conquest, violation, exploitation, possession, or use, or through postures or positions of servility or submission or display. (Indianapolis, Ind., Code § 16-3(q) (1984).)

68. Indianapolis, Ind., Code § 16-3(g)(7) (1984).

69. Indianapolis, Ind., Code § 16-17(b) (1984).

70. *See supra* note 67.

71. Catharine A. MacKinnon, "Pornography, Civil Rights, and Speech," 20 *Harv. C.R.-C.L. L. Rev.* 1, 21 (1985).

72. *Id.* at 18.

73. *See* Catharine A. MacKinnon, "Pornography as Defamation and Discrimination," 71 *Boston Univ. L. Rev.* 793, 802 (1991).

74. 771 F.2d 323 (7th Cir. 1985), *aff'd*, 475 U.S. 1001 (1986).

75. 771 F.2d at 325 (citation omitted).

76. *See* 771 F.2d at 328.

77. *Id.*

78. 771 F.2d at 330.

79. 771 F.2d at 330–31.

80. Richard Herrnstein & Charles Murray, *The Bell Curve: Intelligence and Class Structure in American Life* (New York: Free Press, 1994).

81. For a discussion, *see* Bernie Devlin, Stephen E. Fienberg, Daniel P. Resnick & Kathryn Roeder, eds., *Intelligence, Genes, and Success: Scientists Respond to* The Bell Curve (New York: Springer-Verlag, 2007); Russell Jacoby & Naomi Glauberman, *The Bell Curve Debate: History, Documents, Opinions* (New York: Three Rivers, 1995).

82. The case is Doe v. University of Michigan, 721 F.Supp. 852 (E.D. Mich. 1989).

83. *See, e.g.,* Whitney v. California, 274 U.S. 357, 377 (1927) (Brandeis, J., concurring).

84. 418 U.S. 87 (1974).

85. 418 U.S. at 119 (quoting 18 U.S.C. § 1461).

86. 418 U.S. at 123–24.

87. 418 U.S. at 124 (quoting United States v. Wurzbach, 280 U.S. 396, 399 (1930)).

88. 513 U.S. 64 (1994).

89. 18 U.S.C. § 2252 (1988 ed. & Supp. V).

90. *See* 513 U.S. at 69.

91. 513 U.S. at 70.

92. 513 U.S. at 78.

NOTES TO CHAPTER 8

1. The facts of the case are presented in Dambrot v. Central Michigan University, 55 F.3d 1177 (6th Cir. 1995); in the lower-court opinion of the same name found at 839 F.Supp. 477 (E.D. Mich. 1993), an opinion that was affirmed in the Sixth Circuit opinion; and in Randall Kennedy, *Nigger: The Strange Career of a Troublesome Word* (New York: Pantheon Books, 2002).

2. 55 F.3d at 1180.

3. There appears to be some lack of clarity regarding the pronunciation of the word used:

> According to testimony from some of the players and assertions of plaintiff's counsel at oral arguments, there is some confusion about the actual language used. The term may have been "nigger," a word pronounced with a concluding "r" sound and commonly thought of as insulting, . . . "a racial epithet" or "racial slur," as defendants cast it in their representations to the Court and the public. It may also have been something like "nigga" or "niggah," a pronunciation which carries with it a much different, and non-insulting, connotation especially when used by blacks themselves.

839 F.Supp. at 479 n.1. For purposes of the matter before the court, the trial judge found it unnecessary to resolve the issue.

4. 55 F.3d at 1181.

5. *Id.*

6. *See, e.g.,* Connick v. Myers, 461 U.S. 138 (1983).

7. 55 F.3d at 1187–88.

8. Randall Kennedy, *supra* note 1, at 146–47.

9. *See* 839 F.Supp. at 479.

10. 478 U.S. 675 (1986).

11. 416 U.S. 134 (1974).

12. Kennedy does not discuss the classroom comments, so the discussion that follows does not represent a disagreement with the outcome of his analysis.

13. 55 F.3d at 1181 (citing Joint Appendix at 504).

14. Randall Kennedy, *supra* note 1, at 52.

15. *See id.* at 53.

16. *Id.* at 120.

17. *Id.* at 121 (citing the columnist Debra Dickenson).

18. *Id.* at 52.

19. *Id.* at 130–33.

20. *Id.* at 132–33.

21. *Id.* at 133.

22. 721 F.Supp. 852 (E.D. Mich. 1989).

23. 721 F.Supp. at 856. The policy also addressed "[s]exual advances, requests for sexual favors, and verbal or physical conduct that stigmatizes or victimizes an individual on the basis of sex or sexual orientation" and that raised the same problems.

24. The university later withdrew the guide because of perceived inaccuracies, but the fact of the withdrawal did not seem to be widely known. *See id.* at 860.

25. 721 F.Supp. at 863.

26. *Id.*

27. 721 F.Supp. at 865.

28. 721 F.Supp. at 858.

29. 721 F.Supp. at 860.

30. 774 F.Supp. 1163 (E.D. Wisc. 1991).

31. 774 F.Supp. at 1165.

32. 774 F.Supp. at 1166.

33. 2000 S.C.C. 69 (2000).

34. Ronald J Krotoszynski, *The First Amendment in Cross-Cultural Perspective* 72 (New York: New York University Press, 2006).

35. *Id.* at 74.

NOTES TO CHAPTER 9

1. Richard Delgado & Jean Stefancic, *Understanding Words That Wound* 93–109 (Boulder, CO: Westview, 2000).

2. *Id.* at 93.

3. *Id.* at 95.

4. Richard Rodgers & Oscar Hammerstein, "You've Got to Be Carefully Taught," *South Pacific* (1949).

5. *See infra* notes 55–75 and accompanying text.

6. *See infra* notes 27–38 and accompanying text.

7. The quotation may be found in various places, including in Richard Hornik, "Essay: Communism Confronts Its Children," *Time.com,* May 22, 1989, http://www.time.com/time/magazine/article/0,9171,957700-1,00.html (accessed Nov. 18, 2009).

8. This quotation also may be found in a variety of places, including at the website for LEARN (Lynn's Education and Research Network): http://www.learn-usa.com/of_relevance/~quotable_quotes.htm (accessed Nov. 18, 2009).

9. The quotation may be found at the QuotationsBook website: http://quotationsbook.com/quote/6450 (accessed Nov. 18, 2009).

10. Again, there are a number of sources for this quotation, including the BrainyQuote website: www.brainyquote.com/words/tw/twig233544.html (accessed Nov. 18, 2009).

11. 383 U.S. 502 (1966). The concept had seen its academic genesis in William B. Lockhart & Robert McClure, "Censorship of Obscenity: The Developing Constitutional Standards," 45 *Minn. L. Rev.* 5 (1960).

12. 383 U.S. at 961–62. The nature of the material was also indicated by the titles of the books, which included *Mistress of Leather, The Whipping Chorus Girls, Dance with the Dominant, Fearful Ordeal in Restraintland, Screaming Flesh, Columns of Agony,* and *Mrs. Tyrant's Finishing School.*

13. 354 U.S. 476 (1957).

14. 383 U.S. at 508.

15. (1868) L.R. 3 Q.B. 360.

16. 383 U.S. at 508.

17. *See* 383 U.S. at 510 ("to be certain that authors fulfilled his purpose, appellant furnished them with such source materials as Caprio, *Variations in Sexual Behavior,* and Krafft-Ebing, *Psychopathia Sexualis*").

18. 390 U.S. 629 (1968).

19. The law, New York Penal Law s 484-h, as enacted by L. 1965, c. 327, is set out in an appendix to the opinion. *See* 390 U.S. at 645–46. It defines nudity as "the showing of the human male or female genitals, pubic area or buttocks with less than a full opaque covering, or the showing of the female breast with less than a fully opaque covering of any portion thereof below the top of the nipple, or the depiction of covered male genitals in a discernibly turgid state." Section 484-h(1)(b), quoted at 390 U.S. at 645.

20. 484-h(1)(f), quoted at 390 U.S. at 646. The test for obscenity in that period was to be found in Memoirs of a Woman of Pleasure v. Massachusetts, 383 U.S. 413 (1966).

21. 390 U.S. at 636 (quoting William B. Lockhart & Robert McClure, *supra* note 11 at 85).

22. 390 U.S. at 639 n.6 (quoting Thomas Emerson, "Toward a General Theory of the First Amendment," 72 *Yale L.J.* 877, 938–39 (1963)).

23. 390 U. S. at 639 n.7 (quoting Louis Henkin, "Morals and the Constitution: The Sin of Obscenity," 63 *Colum. L. Rev.* 391, 413, n. 68 (1963)).

24. The Court noted that parents were not prohibited from providing the materials in question to their own children. *See* 390 U.S. at 639.

25. 390 U.S. at 642.

26. *See infra* notes 40–75 and accompanying text.

27. The hate-music industry is tracked by the Anti-Defamation League. Much of what follows is derived from, or at least influenced by, the ADL's website, www.adl.org. Another good source of information on hate groups is the website of the Southern Poverty Law Center, www.splcenter.org.

28. The lyrics can be found at "Angry Aryans Lyrics: Browntown Burning Down Lyrics," LyricsOnDemand website, www.lyricsondemand.com/a/angryaryanslyrics/browntownburningdownlyrics.html (accessed Nov. 18, 2009).

29. "Angry Aryans Lyrics: Racially Debased Lyrics," LyricsOnDemand website, www.lyricsondemand.com/a/angryaryanslyrics/raciallydebasedlyrics.html (accessed Nov. 18, 2009).

30. "Nordic Thunder Lyrics: United, White, & Proud Lyrics," LyricsOnDemand website, www.lyricsondemand.com/n/nordicthunderlyrics/unitedwhiteproudlyrics.html (accessed Nov. 18, 2009).

31. "Rahowa Lyrics: White Revolution Lyrics," LyricsOnDemand website, www.lyricsondemand.com/r/rahowalyrics/whiterevolutionlyrics.html (accessed Nov. 18, 2009).

32. "Blue Eyed Devils Lyrics: Final Solution Lyrics," LyricsOnDemand website, http://www.lyricsondemand.com/b/blueeyeddevilslyrics/finalsolutionlyrics.html (accessed Nov. 18, 2009).

33. "Blue Eyed Devils Lyrics: Murder Squad Lyrics," LyricsOnDemand website, www.lyricsondemand.com/b/blueeyeddevilslyrics/murdersquadlyrics.html (accessed Nov. 18, 2009).

34. "Extremism in America: William Pierce," ADL website, www.adl.org/learn/ext_us/Pierce.asp?LEARN_Cat=Extremism&LEARN_SubCat=Extremism_in_America&xpicked=2&item=wp (accessed Nov. 18, 2009).

35. Its website is www.resistance.com.

36. "Neo-Nazi Hate Music: A Guide: Distributors and Labels," ADL website, www.adl.org/main_Extremism/hate_music_in_the_21st_century.htm?Multi_page_sections=sHeading_6 (accessed Nov. 18, 2009).

37. *See* "Panzerfaust Records: Distributor of Hate Music," ADL website, www.adl.org/extremism/panzerfaust_records.asp (accessed Nov. 18, 2009). If the company has in fact gone out of business, there are still others willing to fill the gap. The Anti-Defamation League lists a number of hate-music distributors in the United States: Diehard Records, Micetrap Records & Distribution/RAC Records, MSR Productions, Vinland Winds Records, White Power Records, and Final Stand Records.

38. "Ethnic Cleansing: The Game," Resistance website, www.resistance.com/ethnic-cleansing/catalog.htm.

39. Again, even if racism is not a mental disorder in the sense of a diagnosable illness, it is still not the sign of a healthy mind.

40. *See* Kevin W. Saunders, *Saving Our Children from the First Amendment* (New York: New York University Press, 2003).

41. Alexander Meiklejohn, *Free Speech and Its Relation to Self-Government* 26–27 (New York: Harper and Brothers, 1948).

42. *See* Winters v. New York, 333 U.S. 507 (1948).

43. *See, e.g.,* Entertainment Software Ass'n v. Swanson, 519 F.3d 768 (8th Cir. 2008); Entertainment Software Ass'n v. Blagojevich, 469 F.3d 641 (7th Cir. 2006); Interactive Digital Software Ass'n v. St. Louis Co., 329 F.3d 954 (8th Cir. 2003).

44. American Amusement Machines Ass'n v. Kendrick, 244 F.3d 572, 577 (7th Cir. 2001), *cert. denied,* 534 U.S. 994 (2001).

45. *See, e.g.,* C. Edwin Baker, *Human Liberty and Freedom of Speech* (New York: Oxford University Press, 1989); C. Edwin Baker, "Scope of the First Amendment Freedom of Speech," 25 *UCLA L. Rev.* 964 (1978): Martin H. Redish, "The Value of Free Speech," 130 *U. Pennsylvania L. Rev.* 591 (1982); David A. J. Richards, "Free Speech and Obscenity Law: Toward a Moral Theory of the First Amendment," 123 *U. Pennsylvania L. Rev.* 45 (1974).

46. *See, generally,* John Stuart Mill, *On Liberty* 31–99 (London: John W. Parker and Son, 1859). Mill argues that suppression of expression may lead to suppression of the truth itself. Even if the suppressed material is false, Mill sees it as having value in providing a test for the received view. He also suggests that it is perhaps most common that the view that might be suppressed and the accepted view are both partially correct and partially incorrect and that not suppressing a dissenting view will lead to improved synthesis.

47. *Id.* at 136.

48. *Id.* at 147–48.

49. 250 U.S. 616, 630 (1919) (Holmes, J., dissenting).

50. 274 U.S. 357, 377 (1927) (Brandeis, J., concurring).

51. *See* Thomas I. Emerson, "Toward a General Theory of the First Amendment," 72 *Yale L.J.* 877 (1963). Lee Bollinger also suggests that a value behind free expression is that it fosters toleration. *See* Lee Bollinger, *The Tolerant Society* (New York: Oxford University Press, 1986). By practicing toleration with regard to expression, we may come to be more tolerant of others more generally. It seems unlikely that hate speech will, in fact, foster toleration, and there is not really any reason for us to want to develop more toleration of the acts of others toward our children.

52. 393 U.S. 503 (1969).

53. Of course, the determination of what ideas to convey to children would still be the subject of debate in the adult world. Nonetheless, insistence on the conveyance of a particular set of ideas, without leave for the parents to convey conflicting views, would allow a majority in one generation to limit too severely the variety of ideas in the next.

54. It is, of course, quite possible that children will bring those views to their contemporaries while they are all still children. That seems simply to be a price worth bearing to avoid regimentation by society.

55. *See* Jean Piaget, *The Moral Judgment of the Child* (London: Routledge and Kegan Paul, 1932). Piaget's work is discussed in Danuta Bukatko & Marvin W. Daehler, *Child Development: A Topical Approach* 535–73 (Boston: Houghton Mifflin, 1992).

56. *See, e.g.,* Lawrence Kohlberg, "Stage and Sequence: The Cognitive-Developmental Approach to Socialization," in D. A. Goslin, ed., *The Handbook of Socialization Theory and Research* (Chicago: Rand McNally, 1969); Lawrence Kohlberg, "Moral Stages and Moralization: The Cognitive Developmental Approach," in T. Lickona, ed., *Moral Development and Moral Behavior: Theory, Research, and Social Issues* (New York: Holt, Rinehart and Winston, 1976); Lawrence Kohlberg, *Essays on Moral Development, Vol. 2: The Psychology of Moral Development* (San Francisco: Harper and Row, 1984).

57. A discussion of these stages may be found in Danuta Bukatko & Marvin W. Daehler, *supra* note 55, at 544–46.

58. *See id.* at 535–73.

59. *See* Lawrence Kohlberg, Charles Levine & Alexandra Hewer, "The Current Formulation of the Theory," in Lawrence Kohlberg, *Essays on Moral Development, supra* note 56, 212, 212.

60. *Id.*

61. *See* Carol Gilligan, *In a Different Voice: Psychological Theory and Women's Development* (Cambridge, MA: Harvard University Press, 1982).

62. For a discussion of the development of the teenage brain, see Barbara Strauch, *The Primal Teen: What the New Discoveries about the Teenage Brain Tell Us about Our Kids* (New York: Doubleday, 2003). For a discussion of other work in the area and for its application to media issues, see Kevin W. Saunders, "A Disconnect between Law and Neuroscience: Modern Brain Science, Media Influences and Juvenile Justice," 2005 *Utah L. Rev.* 695.

63. *See* Peter R. Huttenlocher & Arun S. Dabholkar, "Regional Differences in Synaptogenesis in Human Cerebral Cortex," 387 *Journal of Comparative Neurology* 167, 176–77 (1997).

64. The relatively low mortality rate for preteens and teenagers, compared to infants and adults, had limited the availability of brains from that group for study. The MRI has also allowed the longitudinal study of individual brains, rather than comparative study of brains obtained from autopsies of different individuals of various ages, so the changes an individual brain undergoes can now be examined.

65. *See* Jay N. Giedd, Jonathan Blumenthal, Neal O. Jeffries, F. X. Castellanos, Hong Liu, Alex Zijdenbos, Tomas Paus, Alan C. Evans & Judith L. Rapoport, "Brain Development during Childhood and Adolescence: A Longitudinal MRI Study," 2 *Nature Neuroscience* 861 (1999).

66. *See* Elizabeth R. Sowell, Paul M. Thompson, Colin J. Holmes, Terry L. Jernigan & Arthur W. Toga, "*In Vivo* Evidence for Post-Adolescent Brain Maturation in Frontal and Striatal Regions," 2 *Nature Neuroscience* 859, 860 (1999) (citations omitted). The importance of the area under study to inhibition and judgment was demonstrated by a study of the behavior of individuals who had suffered physical injuries to the cortex, in particular to the prefrontal cortex. *See* Steven W. Anderson, Antoine Bechara, Hanna Damasio, Daniel Tranel & Antonio R. Damasio, "Impairment of Social and Moral Behavior Related to Early Damage in Human Prefrontal Cortex," 2 *Nature Neuroscience* 1032 (1999). The individuals exhibited what was described as "severely impaired social behavior despite normal basic cognitive abilities, were insensitive to the consequences of their behavior and were not amenable to correction of their behavior through punishment." *Id.* at 1032. When such an injury occurs in an adult, the result is behavioral problems, but if the injury is in childhood, there is also a defect in moral reasoning ability. *Id.* at 1033.

67. *See* Linda Patia Spear, "Neurobehavioral Changes in Adolescence," 9(4) *Current Directions in Psychological Science* 111, 112–13 (2000).

68. *Id.* at 113 (emphasis in original).

69. Barbara Strauch, *supra* note 62, at 203–04.

70. *See* Eric Jensen, *Teaching with the Brain in Mind* 30 (Alexandria, VA: Association for Supervision & Curriculum Development, 1998).

71. *See id.* at 32.

72. *See* Barbara Strauch, *supra* note 62, at 212.

73. *See* Abigail M. Baird, Staci A. Gruber, Deborah A. Fein, Luis C. Maas, Ronald J. Steingard, Perry F. Renshaw, Bruce Cohen & Deborah A. Yurgelun-Todd, "Functional Magnetic Resonance Imaging of Facial Affect Recognition in Children and Adolescents," 38 *Journal of the American Academy of Child & Adolescent Psychiatry* 195 (1999).

74. *Id.* at 195.

75. *Id.* at 198.

76. 393 U.S. 503 (1969).

77. 393 U.S. at 506.

78. 393 U.S. at 509.

79. *Id.*

80. 393 U.S. at 508.

81. 478 U.S. 675 (1986).

82. 478 U.S. at 677–78.

83. 478 U.S. at 681.

84. 127 S.Ct. 2618 (2007).

85. *See* 127 S.Ct. at 2625 ("this is plainly not a case about political debate over the criminalization of drug use or possession").

86. 127 S.Ct. at 2626.

87. *Id.* (quoting Virginia v. Black, 538 U.S. 343, 365 (2003)).

88. *Id.*

89. *Id.* (quoting *Fraser*, 478 U.S. at 680, 683).

90. 127 S.Ct. at 2626–27 (citations omitted).

91. *See* 127 S.Ct. at 2629.

92. 347 U.S. 483 (1954).

93. *Id.* at 493.

94. *Id.* at 494.

95. 478 U.S. at 683.

96. The original opinion had been the appeal of a denial of a motion for preliminary injunction. That denial was upheld, but by the time the case went on to the Supreme Court, the district court had come to its final resolution of the case, and the appellate opinion had become moot. Thus, the status of the opinion may prevent it from having value as precedent, but it still has whatever intellectual strength the reader thinks it demonstrates.

97. 445 F.3d 1166 (9th Cir. 2006), *vacated,* 127 S.Ct. 1484 (2007).

98. The court explained the day's activities:

> On the "Day of Silence," participating students wore duct tape over their mouths to symbolize the silencing effect of intolerance upon gays and lesbians; these students would not speak in class except through a designated representative. Some students wore black T-shirts that said "National Day of Silence" and contained a purple square with a yellow equal sign in the middle. The Gay-Straight Alliance, with the permission of the School, also put up several posters promoting awareness of harassment on the basis of sexual orientation. (445 F.3d at 1171 n.3.)

99. 445 F.3d at 1177 (quoting *Tinker,* 393 U.S. at 508).

100. 445 F.3d at 1178 (citation omitted).

101. 445 F.3d at 1180.

102. 324 F.3d 1246 (11th Cir.), *cert. denied,* 504 U.S. 824 (2003).

103. 324 F.3d at 1247 (emphasis added).

104. 619 F.Supp.2d 517 (N.D. Ill. 2007), *rev'd and remanded sub nom.,* Nuxoll v. Indian Prairie Sch. Dist. #204, 523 F.3d 668 (7th Cir. 2008).

105. 619 F.Supp.2d at 527.

106. *See id.*

107. *Id.*

108. Nuxoll v. Indian Prairie Sch. Dist., 523 F.3d 667 (7th Cir. 2008).

109. 523 F.3d at 675.

110. 523 F.3d at 676.

111. *Id.*

112. 523 F.3d at 671.

113. *Id.* (citing David M. Huebner et al., "Experiences of Harassment, Discrimination, and Physical Violence among Young Gay and Bisexual Men," 94 *Am. J. Public Health* 1200–01 (July 2004); Michael Bochenek & A. Widney Brown, "Hatred in the Hallways: Violence and Discrimination against Lesbian, Gay, Bisexual, and Transgender Students in U.S. Schools," *Human Rights Watch* 1–3 (2001), available at www.hrw.org/reports/2001/uslgbt/toc.htm; American Association of University Women Educational Foundation, "Hostile Hallways: Bullying, Teasing, and Sexual Harassment in School" 37 (2001), available at www.aauw.org/research/upload/hostilehallways.pdf).

114. 523 F.3d at 672.

1. *See, e.g.,* Devlin Barrett, "Atty. General Urges Conversations about Race," *St. Louis Post-Dispatch* A3 (Feb. 19, 2009), available at 2009 WLNR 3209969.

2. *Id.*

3. Charles M. Blow, "A Nation of Cowards?" *New York Times* A21 (Feb. 21, 2009), available at 2009 WLNR 3401110

4. Dawn Turner Trice, "On Different Pages When It Comes to Race," *Chicago Tribune* 13 (Feb. 23, 2009, available at 2009 WLNR 3488133.

Index

Fables: Aesop's, 18–20; and relationship between humans and animals, 18–20, 44–45
Fanny Hill. See Memoirs of a Woman of Pleasure
Fassler, David, 183
Fertility, 11, 20, 38–39, 83, 91
First Amendment: in the employment context, 148–49. *See also* Children and the First Amendment; Hate speech law in the United States, and fighting words; . . . and political speech; . . . and true threat; Obscenity; Schools and hate speech
Forbidden list, 41, 43–45, 206n116
Fox, Robin Lane, 30, 32, 34–35, 39
French Revolution, 53–54, 59

Galileo, 50
Geishas, 85
Genesis, 65
George III, 56, 59, 63
Gerhard, Paul, 8, 84–85
Gilligan, Carol, 180
Ginsberg v. New York, 170–72
Gluttony, 29–30
Gnostics, 29
God or gods and humans, separation from. *See* Humans and God or gods, separation from
Gods and goddesses. *See* Greek gods and goddesses; Hinduism; Japan; Rome; Scandinaviad
Good faith, doctrine of, 38. *See also* Confession
Greece, 7–20: arts, 7–11; pottery, 7–8, 198n10; ruling houses as descended from the gods, 17–18; sex attitudes and practices, 11–13, 199n42, 199n52, 200nn58, 59. *See also* Greek gods and goddesses
Greek gods and goddesses, 13–20, 24–25, 200n69: sex life of, 14–16; virginity of, 14, 24–25
Gregerson, Edgar, 70

Hamilton, Edith, 86–87
Hamling v. United States, 141–42

Harmful to minors. *See* Children; Obscenity, variable
Harper v. Poway Unified School District, 187–89
Harris v. Forklift Systems, 118–19
Hate Speech: definition, 133–36; as degradation, 6, 73, 99–100, 128, 132, 151, 153–54, 165–66, 168–69, 175; and disability, 223n91; impact of, 1–2, 128–29, 132, 175, 221n55; metaphors for, 1–2; by minorities, 108; as obscenity, 100–103; and suicide, 2. *See also* Adapting the *Miller* test to hate speech; Applications of the test for hate speech; Assault and hate speech; Children; Hate speech international agreements; Hate speech law in other countries; Hate speech law in the United States; Homophobic speech and hate speech; Schools and hate speech
Hate speech international agreements, 104, 108, 120–21, 133–34: Committee of Ministers of the Council of Europe protocol on hate speech and computers, 105, 120–21, 133–34; Discrimination against women, 222n88; European Convention for the Protection of Human Rights and Fundamental Freedoms, 108; International Covenant on Civil and Political Rights, 104, 133; International Convention of the Elimination of All Forms or Racial Discrimination, 104, 120, 133
Hate speech law in other countries, 105–11: Austria, 110; Canada, 105–7; France, 110–11; Germany, 108–10, 112; Norway, 121–22, 223n91; Spain, 110; United Kingdom, 107–8
Hate speech law in the United States, 111–18: and breach of the peace, 113; and employment, 118–20; and fighting words, 114–17; and migration of hate internet sites to the United States, 116; and political speech, 115; and true threats, 114–15
Henkin, Louis, 172
Heresy and political subversion or dissent, 45, 51, 60–61
Hetaerae, 8, 10, 12–13, 21, 80, 85, 214n52

Hinduism, 75–81; and the cow, 214n36; gods, 76–79; sex life of the gods, 76–78, 213n27. *See also* India

Holder, Eric, 193

Holmes, Oliver Wendell, Jr., 178

Holocaust, 109, 120–21, 160; denial, 109

Homophobic speech and hate speech, 120–22. *See also* Schools and hate speech

Homosexuality: in Greece, 13; in Rome, 22

Hughes, Langston, 154, 200n58

Humans and animals: *see* Animals and humans

Humans and God or gods, separation from, 4–5, 15, 18, 22, 24–26, 27–30, 45, 48, 57, 80–81, 83, 86, 88–89, 91–95, 97, 131–32, 202n1; pornography as contributing to separation, 57

Hunt, Lynn, 50, 53, 59

Hurley v. Irish-American Gay, Lesbian and Bisexual Group of Boston, 121

Huttenlocher, Peter, 181

Huxley, Thomas, 67

Hyde, H. Montgomery, 8, 11, 13, 21, 43, 46, 51, 59

India, sex and the arts in, 79–80. *See also* Hinduism

Industrial Revolution, 50, 60

Intelligent design, 64, 72

Intyre, Cathy Jorgensen, 89

Irving, David, 109

Islam, 95–97, 218n154; sex attitudes and practices, 95–96, 218n141

Jacobsen, Grethe, 89

Japan, 83–86: sex and the gods, 83–84; sex practices and attitudes, 84–85; sexual representation, 84–85, 216n84

Jesus. *See* Christ

Jochens, Jenny, 89

Judaism, 90–95: changes in sexual attitudes in development of monotheism, 91–92, 217n130; historic leaders, 94; marriage, 92–93, 217n131; religious precursors, 91–92; sex practices, 90–93, 202n2, 217nn129, 130

Kellogg, John Harvey, 69

Kennedy, Randall, 147, 149–50, 154, 156–59

King v. Sir Charles Sedley, 54–55

Knowles, John, 100–103

Knowles v. Connecticut. See Knowles, John

Kohlberg, Lawrence, 180

Kraft-Ebing, Richard von, 70

Krotoszynski, Ronald, 109, 112, 165

Lamarck, John Baptist Pierre Antoine de Monet de, 64, 70

Lawrence, Charles, 1–2

Lawrence, D. H., 8–9

Lecky, William, 23

Leclerc, George-Louis, 63

Lee, Spike, 158–59

Levine, George, 211n128

Levy, Leonard, 54–55

Lewis, Felice Flanery, 54

Linnaeus, Carl, 63, 70

Little Sisters Book & Art Emporium v. Canada, 165

Lockhart, William, 171

Loth, David, 7, 13, 38–41, 90

Luther, Martin, 37, 39–40, 204n39

MacKinnon, Catharine, 139

Mahoney, Kathleen, 111

Marie Antoinette, 53

Marie of France, 44

Marriage: China, 81; and Christianity, 31; Greece, 11–13; Hinduism, 80; Islam, 95–96; Rome, 21–22. *See also* Sex

Marshall, Thurgood, 126

Masturbation, 49, 68–70: impact on evolution, 70–71; physical effects of, 68–70; tie to pornography, 71

Matsuda, Mari, 2, 111

McClure, Robert, 171

Meiklejohn, Alexander, 175–76

Memoirs of a Woman of Pleasure, 52, 57

Memoirs v. Massachusetts, 52

Meritor Savings Bank, FSB v. Vinson, 118

Metamorphosis: gods to animals, 15–16; humans to animals, plants or gods, 16, 30

Mill, John Stuart, 177–78, 230n46

About the Author

KEVIN W. SAUNDERS holds the Charles Clarke Chair in Constitutional Law at Michigan State University and is the author of *Saving Our Children from the First Amendment* (2003, also available from NYU Press) and *Violence as Obscenity: Limiting the Media's First Amendment Protection* (1996).